Oxford Revision Guides

AS & A Level

ECONOMICS

Through Diagrams

Andrew Gillespie

OXFORD
UNIVERSITY PRESS

Great Clarendon Street, Oxford OX2 6DP

Oxford University Press is a department of the
University of Oxford. It furthers the University's objective
of excellence in research, scholarship, and education by
publishing worldwide in

Oxford New York

Auckland   Cape Town   Dar es Salaam   Hong Kong   Karachi
Kuala Lumpur   Madrid   Melbourne   Mexico City   Nairobi
New Delhi   Shanghai   Taipei   Toronto

With offices in:

Argentina   Austria   Brazil   Chile   Czech Republic   France   Greece
Guatemala   Hungary   Italy   Japan   Poland   Portugal   Singapore
South Korea   Switzerland   Thailand   Turkey   Ukraine   Vietnam

Oxford is a registered trade mark of Oxford University Press
in the UK and in certain other countries

© Andrew Gillespie 1998, 2002, 2009

The moral rights of the author have been asserted

Database right Oxford University Press (maker)

First published 1998
Second Edition 2001
Reprinted with correction 2002
Third Edition 2009

British Library Cataloguing in Publication Data

Data available

ISBN-13: 9780199180899

10 9 8 7 6 5 4 3 2 1

Printed in Great Britain by Bell & Bain Ltd., Glasgow

To Ali, Clemency, Romily and Seth, with love

CONTENTS

How Economics is assessed and examined

AQA
AS examinations
Unit 1: Markets and Market Failure
50% of AS and 25% of A level.
1 hour 15 minutes; 75 marks.
Section A: 25 compulsory objective text items (25 marks).
Section B: two optional data response questions; candidates answer one (50 marks).

Unit 2: The National Economy
50% of AS and 25% of A level.
1 hour 15 minutes; 75 marks.
Section A: 25 compulsory objective text items (25 marks)
Section B: two optional data response questions; candidates answer one (50 marks)

A2 examinations
Unit 3: Business Economics and the Distribution of Income
25% of A level.
2 hour examination; 80 marks.
Section A: two optional data response questions are set; candidates answer one (40 marks). One question will always relate to the global context and the other to the European Union context. *Section B*: three optional essay questions; candidates answer one.

Unit 4: The National and International Economy
25% of A level.
2 hour examination; 80 marks.
Section A: two optional data response questions are set; candidates answer one (40 marks). One question will always relate to the global context and the other to the European Union context.
Section B: three optional essay questions; candidates answer one.

All units are available in January and June.

Edexcel
AS
Unit 1: Competitive Markets – How They Work and Why They Fail
50% of the total AS marks; 25% of the total A level marks.
An introduction to the nature of economics, and how the price mechanism allocates resources in markets. The nature of market failure, its causes and possible policy remedies.
1 hour 30 minutes, consisting of supported multiple-choice questions and one data response question out of a choice of two questions.

Unit 2: Managing the Economy
50% of the total AS marks; 25% of the total A level marks.
Key measures of economic performance and the main objectives and instruments of economic policy. Involves use of basic AD/AS model. 1 hour 30 minutes, consisting of one data response question out of a choice of two questions.

A2
Unit 3: Business Economics and Economic Efficiency
40% of the total A2 marks; 20% of the total A level.
Develops the content of Unit 1 and examines how the pricing and nature of competition between firms is affected by the number and size of market participants. 1 hour 30 minutes; supported multiple-choice questions and one data response question out of a choice of two questions.

Unit 4: The Global Economy
60% of the total A2 marks; 30% of the total A level marks.
Develops the knowledge and skills gained in Unit 2 so that they can be applied in a global context.
2 hours exam; one essay question with two parts from a choice of three topic areas, and one data response question out of a choice of two questions.

OCR
Two mandatory units at AS and **two** further units at A2. These A2 units are also externally assessed.
Candidates choose **one** of **two** options for A2 Unit 3 – **either** A2 F583: *Economics of Work and Leisure* or A2 F584: *Transport Economics*, together with A2 F585: *The Global Economy.*

AS units
Unit F581 Markets in action
50% of AS marks.
1 hour 30 minutes; 60 marks.
Questions based on a particular theme or case study including some short answer and data interpretation plus one question that requires an answer written in continuous prose.
Unit F582 The national and international economy
50% of AS marks.
1 hour 30 minutes; 60 marks.

Questions based on a particular theme or case study including some short answer and data interpretation plus one question that requires an answer written in continuous prose.

A2 units
Either **Unit F583 Economics of work and leisure** *or* **Unit F584 Transport economics**
These papers comprise: *Section A*; candidates are required to answer one data response question.
Section B: candidates are required to answer one structured question from a choice of three. Each structured question is split into two parts.
Plus **Unit F585 The global economy**
Candidates are required to answer questions based on pre released stimulus material. Some questions may involve data interpretation. Most questions will require an essay style answer of varied lengths written in continuous prose.
Each paper is 25% of the total A level.
2 hours, Written paper; 60 marks.

WJEC

AS

Unit 1

1 hour, Written Paper; 50 marks.
20% of A level; 40% of AS level
Compulsory short-answer questions to assess all of the AS content.

Unit 2

2 hours, Written Paper; 80 marks.
30% of A level; 60% of AS level
One compulsory data response question (40 marks) and two, two-part essays (20 marks each) to assess all of the AS content. One of the essays from a choice of three will assess essentially microeconomics and one essay from a choice of three will assess essentially macroeconomics.

A2

Unit 3

1 hour and 45 minutes, Written Paper; 60 marks.
25% of A Level.
Compulsory short-answer questions (40 marks) and one synoptic essay (20 marks) from a choice of three to assess all of the A level content.

Unit 4

2 hours, Written Paper; 60 marks.
25% of A Level.
One data response question from a choice of two (40 marks) and one synoptic essay (20 marks) from a choice of three to assess all of the A level content.

Specification contents

AQA

Specification contents continued

Specification contents continued

Specification contents continued

OCR

Specification contents continued

WJEC

How to revise and succeed in the exam

How to revise: Get hold of the specification. Break it down into manageable sections. Produce a revision timetable. Tick off items as you cover them. Summarize your notes into brief, memory jogging revision notes. Learn: What do the terms mean? What is the relationship between the different variables? What are the relevant diagrams? What is the significance of the topic – why have you studied it? Take 'investment', for example – What is it? What affects it? What are the consequences of it changing? Also, make sure you get hold of past papers – see how examiners have asked about topics in recent years. Practise!

Taking the exam:

- **When you get into the exam room:** Check you know exactly how much time you have, what you have to do and how many questions you must answer. Write down when you must move on to the next question. Quickly read through the whole paper a couple of times. Think before writing. Watch your time. Do not get carried away with the topics you know well and delay starting questions where you are more uncertain. Plan your answers to make sure you are answering the question properly.

- **Read the question:** Then read it again! One of the major mistakes that candidates make is that they fail to answer the question set. Once you get started on an answer it is very difficult to change it, so make sure you answer the question correctly first time. Read the question thoroughly, think about how you will answer it *before* you begin.

- **Look for trigger words:** Make sure you check which skills are needed to answer the question. For example, if it asks you to 'explain', this requires lower level skills than a question asking you to 'analyse'. Similarly a question asking you to 'examine' requires lower skills than one which asks you to 'evaluate'. You must match your answer to the type of question – a 'discuss' question, for example, requires you to develop the arguments and come to a conclusion. 'State' simply requires you to make a number of relevant points and show knowledge.

- **Timing:** You cannot *lose* marks in an exam, in the sense that marks are not deducted if you make a mistake. However, you can penalise yourself by taking too long over a question and failing to finish the exam. Make sure you know how long you have for each part of the exam and that you move on to the next question at the appropriate time. If you fail to finish, you are obviously reducing your chances of doing well.

- **Look for specific words:** Check whether the question wants examples or refers to a *specific* situation, such as a 'dramatic', 'sudden', 'long term', or 'short term' change. Any extra words in the question need to be referred to in your answer.

- **Avoid:**
  i) answering too many or too few questions(!), believe it or not this does happen; make sure you know what to do on each paper,

  ii) being too descriptive – develop your ideas,

  iii) answering the question you wish they had set instead of the one they did set.

Good luck!

Answering Economics questions

The skills you will need:
The skills involved in answering Economics questions at AS and A level are:

- **Knowledge:** i.e. you must demonstrate you know what different terms means and what the key points in an argument are. You may have to explain terms or concepts.
  Questions which begin 'define', 'identify', 'state', 'describe' or 'list' typically require knowledge.

- **Application:** this means you must use your knowledge in the context of the market or the data facing you. The price elasticity in the market for oil is likely to be different from the price elasticity for a mobile phone, for example. To apply knowledge you need to think about how your points relate to the actual situation in the question.
  Questions asking you to 'apply', 'calculate' or 'explain' usually require application.

- **Analysis:** this involves developing your ideas and bringing in economic theory. It may also involve identifying a trend in a series of data and linking this to economic theory, i.e. showing why a trend has occurred or showing the possible implications of such a trend.
  Questions which begin 'analyse' or 'examine' require analysis.

- **Evaluation:** this occurs when you show judgement, e.g. you make conclusions about the most important factor, or the most likely course of action in these circumstances. It requires you to reflect on your earlier arguments and consider issues such as :
  - which is the most likely effect?
  - what is the most significant implication?
  - what is the most likely reaction?

  Evaluation can be demonstrated in various ways; for example, you may weigh up your arguments (which one is more important and why) or you may question the validity of the data (how likely is this to be appropriate? How reliable is it? Is it still relevant?)
  Questions which begin 'evaluate', 'assess', 'critically assess', 'discuss' or 'to what extent ...' require evaluation.

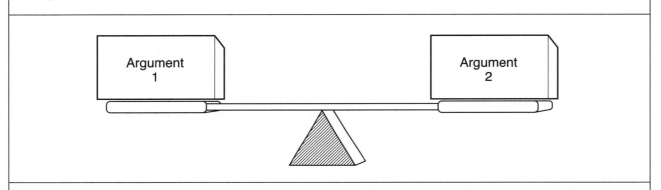

Levels of response and marking
Your exams are likely to be marked using a levels of response marking scheme. This means that examiners look for the quality of the skill you demonstrate rather than the number of points you make. It is quality not quantity which matters. For example it is better to analyse two points effectively than to analyse four points weakly: what matters is the quality of your analysis not how many times analysis occurs. Similarly, one well argued point of evaluation is better than many evaluative points left undeveloped.

Using diagrams
It is a good idea to use diagrams when you can to illustrate your points and to demonstrate and apply economic theory.
To use diagrams effectively:
- make sure they are accurate!
- label them fully; remember that if the axes are not labelled properly most diagrams make little sense
- make them legible: make sure it is easy to read the diagram.

Key terms in Economics

Resources: the resources in an economy provide the inputs for production: They include:
- Land: this include the amount of land available plus minerals and raw materials
- Labour: this includes the numbers and skills of employees
- Capital: this refers to inputs that have themselves been produced such as machinery; the quality of capital will depend on the level of technology
- Enterprise: this refers to the ability of people to see business opportunities and act to take advantage of these; entrepreneurs are willing to take risks to gain rewards such as profit.

Sustainable (renewable) resources: these can be replenished if used up, e.g. water resources are replenished by rain, the soil can continue to grow crops if treated properly, forests can be replaced.

Non-sustainable (non-renewable) resources: these cannot be replenished, e.g. oil.

Scarcity: the limited number of resources in the economy creates the fundamental economic problems. What should these resources be used to produce? How should they be combined for efficient production? And once produced, how should we decide who gets what?

- **Revenue:** the value of a firm's sales.
  Total revenue = price × quantity
- **Costs**
  - Total costs = Fixed costs + variable costs
  - Unit cost = $\dfrac{\text{Total cost}}{\text{Output}}$ = Average cost
- **Profit = Revenue − Costs**
- **Normal profit:** the level of profit which will keep resources in their present usage in the long run. It occurs when total revenue equals total costs
- **Abnormal or super-normal profit:** profit additional to normal profit
- **Profit maximization:** a fundamental assumption of classical economics is that firms seek to maximize profits (i.e. the difference between total revenue and total costs). This occurs where marginal cost equals marginal revenue, i.e. there is no extra profit to be made because the profit is now maximized.

Specialization occurs when an individual, business or country focuses on a limited range of tasks. The argument is that by specializing it is possible to become more skilled and efficient. You can then sell the output to others in return for their goods. They will want to buy your goods because you can make them and sell them at a profit more cheaply than they could make them themselves, because you are a specialist. Similarly it is cheaper for you to buy other goods from people who specialize in producing these than to try and make them yourself.
Specialization is the basis for trade.

Division of labour: occurs when a process is divided up into small, narrowly defined tasks. Individuals specialize in particular parts of the process. First described by Adam Smith in *The Wealth of Nations* in 1776, it basically involves a production line approach.

Division of labour:

- should increase productivity because individuals become more skilled through repetition
- saves time as individuals only have to be trained for one job and do not have to keep moving around
- makes it easier to replace staff as newcomers only have to be trained in one job – and there is a shorter training period. However, overspecialization can lead to boredom in employees because their jobs lack variety. This demotivation can lead to a fall in productivity.

Markets: involve an exchange process between buyers and sellers. In a free market the desires of buyers and sellers are brought into equilibrium by the price mechanism.

Equilibrium: occurs when there is a match between supply and demand. This equilibrium can be stable, which means there is no incentive to move from this position. Alternatively it may be unstable and the market may move from this position into disequilibrium.

Opportunity costs: the use of any resource involves an opportunity cost, i.e. it could be being used for something else. Individuals and governments should always consider what else their resources could be used for when making decisions.

Short term/long term: in economics the short term is defined as the period of time when at least one factor of production is fixed. The long term is a period over which all factors are variable. In the long term a firm can completely change its production system because it is not limited by a fixed factor. Also, in the long term, entry and exit is possible into and out of a market.

How long the short term is depends on the industry; e.g. in the oil industry, changing all the factors of production may take years; in a local café it may be a matter of months.

Market share measures the sales of a product or brand as a percentage of total sales in the market.

Market share = $\dfrac{\text{sales of a product}}{\text{market sales}} \times 100$

Concentration ratio: the N firm concentration ratio measures the market share of the largest N firms in a market, e.g. if the 4 firm concentration ratio is 80% this means the largest four firms have 80% of the sales in the market.

Key terms in Economics continued

Types of market

	Number of firms	Freedom of entry in long run?	Nature of the product	Example
Perfect competition	many	yes	the same	wheat
Monopolistic competition	many	yes	differentiated	restaurants; shoes
Oligopoly	a few	no	differentiated	airlines; supermarkets; dominant newspapers
Monopoly	one	no	unique	Intel dominates the microprocessor market; Durex used to have over 90% of the condom market; Microsoft dominates the market for PC operating systems (e.g. 'Windows 2000)

	Abnormal profits?	Barriers to entry
Perfect competition	short run only	no
Monopolistic competition	short run only	no
Oligopoly	depends on the model	yes
Monopoly	short run and long run	yes

Economic agents or actors: these are the different groups within an economy, i.e.:
- consumers: want to maximize their satisfaction (utility) from consumption
- firms: want to maximize their profits (revenue–costs)
- workers: want to maximize their welfare at work
- governments: want to maximize the welfare of their citizens

Nominal and real values: values that are unadjusted for inflation are called nominal values. These values are stated at current prices (i.e. measured at the level of prices existing at the time period covered).
Values that are adjusted for inflation are called real values. These are values stated at constant prices. This involves taking one period as a base year and then adjusting the following values, removing the effect of inflation.

Types of products

- **Complements** are products in joint demand, i.e. customers buy them together, e.g. DVD recorders and disks
- **Substitutes** are products in competitive demand, i.e. consumer may switch from one product to another, e.g. Coca Cola and Pepsi

Principals and agents
A principal or owner may delegate decisions to an agent. If it is costly for the principal to monitor the agent, the agent has inside information about its own performance, causing a principal agent problem.

The principal agent problem: the principal is the individual or organization that benefits or loses from a decision. The agent is the individual or organization that acts on behalf of the principal. In a company, for example, the principal is the shareholder and the agent is the manager(s). On occasion the agent may not reveal everything to the principal and may not work fully on the principal's behalf, e.g. managers may pursue a particular deal because they want to do it rather than because it is necessarily the best decision for the owners.

The stakeholders of a business are the individuals and organizations affected by its actions. These include:
- Employees (their employment, terms and conditions, job satisfaction and quality of working life all depend on the business)
- Suppliers (they sell to the business and rely on it for orders and payment)
- The local community (employees will spend money in the area; the business may hire people from the area)
- Investors (have put their money at risk and will generally expect the business to grow and dividends to be paid)
- The government (will expect firms to behave legally and to pay their taxes)
- The customer (will expect good value for money and a safe product)

Supply side policies
A supply side policy is a government scheme to promote market forces, cut costs and to raise the full employment level of output. The main categories for a supply side policy are:
- improve price flexibility and signalling within a market
- increase competition
- improve incentives.

Introduction to Economics

Types of economics

- **Positive economics** is based on testable theories, e.g. the idea that higher interest rates lead to a fall in aggregate demand can be tested by looking at past data. Similarly we can test whether lower income tax rates leads to more spending.

V

- **Normative economics** is based on opinion, e.g. the idea that the Government should make the reduction of unemployment its priority, is one person's view; another person might think it is more important to increase growth. Normative statements often have 'should' or 'ought to' in them; they involve value judgements.

- **Microeconomics** focuses on individual markets and decisions by individual households and firms.

V

- **Macroeconomics** focuses on the economy as a whole, e.g. it considers the price level for the economy as a whole, rather than for one market.

Sectors of the economy

- **Private sector:** resources owned by private individuals
- **Public sector:** resources owned by the State
- **Primary sector:** extractive industries, e.g. forestry, fishing, coal
- **Secondary sector:** converts materials into goods, e.g. manufacturing
- **Tertiary sector:** service sector, e.g. finance, tourism

In the UK, the service sector has been growing and the primary sector has been declining for some time.

Factors of production (or resources)

| FACTORS OF PRODUCTION | TRANSFORMATION PROCESS | OUTPUT (GOODS / SERVICES) |

- **Land:** natural resources, e.g. land itself, minerals, the sea
- **Labour:** human resources; this depends on the population size, the working age, people's skills and the level of training
- **Capital:** man-made aids to production, e.g. factories and equipment
- **Entrepreneurship:** this is the ability to combine factors of production and take risks in establishing new ventures

Types of production
- **Capital intensive:** uses relatively high amounts of capital compared to other factors of production, e.g. oil refining
- **Labour intensive:** uses relatively high amounts of labour compared to other factors of production, e.g. hairdressing

Scarcity and choice

At any moment in time output in an economy is limited by the resources and technology available. However, consumers' wants are unlimited and so decisions must be made about:

- **What to produce?** What goods and services should be made with the resources available?

- **How to produce?** What is the most efficient means of using the resources?

- **For whom to produce?** How are the goods and services allocated amongst consumers?

These are the three basic economic problems. Different economic systems solve them in different ways.

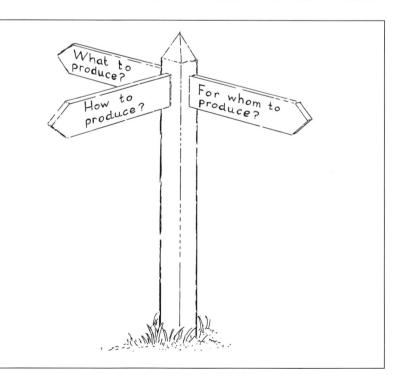

Introduction to Economics continued

Types of economy

Free market: the allocation of resources is left to market forces of supply and demand.

Mixed economy: some of the decisions are made by the Government and some are made by market forces.

Command or planned economy: the Government decides what is produced, how it is produced, and for whom.

Private sector ← → **Public sector**

In reality, all economies are mixed to some degree, but vary in the extent to which the Government intervenes. Since the 1980s the UK Government has reduced its provision of goods and services (e.g. through privatization) and increased the role of the private sector. This trend has been followed in many other countries, e.g. following the decline of Communism in Eastern Europe. UK privatizations include British Gas and British Telecom. However, in 2008 the UK government nationalised Northern Rock and Bradford & Bingley banks.

Opportunity cost is the sacrifice made in the next best alternative. If a firm invests in project A rather than project B, for example, then project B is the opportunity cost. If we use our income to buy X not Y, Y is the opportunity cost.

Types of goods
- **Capital goods (producer goods):** used to produce consumption goods in the future, e.g. machinery and equipment; not bought for final consumption.
- **Consumption goods:** bought for final consumption, e.g. washing machines, videos. Consumer non-durables (e.g. food) are immediately consumed; consumer durables are not consumed immediately, e.g. televisions.
- **Free goods:** involve no opportunity cost, e.g. air. (Note: nowadays <u>clean</u> air may have an opportunity cost because resources are needed to remove pollution.)
- **Economic goods:** products that are scarce and have an opportunity cost, e.g. to produce more cars you need to take resources away from some other production.

Production Possibility Frontier (PPF) or Production Possibility Curve (PPC)
Shows the maximum combination of goods and services which can be produced given the existing level of resources.

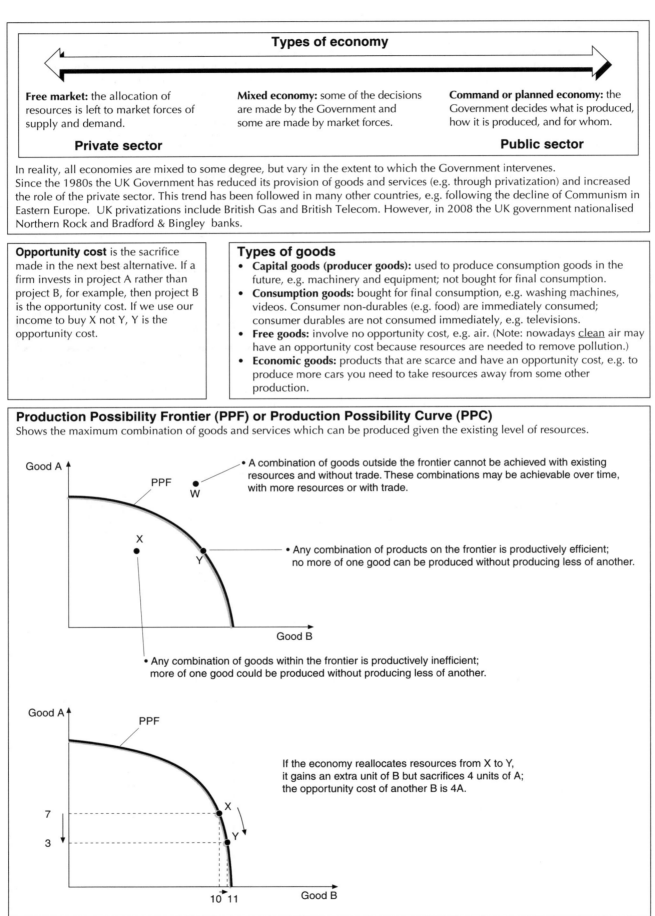

• A combination of goods outside the frontier cannot be achieved with existing resources and without trade. These combinations may be achievable over time, with more resources or with trade.

• Any combination of products on the frontier is productively efficient; no more of one good can be produced without producing less of another.

• Any combination of goods within the frontier is productively inefficient; more of one good could be produced without producing less of another.

If the economy reallocates resources from X to Y, it gains an extra unit of B but sacrifices 4 units of A; the opportunity cost of another B is 4A.

Introduction to Economics continued

Shape of the production possibility frontier

Usually convex to the origin due to the law of diminishing returns – as resources are transferred from Good A to Good B, the extra output of B becomes successively smaller, whilst the amount being sacrificed in A become successively larger.

If returns are constant, the PPF is a straight line – as resources are transferred from one good to another, the amount of output sacrificed by one good and gained by the other is constant.

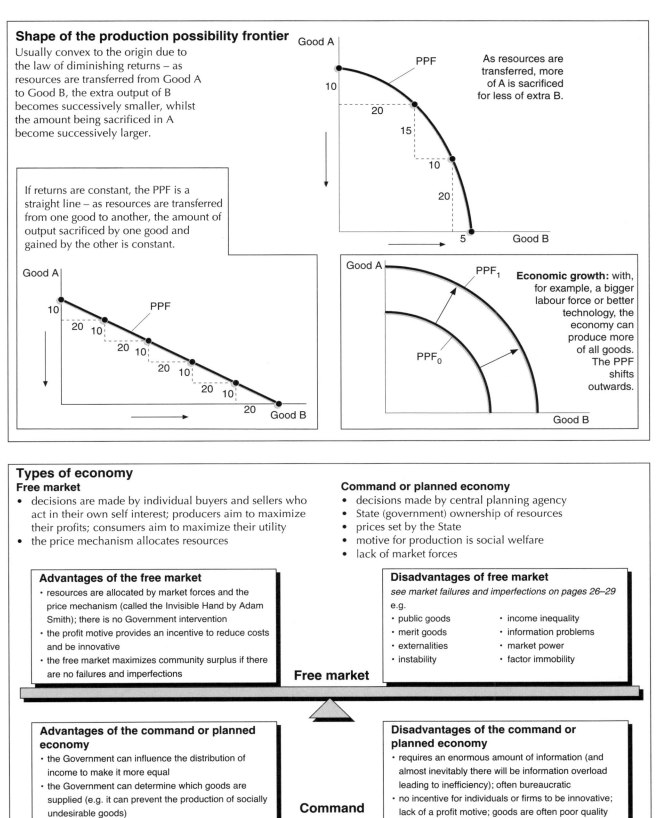

As resources are transferred, more of A is sacrificed for less of extra B.

Economic growth: with, for example, a bigger labour force or better technology, the economy can produce more of all goods. The PPF shifts outwards.

Types of economy

Free market
- decisions are made by individual buyers and sellers who act in their own self interest; producers aim to maximize their profits; consumers aim to maximize their utility
- the price mechanism allocates resources

Command or planned economy
- decisions made by central planning agency
- State (government) ownership of resources
- prices set by the State
- motive for production is social welfare
- lack of market forces

Advantages of the free market
- resources are allocated by market forces and the price mechanism (called the Invisible Hand by Adam Smith); there is no Government intervention
- the profit motive provides an incentive to reduce costs and be innovative
- the free market maximizes community surplus if there are no failures and imperfections

Disadvantages of free market
see market failures and imperfections on pages 26–29 e.g.
- public goods
- merit goods
- externalities
- instability
- income inequality
- information problems
- market power
- factor immobility

Free market

Advantages of the command or planned economy
- the Government can influence the distribution of income to make it more equal
- the Government can determine which goods are supplied (e.g. it can prevent the production of socially undesirable goods)

Disadvantages of the command or planned economy
- requires an enormous amount of information (and almost inevitably there will be information overload leading to inefficiency); often bureaucratic
- no incentive for individuals or firms to be innovative; lack of a profit motive; goods are often poor quality and usually a limited choice
- liable to lead to allocative and productive inefficiency due to lack of competition and no profit motive

Command or Planned economy

Demand

A demand curve shows the quantity that consumers are willing and able to purchase at each and every price, all other things unchanged. If other things do change (e.g. the consumers' incomes rise) the consumers are likely to want more or less at each and every price and the demand curve shifts.

The law of demand states that a higher quantity will be demanded at a lower price assuming all other factors remain constant.

The demand for a product or service depends on factors such as the price, consumers' income, the price of other goods, advertising, the consumers' tastes.

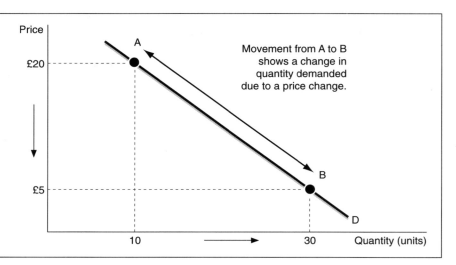

Movement from A to B shows a change in quantity demanded due to a price change.

Movements along the demand curve: extensions and contractions

A change in the price will lead to a 'change in the quantity demanded'. This is shown by a movement along the demand curve.

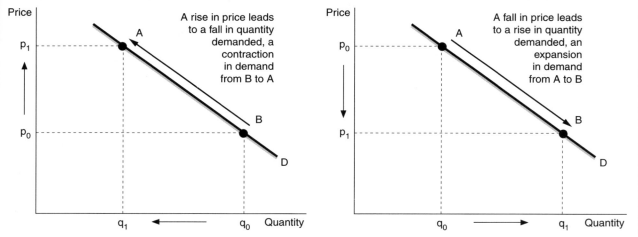

A rise in price leads to a fall in quantity demanded, a contraction in demand from B to A

A fall in price leads to a rise in quantity demanded, an expansion in demand from A to B

Shift in demand

A change in any of the factors affecting demand, except price, leads to a shift in demand. At each and every price there is an increase or decrease in the quantity demanded, so the demand curve shifts.

For example, if B is originally demanded at p_0, a fall in demand leads to the quantity demanded falling to A. With an increase in demand the quantity demanded increases to C.

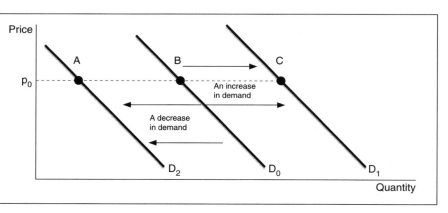

An increase in demand

A decrease in demand

Outward shifts of the demand curve

The demand curve will shift outwards when more is demanded at each and every price. This could be because:

- real incomes have risen (assuming the good is normal)
- the price of a substitute product has gone up, e.g. higher prices for coffee might increase demand for tea
- the price of a complement product has gone down, e.g. a fall in the price of cars might increase demand for petrol

- the product has been advertised more effectively
- the population has grown so there are more consumers
- tastes have changed so more people want the product
- more credit is available so people can borrow more money

Demand continued

Downward sloping demand curves

The demand curve is downward sloping because of the law of diminishing marginal utility. Each extra unit of a good or service will eventually give less extra satisfaction (utility); therefore the consumer will only be willing to pay less for more goods.

Note: although the consumer gets less extra satisfaction from each additional unit, his or her total satisfaction is rising.

Market demand curve: the horizontal summation of individuals' demand curves.

The price, income, and cross elasticity of demand (also see pages 9–11)

- The size of the change in the quantity demanded following a price change depends on the price elasticity of demand.
- The increase or decrease in demand following a change in income depends on the income elasticity of demand.
- The increase or decrease in demand following a change in the price of other goods depends on the cross elasticity of demand.

Upward sloping demand curves

The demand curve can slope upwards. This means more is demanded when the price increases. This can occur with:

- 'ostentatious goods' – people want to be seen buying more expensive goods. Also called Veblen goods.
- Giffen goods – these are very inferior goods and, when they become more expensive, consumers cannot afford any other products, so spend what money they have on these.

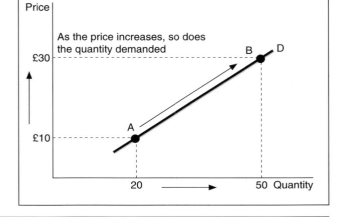

Income and substitution effects

If the price of a good falls, the quantity demanded will usually increase. This is because of:

- a substitution effect – with the fall in price of good A, A becomes relatively cheaper than other goods and inevitably there is a desire to buy more. Consumers inevitably switch to the relatively cheaper good.
- an income effect – with a lower price of good A, the consumer has more real income. If he/she bought the same amount of goods as before, there would be money left over. This means the consumer has more purchasing power because good A is cheaper. This leads to an income effect. **If the good is normal**, the consumers will want to buy more because of the income effect. This

means both the income and substitution effects make the consumer want to buy more.

If the good is inferior, i.e. a basic own-brand product, the consumer will actually want to buy less; now that they have more real income they will want to switch away to buy more luxurious goods. The income effect therefore works against the substitution effect. However, the substitution effect is larger and so overall the consumers do buy more.

If the good is a Giffen good, the income effect again works against the substitution effect and actually outweighs it. This means that overall the quantity demanded falls when the price falls and so the demand curve is upward sloping.

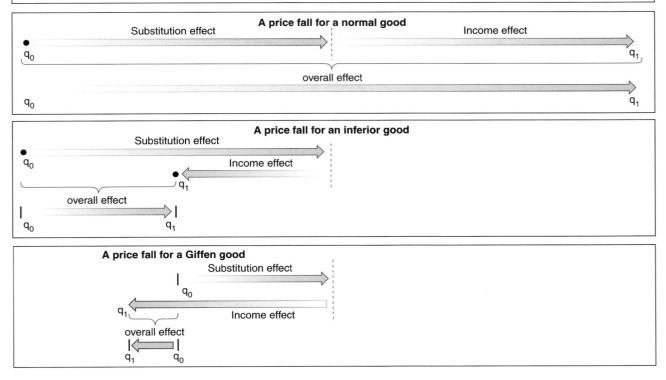

Demand continued

Utility
Utility is another word for satisfaction.

Marginal and total
Marginal utility (MU) is the extra satisfaction gained from consuming another unit of a good.
Total utility (TU) is the total satisfaction gained from consuming a given number of goods.

Law of diminishing marginal utility
states that successive units of consumption will eventually lead to a fall in their marginal utility.

Maximizing utility
We assume the aim of rational consumers is to maximize their utility, given the following constraints: a) limited income b) a given set of prices c) constant tastes.

To maximize utility, consumers will consume up to the point where

$$\frac{MU_A}{P_A} = \frac{MU_B}{P_B} = \frac{MU_C}{P_C} = \ .....$$

This is known as the equi-marginal condition. MU_A = Marginal utility of good A, P_A = Price of A, etc.

This means that the extra satisfaction per £ on the last unit of good A equals the extra satisfaction per £ on the last unit of good B and that of C and D and so on. If this was not the case, consumers would reorganize their spending and increase their satisfaction. For example, if the last A per £ was more satisfying than the last B, the consumers would buy more As and fewer Bs. (They could not have more of both because they are constrained by income.)

Paradox of value
Water is much more essential than diamonds but people are willing to pay more for diamonds. This is because there are relatively few of them and the marginal utility of another one is high. The total utility for them is quite low. However there is a large amount of water and so the extra utility of another unit is low. The total utility, however, is high.

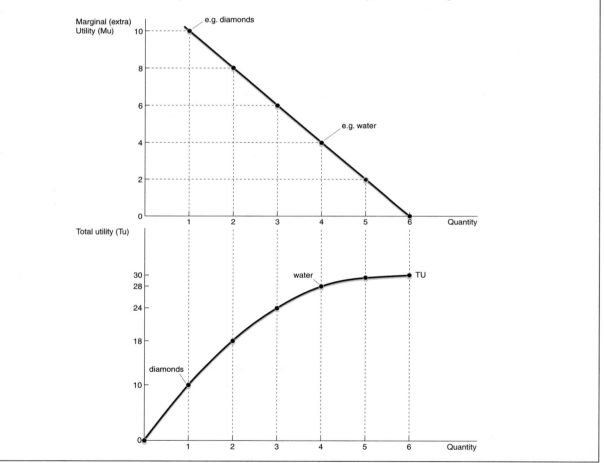

Types of demand
Joint demand
Occurs when complements are bought together e.g. computer consoles and games.

Composite demand
Occurs when a good is demanded for two or more uses, e.g. land may be demanded to build shops, to build houses or to build a factory. An increase in demand for one use leads to a fall in supply for the other, e.g. milk can be used for cheese or butter; if more is used for cheese, less is available for butter.

Derived demand
Occurs when demand for one good occurs as a result of demand for another, e.g. labour is demanded because there is demand for the final product.

Elasticity of demand (price, income and cross)

The elasticity of demand measures the sensitivity of demand to a change in a variable. The variable might be the price of the good, the price of other goods, or income.

The sign of the answer depends on the direction in which the two parts of the equation move. If both demand and the variable move in the same direction (e.g. they both increase or both fall) the sign will be positive. If they move in different directions the answer will be negative, e.g. if demand rises when income rises, the answer will be positive; if demand falls when income rises, the answer will be negative.
The sign shows the direction of movement; it does not show the actual elasticity; this is shown by the size of the number (i.e. whether it is greater or less than one).

The size of the answer (ignoring the sign)

- If demand is elastic this means that the percentage change in demand is greater than the percentage change in the variable. The value of the answer (ignoring the sign) will be greater than one.
- If demand is inelastic this means that the percentage change in demand is less than the percentage change in the variable. The value of the answer (ignoring the sign) will be less than one.
- If demand is unit elastic the percentage change in demand is the same as the percentage change in the variable. The value of the answer (ignoring the sign) is equal to one.

Elasticity of demand

	Value (ignoring the sign)	Description
Perfectly elastic	infinity	the percentage change in the quantity demanded is infinite
Elastic	>1	the percentage change in the quantity demanded is greater than the percentage change in the variable
Unit elastic	=1	the percentage change in the quantity demanded is equal to the percentage change in the variable
Inelastic	<1	the percentage change in the quantity demanded is less than the percentage change in the variable
Perfectly inelastic	0	there is no change in the quantity demanded

Price elasticity of demand

Measures the sensitivity of demand to a change in price.

$$\frac{\text{percentage change in quantity demanded}}{\text{percentage change in price}}$$

The sign

The price elasticity will usually be negative: when the price goes up, the quantity demanded falls, and vice versa. However, for a Giffen good or Veblen good, the price elasticity is positive. When price increases, the quantity demanded also rises.

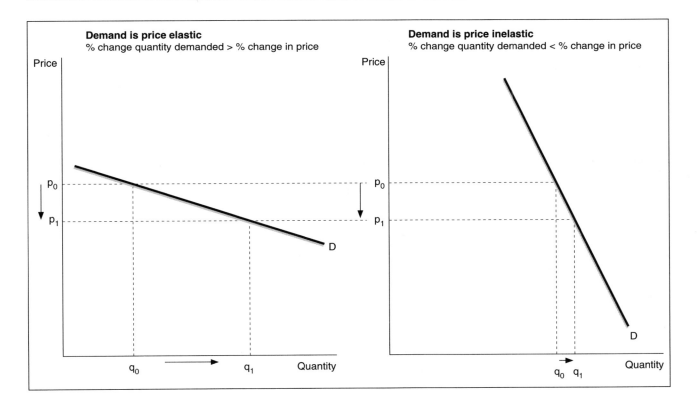

Demand is price elastic
% change quantity demanded > % change in price

Demand is price inelastic
% change quantity demanded < % change in price

Elasticity of demand (price, income and cross) continued

The size of the price elasticity of demand depends on:
- the number and availability of substitutes. If there are many substitutes available, consumers can easily switch away if the firm increases its price. Demand will be more price elastic.
- the time horizon. In the short run it may not be easy to find alternatives and so demand is likely to be price inelastic. Over time, consumers can shop around and search for more substitutes and so demand is likely to be more price elastic.
- the percentage of income spent on the good, e.g. consumers only spend a small percentage of their income on salt and so are not very sensitive to price changes in this product. Demand is price inelastic. By comparison, washing machines, personal computers, and holidays take

a greater percentage of income and households are more likely to look around for the best price. These goods are more price sensitive.
- the type of good. Some goods are habit forming and so tend to be price inelastic. In the extreme case this could be drugs, but is also true of items such as newspapers and brands of coffee.
- the width of the definition. If we define the category of goods and services we are interested in very widely, demand will be more price inelastic, e.g. if we look at the demand for one brand of butter or margarine, consumers can switch easily to another brand if the price goes up; if we look at all brands, consumers are less likely to give up the product altogether.

Price elasticity and a straight line demand curve

Price elasticity will vary on a downward sloping straight line demand curve from being elastic on the top left, unit elastic in the middle and inelastic at the bottom right.

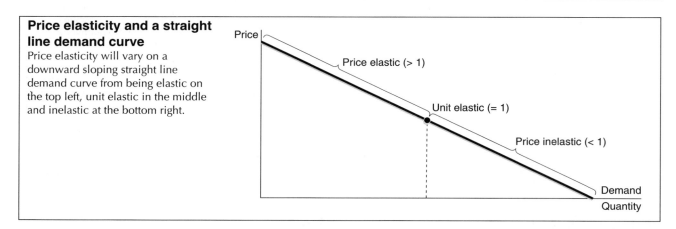

Extreme cases of price elasticity of demand

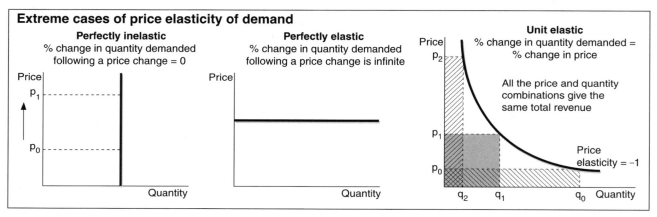

Price elasticity and revenue

If demand is price elastic, a fall in price will lead to an increase in revenue. Although each good is cheaper, the increase in the number demanded more than compensates for this and revenue increases overall.

If demand is price inelastic, a fall in price leads to a fall in revenue. The increase in the quantity demanded does not compensate for the fact that each unit is selling for less.

To increase revenue when demand is price inelastic, the firm should increase price.

If demand is unitary elastic the revenue does not change when price is changed.

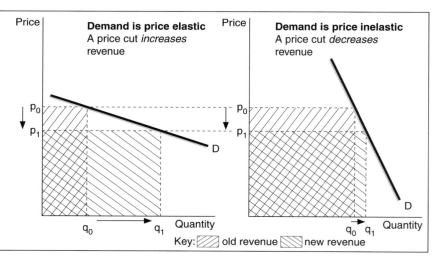

Elasticity of demand (price, income and cross) continued

Cross price elasticity of demand

Measures the sensitivity of the demand for one good to a change in price of another.

Cross price elasticity of good A with respect to good B =
percentage change in quantity demanded of good A
percentage change in the price of good B

If the two goods are substitutes, the cross price elasticity will be positive. If good B increases in price, people switch to good A and demand for A rises. If the goods are complements, such as golf clubs and golf balls, the sign will be negative. As the price of golf clubs rises, fewer people buy clubs and fewer people buy golf balls.

Income elasticity of demand

Measures the sensitivity of demand to a change in income.

percentage change in the quantity demanded
percentage change in income

The sign

If the good is normal, the income elasticity will be positive. As income rises, the quantity demanded rises. If the value is greater than 1, demand is income elastic, e.g. holidays abroad; these are often called 'luxuries', e.g. private health care. If the value is less than 1, demand is income inelastic, e.g. demand for bread; these are often 'necessities'.

If the good is inferior or Giffen, the income elasticity will be negative. With more income people switch from this good to a more superior good, e.g. they switch from supermarket branded products to a more exclusive brand name; from using buses to buying a car.

The size

The higher the figure (ignoring the sign), the greater the relationship between demand and income.

An Engels curve shows the relationship between income and quantity demanded (see diagram on right).

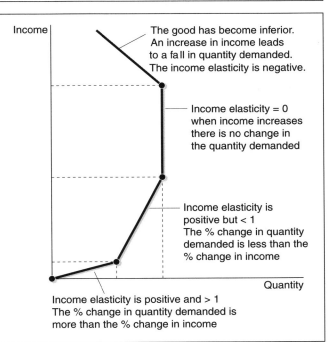

The good has become inferior. An increase in income leads to a fall in quantity demanded. The income elasticity is negative.

Income elasticity = 0 when income increases there is no change in the quantity demanded

Income elasticity is positive but < 1. The % change in quantity demanded is less than the % change in income

Income elasticity is positive and > 1. The % change in quantity demanded is more than the % change in income

Types of goods

	Normal goods	Inferior goods	Giffen goods
Price elasticity	NEGATIVE If price rises, quantity demanded falls. Downward sloping demand curve	NEGATIVE If price rises, quantity demanded falls. Downward sloping demand curve	POSITIVE If price rises quantity demanded rises. Upward sloping demand curve
Income elasticity	POSITIVE When income rises quantity demanded increases	NEGATIVE When income rises quantity demanded falls as consumers switch to more luxurious products	NEGATIVE When income rises quantity demanded falls as consumers switch to more luxurious products

Uses of elasticity

Uses of price elasticity

- used to determine pricing policy: if demand is price inelastic, firms will increase price to raise revenue; if demand is price elastic firms will decrease price.
- firms can use it for planning, e.g. by estimating the effect of a price change, firms can plan the number of goods to produce, the number of people to employ, and the impact on cashflow.
- used when price discriminating to set price in each market.
- used by the Government to estimate the impact of an indirect tax increase in terms of sales and tax revenue.
- used to estimate the impact on consumer spending, producers' revenue, and income of any shift in supply.

Uses of cross price elasticity

- firms can estimate the effect on their demand of a competitor's price cut.
- firms can estimate impact on demand for their product if other firms cut the price of a complement, e.g. if they cut the price of the computer, how much will demand for software increase?

Uses of income elasticity

- can determine what goods to produce or stock, e.g. as the economy grows, firms might want to avoid inferior goods.

- can help firms plan production and employee requirements as the economy grows.
- can help firms estimate any potential changes in demand, e.g. as overseas incomes grow it may create new markets.

Why price elasticity is important to government

Introducing a tax on goods or services will raise the price. This in turn will have an impact on the equilibrium price and quantity. If demand is relatively price inelastic (compared to supply), the burden of the indirect tax will fall on the buyer rather than the supplier. The impact is more on the price in the market than on the quantity consumed. If demand is more price elastic than supply, the burden of the indirect tax falls on the supplier and the impact is on quantity rather than on price.

Taxing products such as cigarettes and petrol has a relatively big effect on the final price paid by consumers compared to the quantity consumed.

Why income elasticity is important to government

If the government changes income tax this alters the disposable income of households, which in turn will affect their spending. The size of the impact depends on the income elasticity of demand; a high positive income elasticity of demand means the impact on spending will be relatively high.

Supply

A **supply curve** shows the quantity that producers are willing and able to supply at each and every price, all other things unchanged.

According to the **law of supply** a higher quantity will be supplied at higher prices, all other things unchanged. The supply curve is derived from the marginal cost curve; as the extra cost of producing a unit increases, producers need a higher price to produce the product.

The supply of a product will depend on factors such as the number of producers, the state of technology, the prices of factors of production, indirect taxes and Government subsidies, and the aims of producers.

Movements along a supply curve: extensions and contractions

A change in the price of a good will lead to a change in the quantity supplied; this is shown as a movement along the supply curve.

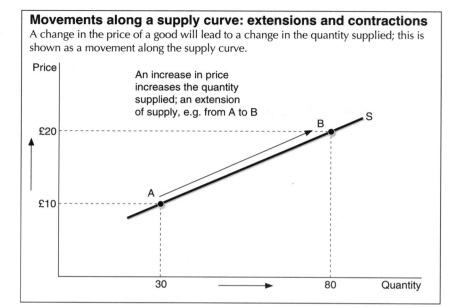

Shifts in supply

If other factors change (apart from the price) then more or less will be supplied at each and every price. This is shown as a shift in the supply curve or change in supply.

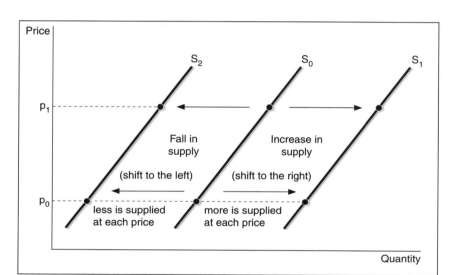

Outwards shifts in supply

If the supply curve shifts outwards, more is supplied at each and every price. This could be caused by:

- an increase in the number of suppliers
- an improvement in technology
- a fall in the prices of factors of production – if labour becomes cheaper, for example, more can be supplied at each price
- a cut in indirect tax or an increase in subsidies to producers
- a change in the prices of other goods, e.g. if good B falls in price, producers may switch their resources into good A, which will increase the supply of A
- other factors, e.g. changes in the weather can increase the supply of agricultural products; better management can improve the productivity of the workforce.

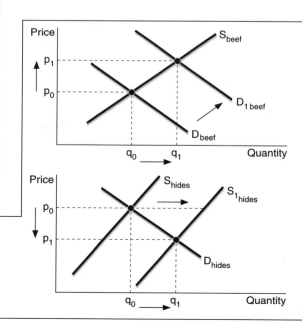

Beef market

An increase in demand for beef leads to more being supplied at a higher price

Hides market

An increase in the quantity of beef increases the supply of cattle hides at the old price p_0 and leads to a fall in the equilibrium price. (<u>Note</u>: Cattle hide is the skin of the cow)

Joint supply

This occurs when two or more goods are supplied together; a change in supply of one will change supply of the other, e.g. beef provides hides and meat. More beef equals more hides and more meat.

Supply continued

The price elasticity of supply

Measures the responsiveness of supply to a change in price.

$$\frac{\text{percentage change in the quantity supplied}}{\text{percentage change in the price}}$$

Size of answer (ignoring the sign)

- If the percentage change in supply is greater than the percentage change in price then supply is price elastic. The answer will be bigger than one.
- If the percentage change in supply is less than the percentage change in price then supply is inelastic.

Any straight line supply curve:
- drawn from the origin has a unit price elasticity of supply
- which would intersect with the price axis is price elastic
- which would intersect with the quantity axis is price inelastic

Price

Supply (price elasticity of supply > 1)

Elastic

Quantity

Price

Supply (price elasticity of supply = 1)

Unit elastic

Unit elastic

Supply (price elasticity of supply = 1)

Quantity

Price

Supply (price elasticity of supply < 1)

Inelastic

Quantity

Extreme cases of the price elasticity of supply

Price

Perfectly elastic (elasticity = infinity)

S

A change in price would lead to an infinite change in supply

Quantity

Price

S

P_1

P_0

Perfectly inelastic (elasticity = 0)

A change in price has no effect on the quantity supplied

Quantity

Determinants of the price elasticity of supply

- **the number of producers.** The more producers there are, the easier it should be for the industry to increase output in response to a price increase.
- **the existence of spare capacity.** The more capacity there is in the industry, the easier it should be to increase output if price goes up.
- **ease of storing stocks.** If it is easy to stock goods, then if the price rises the firm can sell these stocks and so supply is more elastic. In the case of goods such as fresh flowers, it may not be easy to store them and so the supply will not be very flexible.
- **the time period.** Over time the firm can invest in training and more equipment and more firms can join the industry, so supply should be more flexible, i.e. more elastic.
- **factor mobility,** i.e. the easier it is for resources to move into the industry, the more elastic supply will be.
- **length of the production period,** i.e. the quicker a good is to produce, the easier it will be to respond to a change in price; supply in manufacturing is usually more price elastic than agriculture.

Periods of supply

- Momentary: supply totally inelastic
- Short run: constrained by fixed factors; supply usually inelastic
- Long run: all factors are variable, so supply is more elastic

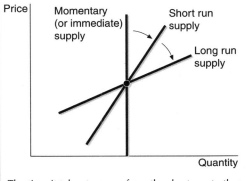

Price

Momentary (or immediate) supply

Short run supply

Long run supply

Quantity

The time it takes to move from the short run to the long run depends on how long it takes to change all the factors of production. This may take years, e.g. in the nuclear power sector, or weeks/months, e.g. for a local market stall.

Demand and supply

In the market system, resources are allocated by the price mechanism. The price will adjust to equate supply and demand.

The price mechanism

Rationing: given that resources are scarce and wants are infinite, the price mechanism rations demand so that it meets supply; e.g. if demand is greater than supply price increases to reduce the quantity demanded until equilibrium is reached.

Incentive: high prices act as an incentive to producers in other markets to leave them and come into this one because of the profits that can be earned.

Signalling: the price acts as a signal to producers; if prices increase this is a signal to produce more.

Equilibrium

Equilibrium occurs when the quantity supplied equals the quantity demanded and there is no incentive for change, i.e. there is a state of rest. This occurs at p_0q_0.

If the price is above the equilibrium price (e.g. p_1) there will be excess supply ($q_1 q_2$); the quantity supplied is greater than the quantity demanded and the price will fall. As it does this, the quantity demanded will increase and the quantity supplied will fall. This will continue until the quantity supplied equals the quantity demanded and equilibrium is reached (p_0q_0). If the price is below the equilibrium price, e.g. p_3, there will be excess demand (q_3q_4); the quantity demanded will be greater than the quantity supplied. In this situation the price will rise. This will increase the quantity supplied and reduce the quantity demanded until equilibrium (p_0q_0).

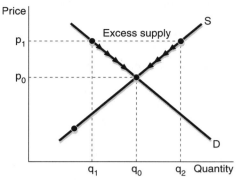

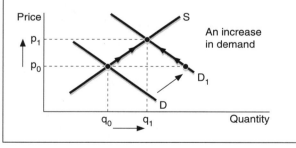

Condition	Description	Effect
quantity demanded > quantity supplied	excess demand/ shortage	price will rise
quantity demanded = quantity supplied	equilibrium	price remains the same
quantity demanded < quantity supplied	excess supply/ surplus	price will fall

The price mechanism: an increase in demand

If demand for a product increases, this will lead to excess demand at the old price. The price will rise reducing the quantity demanded (rationing device), encouraging existing firms to produce more (incentive), and encouraging others to join the industry (signal). This brings resources into this industry and out of another.

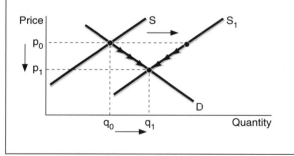

The price mechanism: an increase in supply

With an increase in supply the supply curve shifts to the right. At the old equilibrium price (p_0) there is excess supply. The price will fall, increasing the quantity demanded and decreasing the quantity supplied. The price falls until it reaches the new equilibrium at p_1q_1.

Price controls

A minimum price

This means that the price is not allowed to fall below a set level. If the market price is below this level the effect will be to create excess supply. For example, the Government has introduced a minimum wage rate. If this is set above the market rate, those who are still employed will earn more than before but there will be excess supply, i.e. the higher price will mean more people want to work but fewer are demanded.

Note: if the minimum price is below equilibrium it will have no effect.

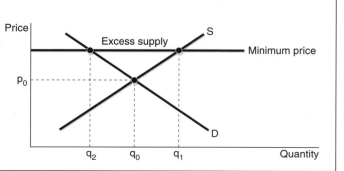

Demand and supply continued

Price controls
A maximum price

This sets a limit for the price, e.g. the Government might fix a maximum rent which can be charged. If the market price is above this level, the effect is to create excess demand. Maximum prices often cause a black market to arise whereby people start trading at the market price rather than the 'official price', e.g. tickets for concerts are sometimes set lower than the market prices, which is why ticket touts buy them at the fixed price and sell them for more.

Note: if the maximum price is above equilibrium it will have no effect.

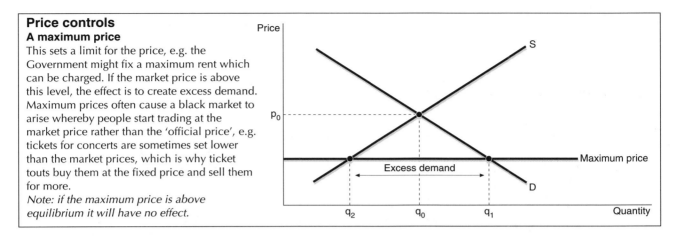

No equilibrium

It may not be possible to supply a good because there is no equilibrium price.

This good will not be produced – the highest price consumers are willing to pay (p_0) is less than the minimum price producers need to supply (p_1)

Indirect taxes

Indirect taxes are taxes placed on the supplier and have the effect of raising costs.

There are two types:

a **ad valorem taxes** which add a certain *percentage* on to the price

b **specific (or per unit) taxes** which add a fixed *amount* of money on to the costs.

Suppliers try to pass these increased costs on to the consumer. Their ability to do this depends on the relative elasticities of demand and supply.

- If demand is more inelastic than supply the consumers will pay the greater proportion (or have the greater incidence of) the taxation
- If supply is more inelastic than demand the producer will pay the greater incidence of taxation.

Tax yield

When an indirect tax is first introduced, the yield (i.e. the revenue generated for the Government) automatically increases because there was none to begin with. When increasing the tax the yield will not necessarily increase:

- when indirect taxes are increased, the yield will increase if demand and supply are relatively inelastic.
- if an indirect tax is increased and demand and supply are relatively elastic, the yield will fall. Although the tax per unit is higher, the fall in the number bought reduces the overall revenue to the Government.

To maximize revenue the Government can widen the tax base, i.e. tax more goods and services; by taxing more goods the consumers will find it less easy to switch to a cheaper alternative and so demand is inelastic.

Ad valorem tax

Specific tax
(per unit tax)

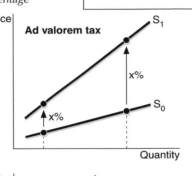

Tax = ab per unit. Consumer pays an additional p_0p_1. Less is paid by the producer because demand is more inelastic than supply

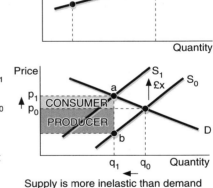

Supply is more inelastic than demand so producers pay the greater incidence of tax

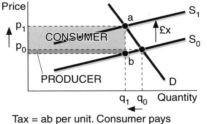

A tax is placed on producers, supply shifts S_0 to S_1. Tax revenue for the Government is $p_1$bfe. Tax is increased, supply shifts S_1 to S_2. Tax revenue is now $p_2$cgh. Revenue for the Government (or yield) has increased because demand is inelastic

Agricultural markets (primary products)

Producers in agricultural markets face two problems:
- long run downward trend in prices
- short run price instability

Short run price instability of agricultural products
- inelastic demand because food is a necessity
- inelastic short run supply (e.g. due to difficulties holding stocks; long production period)
- supply is vulnerable to sudden shifts, e.g. changes in the weather

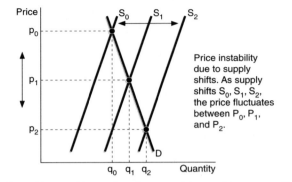

Price instability due to supply shifts. As supply shifts S_0, S_1, S_2, the price fluctuates between P_0, P_1, and P_2.

Note: Commodity markets in general (e.g. gold, wheat, oil and silver) experience major changes in prices due to changes in demand and price inelastic supply and demand.

Long run downward trend of agricultural prices
- supply is increasing due to better technology, e.g. fertilizers, machinery
- demand is not growing fast as demand is income inelastic

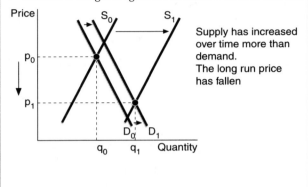

Supply has increased over time more than demand.
The long run price has fallen

Price instability and incomes
Unstable prices also mean unstable incomes for farmers and other producers of primary products. If demand is inelastic it also means that producers earn more in bad years than in good ones; with a fall in supply, prices increase and producers earn more!

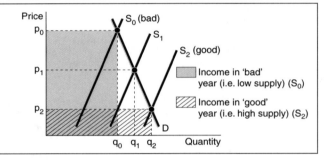

Income in 'bad' year (i.e. low supply) (S_0)

Income in 'good' year (i.e. high supply) (S_2)

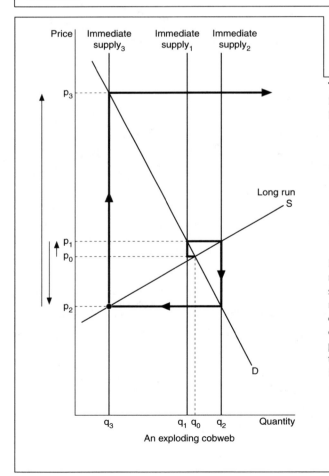

An exploding cobweb

The cobweb model
Highlights price instability in agricultural markets.
It is assumed that
- in the immediate run supply is totally inelastic; farmers cannot increase their output once a crop has been grown and taken to market until next season
- a farmer's decision about how much to produce next season depends on the price this season because it takes one season for the crop to grow, so they must plant it now (this is known as 'adaptive expectations')
- the long run supply is more elastic than the immediate run; this is because over time farmers can decide how many resources to devote to this crop and so can increase or decrease output.

Equilibrium is originally at p_0 q_0 until a sudden supply shock, e.g. a natural disaster reduces the crop available to q_1. Given the fall in supply the price rises to p_1. Farmers then decide how much to plant next year; given the high price p_1 they decide to supply q_2. At the end of the next year q_2 is produced; because this is much more crop than before, the price falls to p_2. Farmers now look at the low price p_2 and decide to cut back on production to q_3. At the end of the next period they produce this and the price increases to p_3. This is a signal to plant much more next period. This process continues.

- If the demand curve is more inelastic than the supply curve this causes an exploding cobweb, i.e. ever greater swings in the price level further and further from the equilibrium price.
- If the demand curve is more elastic than the supply curve it causes an imploding cobweb, where the price gradually moves back towards equilibrium.

Agricultural markets (primary products) continued

Buffer stock schemes

A buffer stock is a safety stock held to help reduce price instability.
Prices are fixed at a given level (or within a specific range); if there is excess supply at this price the Government buys it up; if there is excess demand the Government sells its stocks.

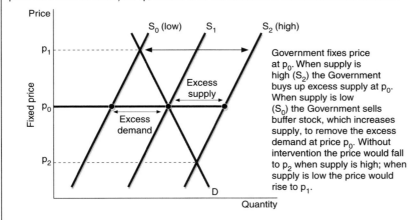

Government fixes price at p_0. When supply is high (S_2) the Government buys up excess supply at p_0. When supply is low (S_0) the Government sells buffer stock, which increases supply, to remove the excess demand at price p_0. Without intervention the price would fall to p_2 when supply is high; when supply is low the price would rise to p_1.

Problems of a buffer stock scheme

- storage costs
- some goods may be perishable
- administration costs
- if the Government sets the price too high (as it has in Europe) it is continually buying up crops – this has led to wine lakes and butter mountains. This is likely to be a continuing problem as technology improves, so the equilibrium price should often be lower than the price originally set
- there may be inadequate supplies if there are many bad years
- to raise finance for this intervention, taxes have to be increased
- intervention in other areas of the economy might be more important

Guaranteed price scheme

The Government guarantees a price, e.g. p_1. Farmers therefore produce q_1. The market clearing price for this quantity is p_2 (i.e. this is the price at which this quantity is demanded) and so the Government pays a subsidy to the farmers equal to p_2p_1 per unit. Total subsidy: p_1abp_2.
Note: by allowing the market to clear, this system means the Government does not have to store the crops.

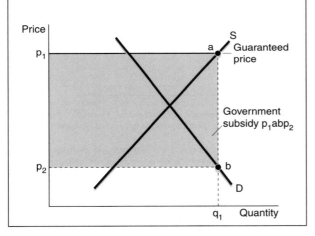

European Common Agricultural Policy (CAP)

Aims to ensure supplies of food to the consumer within Europe and ensure an adequate return to the farmers. The European Union system taxes imported foodstuffs to increase their price to the level of European crops. It also runs a buffer stock scheme.

Set aside policy

This approach by the EU pays farmers for producing cereal crops on their land but insists they do not actually produce anything! This is to prevent excess supplies of grain throughout Europe, which the European Union would have to buy up.

Income support schemes

A scheme which keeps the price that farmers receive constant, still leads to unstable incomes. Alternatively the Government can stabilize income but this means prices will still fluctuate.

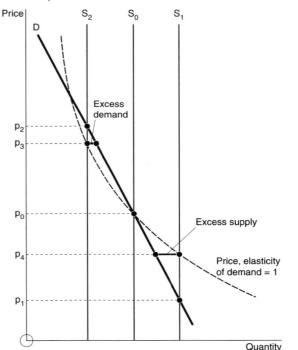

In a free market the price would fluctuate from p_0, p_1 and p_2 and incomes would fluctuate. Government sets prices from the unit elastic demand curve so that farmers' incomes are constant, ie p_3, p_0, p_4. When supply is S_1 Government sets price p_4. At this price there is excess supply; Government buys this up creating a buffer stock. When supply is S_2 Government sets price p_3. There is excess demand so Government sells buffer stock.

High wheat prices

The price of wheat has increased significantly in recent years due to:
- increased demand due to rising incomes and world population
- reduced supply as crops are switched to be used as biofuels
- speculators buying up crops in the hopes that prices will rise even further

Markets: transport

Transport involves the movement of people and goods between destinations.
A mode of transport is the method of moving passengers and freight. The main modes of transport are: road, air, sea and pipelines.
Transport economics deals with the allocation of resources within the transport sector used to move passengers and freight from one place to another. In transport, demand can be measured in various ways, such as numbers of journeys or total distance travelled. Demand decisions include: what journey to make, what mode of transport to choose and when to make the journey.
Supply depends on the capacity of the transport systems to carry passengers. Given the privatization of many transport operators (e.g. coach, bus and train), supply decisions in the UK are increasingly made by private sector firms. The price of travel includes the cost of travelling in money and time terms (i.e. what are you giving up by travelling in this way).
Transport generates positive and negative externalities:
- positive externalities: can increase land values in an area and can stimulate economic activity in a region.
- negative externalities: air pollution, noise pollution, safety hazards and congestion.

Transport and travel
UK transport market
- Transport is a service. It includes rail, road, waterways and pipelines. It involves the movement of people (passenger transport) and goods (freight transport). Output may be measured in terms of how far has been travelled, e.g. passenger miles or how much has been transported, e.g. tonnes.
- Transport is usually regarded as a *derived demand* – you usually travel to get somewhere or to deliver products rather than for the experience of travelling in itself (this is not always the case, e.g. you may choose a cruise ship holiday because you enjoy the experience).

Resources in the transport market are allocated by a combination of Government and the market mechanism
For example, the Government decides:
- what roads to build
- which roads are to be maintained and improved.
- In the UK most roads are provided free at the point of use financed by the Government (in other countries motorways are often run by private companies which charge a toll to users).

However, the market mechanism works in that:
- privately owned bus companies charge for their services as do e.g. taxi companies
- freight companies charge customers
- individuals have to pay for their cars

Deciding how to travel
This may depend on:
- Availability of a particular option. In 2000 problems with the rail network led to increased road usage and more people using air travel within the UK. If you want to go house to house, road is almost the only option.
- Costs. In the short run travellers will compare the marginal cost of a trip, e.g. the cost of a train ticket compared with the cost of petrol used in a car journey. In the long run travellers should consider all the costs, e.g. whether it is worth replacing the car or not.
- Speed. How urgent is the journey? The time taken on a journey involves an *opportunity cost* – this time could be used to do other things. Travellers should consider the cost of each minute spent travelling.
- Reliability. The decision about which method of transport to choose may depend on the reliability of a particular option, e.g. if bad weather causes high levels of train cancellations or delays you may choose to go by car.
- Safety. Travellers will consider the likelihood of an accident before travelling, e.g. following an air disaster the number of people travelling by plane may decline.

PUBLIC SECTOR ➡ **PRIVATE SECTOR**
privatization

Many providers of transport have been privatized in the UK, e.g. in the bus, coach, rail and air sectors. However, through organizations such as the Office of the Rail Regulator (ORR), the Government regulates to monitor private sector transport operators such as Train Operating Companies (TOCs) like Virgin Rail.

Government transport policy objectives
Objectives are likely to include or take into account:
- Efficiency. If the Government can make the transport system more efficient, e.g. reduce congestion, this can reduce the distribution costs for firms and make them more efficient. Poor roads or a poor rail system make distribution slower and expensive. This leads to a poorer service and greater costs which is likely to lead to higher prices for consumers.
- Environmental issues. Transport creates negative externalities. Individuals using the road, for example, do not consider the social costs of their actions. Transport leads to noise and air pollution. Building of roads, airports, etc can also impact on wildlife and the environment. Transport also creates accidents; car drivers do not take into account the costs of such accidents when they decide to use the car.
- Accessibility. It may be argued that everyone should have the ability to travel around their country. On this basis the transport system should

be suitable to enable people to get from A to B. This is vital for a variety of activities such as seeing friends and getting their shopping. People in a rural area should be able to get around as much as people in a city.
- Public finance. The amount that a Government spends on transport obviously has an impact on the amount of tax which needs to be raised or on spending on other areas. Transport spending must therefore be put in context of other Government issues and demands.
- Integrated transport policy. This means that policies in different areas of the transport system are integrated into a coherent whole, e.g. decisions about the rail system are taken in the context of what is happening with the road network. There may be no point building a new railway station, for example, unless it is accessible by road so commuters can get to it.

UK transport facts
- Car access. The percentage of households in Great Britain with access to two cars more than quadrupled between 1971 and 2006, rising from 6% to 26%. The percentage of households with access to one car remained stable at around 45%.
- In 2006, 80% of the distance travelled in the UK was by car. This percentage has remained fairly stable since 1995–97. The average time spent travelling by residents of Great Britain has increased by 4% from 1995–97 to 383 hours per person per year, or just over an hour a day. Of this, around 38 minutes were spent travelling by car.
- Over 4.7 billion journeys were made by local bus in Great Britain in 2005–06, more than double the number of journeys made by rail (2.2 billion).
In terms of passenger journeys, use of both bus and rail declined during the 1970s. Rail use has been increasing, in general, since the early 1980s, while the number of journeys on local buses continued to fall until 1998–99, before increasing slightly. Travel in London accounts for well over a third of all GB passenger journeys on local buses.

Forecasting transport levels
Could:
- use extrapolation: basing future levels on past trends
- consider forecasts, e.g. for population and income, and estimate the possible impact of these on different forms of transport
- use expert opinion
- consider supply issues, e.g. road building projects, as these will affect usage.

Forecasts are important to firms involved in this industry. What is the likely demand for new cars or shipping? Will investment in particular services/routes prove profitable? How much is it worth bidding for particular routes? The Government will also be interested. What is the likely environmental impact? What will be the likely impact on tax revenue?

Markets: transport continued

Degree of competition within the transport industry

- There is some competition *between* different forms of transport, e.g. you can drive somewhere, take a train or take a boat. However, it depends on where you are going, when you want to go and when you want to get there. Within each transport sector there are varying degrees of competition. The amount of competition partly depends on how the market is defined. The bus industry, for example, has a few firms competing across the country and therefore can be seen as an oligopoly. However, within an area only one firm may be providing a particular route and so the provider has a local monopoly.
- The airline industry is relatively competitive both within a country and between countries. However, firms try to brand their products to differentiate their offerings. They also run particular routes – there may not be much competition on a particular route on a particular day. Entry into the airline market can be a problem because it can be difficult gaining landing slots at the major airports. Also it can be difficult getting permission to fly to particular countries which control the number of foreign airlines coming into their country. There is an 'open skies' policy within the EU, i.e. any airline of an EU member country can fly anywhere within the EU, but this is not generally true elsewhere.
- Shipping. For freight this is a relatively competitive market with many providers offering similar services. For passengers there are often only one or two providers on a particular route.

The potential abuse of monopoly power within the transport sector depends on the degree of regulation, e.g. the rail companies which have a franchise for a particular route are regulated by the Government.

Road

External costs of road transport
Road traffic causes external costs:
- noise pollution
- congestion: increasing journey time
- air pollution
- impact on buildings caused by vibration
- impact on local environment, e.g. accidents with wildlife
- blight, i.e. roads can destroy the view and scenery
- stress, i.e. it can cause frustration if caught up in congestion (road rage)

The divergence between the social and private costs of motoring can lead to a misallocation of resources.

	Advantage	Disadvantage
Road	Convenient and flexible: can go door to door, can travel when you want; comfortable; you can get a seat	High on pollution; stressful for drivers; can be expensive and slow, e.g. if congestion; possible road charges
Rail	Fast over long journeys; safe; relatively environmentally friendly compared to cars; can use work while travelling	Limited routes; lack of flexibility, e.g. timetables; can be busy on certain routes
Air	Fast for long distances	Expensive; limited routes and timetables; airport taxes; pollutes
Sea	Cheap for transporting large volumes	Slow; limited number of ports; port taxes; requires transportation to and from ports
Bus	Better for the environment than car, for example; can be relatively cheap	May not go when or exactly where you want to travel; may be crowded and uncomfortable

Rail
The rail industry now consists of:
- *Railtrack* This is the owner of the existing rail infrastructure. Responsible for upgrading and maintaining all the elements of the system such as track and bridges.
- *Train-operating companies* These provide the service itself, e.g. Virgin. These companies have a franchise to run a service for several years.
- The trains themselves are rented from *leasing companies*.
- Goods are transported by *freight companies*.

Transport systems
- Enable goods to be sold in new markets.
- Enable customers and employees to travel to more places creating new purchase and job opportunities.
- Enable businesses to choose from a wider range of suppliers.

Transport substitutes
The different forms of transport available may be substitutes for each other (although there may be cases where not all forms of transport are actually available).

Factors affecting the choice of the mode of freight transport
- speed
- convenience
- network coverage
- cost
- environmental impact

Demand for transport
Composite demand: the demand for roads is a composite demand in that it is demanded by private and commercial users; when the demand from these different groups is high this can lead to congestion.
Peak demand: there are times of the day, week, month and year where demand for transport systems is particularly high – these are peak periods (e.g. on commuter trains before 9 am). This often creates congestion as the supply cannot cope with this volume of traffic.

Government influences on transport
- Taxes, e.g. on airline travel and fuel, and subsidies, e.g. public transport
- Regulation and deregulation
- Direct provision

Evaluating government policies to reduce congestion
Consider the following.
- Who will pay – is it fair?
- Administrative costs
- Costs of monitoring and policing
- Political impact, e.g. likely impact on votes
- Funding implications (e.g. if subsidising public transport)
- Accuracy of estimates of external costs

Should the government subsidize public transport?
- Makes public transport cheaper, which should encourage people to switch to this from private transport; this is better for the environment.
- May help lower income groups and therefore be socially desirable.
But
- May subsidize inefficiency; may remove motivation to keep costs down.
- How will subsidies be used? Is it better to improve the quality and comfort of the service or reduce the price (how price sensitive is demand?).
- Opportunity cost of government funding – will this create distortions through tax elsewhere? Could the money be better used elsewhere?

Promoting sustainable transport
Sustainable transport tries to ensure that resources are available for the next generation; in transport we need to consider issues such as how far food has travelled to get to the consumer – what has the impact been on the environment?

Evaluating regulation as a means of reducing road usage
Consider the following.
- The cost of enforcing and monitoring the regulation; this may mean that the costs exceed the possible benefits.
- May be difficult to determine what level of regulation is actually needed in the first place to achieve the socially optimal level of production/consumption.
- The effectiveness of regulation will depend on how it is monitored and policed, e.g. how much is the fine and what is the probability of getting caught?
- It may take time to introduce because of the time lag of introducing the legislation.

Markets: transport continued

Examples of UK government transport aims
- Improved/new bus services
- Incentives for drivers to leave their cars at home
- Better train services
- Joined-up thinking on transport
- Anti-congestion measures
- Light rail systems
- Road pricing

Transport demand
Demand for passenger transport depends on:
- Prices. The average price of transport in the UK has risen in line with inflation. However, the price of rail, bus and coach has increased much faster than inflation in the 1980s and 1990s; this is mainly due to lower subsidies and more private operators seeking to increase profits. Changes in price lead to a movement along the demand curve.
- Real incomes. With more income the demand for travel will increase.
- Population trends. An increase in population is likely to increase demand for travel.
- Social trends. If families are more geographically divided and more people commute to work, the demand for travel will increase.
- Government policies. E.g. subsidies, town planning, spending on the infrastructure.

The amount of passenger transport has almost quadrupled over the past 50 years. This is mainly due to car travel. Over 90% of passenger kilometres and over 60% of freight tonnage kilometres in the UK are by road.

Demand for road travel
The demand for road space:
- Depends on individual decisions to travel.
- Is derived – people do not want the journey itself but to get to somewhere. The greater the benefit of getting somewhere the greater the demand for road space.

Demand depends on:
- The marginal (extra) costs of a journey, e.g. petrol, maintenance and depreciation. The price elasticity for road travel is low and so attempts to reduce usage purely by higher charges are not likely to have major effects on the quantity demanded.
- Income. As incomes rise, car ownership and usage increase significantly as the income elasticity of demand. This means that continued economic growth will increase car ownership and usage.
- Price of substitutes. If prices of alternatives such as buses and trains come down, people may switch to these. However, the cross price elasticity of demand is relatively low as people tend to regard these as poor substitutes for car travel. The speed and relative comfort of the journeys will be factors in the decision to switch.
- Price of complements. The demand for road space will depend on the price of vehicles and the price of parking.

Possible reasons for demand for cars rising
- Price of substitute increasing, e.g. bus, coach, train fares.
- Fall in own price; cost of motoring falling.

Supply of road space
- In the short run, supply is fixed (inelastic); roads cannot be built quickly. The demand will fluctuate according to the time of day and in peak periods there can be congestion as demand is high relative to supply. At other times of day demand may be much lower than supply.
- In the long run, supply depends on the road building programme by the authorities. This will depend on an assessment of the costs and benefits of each proposal. Many road building projects are opposed by pressure groups because of the damage to the environment or community.

Costs of traffic congestion
- Costs of running the vehicle
- Costs if there is an accident
- Slower journey time
- Increased negative externalities such as noise and air pollution

The optimal level of road usage
A socially efficient level of road usage occurs when the marginal social benefit equals the marginal social cost of a journey.
The marginal social benefit is mainly the benefit to the individual car driver plus any benefits to others travelling with them.
The marginal social cost includes private costs (such as depreciation and petrol) plus external costs such as the costs of pollution and congestion in terms of, for example, other people's time and the environment.

Should the government increase the price of motoring?
The increase in demand for transport is mainly due to motoring so increasing the price might reduce the amount of car travel (e.g. by increasing the tax on car ownership or on petrol).
However, demand for car travel is price inelastic and therefore the fall in demand is proportionately less than the increase in price (for many journeys there are few or no options other than car travel).

How can the government improve the allocation of resources for road travel?
Direct provision
Build more roads. However, this does have equity effects, e.g. the impact on those living next to motorways, the effect of greater private transport in terms of reducing public transport provision (e.g. what if you are poorer and want public transport). Also, more roads may simply generate more traffic (e.g. more journeys made or less public transport used). More roads also have a negative impact on the environment.
Greater provision of public transport to encourage people to switch from cars. This would require frequent, cheap and comfortable services.

Changing market signals to achieve the socially efficient level of transport and prevent too much damage to the environment
This involves using the price mechanism to affect demand:
- use more taxes, e.g. fuel tax, taxes on new cars and car licences. The last two increase the fixed costs of having a new car but not the marginal cost, so do not discourage extra journeys once you have a car. Fuel taxes do increase the marginal cost; however, given the price inelasticity of demand a big increase in fuel tax would be needed to discourage travel. This would affect all drivers and not just those using roads in peak times in congested areas, so may be seen as unfair. Also higher car tax is politically unpopular so governments are reluctant to increase it.
- Road pricing: taxes could be placed at set times in set locations and the price could change according to the level of congestion. This would target specific users, unlike fuel tax. Methods include:
  – variable tolls on roads
  – charges to enter certain areas at certain times
  – electronic road pricing systems; the greater the congestion the greater the price paid by motorists using those roads. Systems include reading sensors fitted into cars or scanning number plates. Issues include the costs of installing, how politically popular it will be, the optimum charges and how to inform motorists in advance so they can choose when they travel.
- Subsidizing alternative means of transport; this probably requires not just cheaper fares but investment in the facilities and systems to improve the quality of service.
- Regulation and legislation:
  – Local or central government could intervene in the market to try and reduce road travel, e.g. by restricting car access (e.g. having bus lanes, preventing car access to city centres). The danger here is that this simply moves congestion from one area to another.
  – Parking restrictions, e.g. prevent parking in busy streets to help traffic flow. This may lead to problems such as people driving around looking for spaces, thus adding to congestion, and illegal parking causing safety hazards.

Evaluating the use of government subsidies to promote public transport
Consider the following.
- The financial cost to the government
- Opportunity cost
- The success of the subsidy depends upon the level at which it is set (is it set equal to the external benefits of public transport?)
- Effectiveness depends on the price elasticity of demand; a given subsidy has less effect if demand is price inelastic
- May encourage inefficiency if firms become reliant on the subsidies
- Depends what the subsidy is used for, e.g. does it improve the quality and convenience of public transport?

Air travel
Demand for air transport in the UK and in Europe is growing faster. This is causing severe concerns over the environmental damage caused by air travel. The main features of UK air travel in recent years are:
- the growth of budget airlines such as EasyJet and Ryanair
- increased capacity at UK's airports, e.g. Terminal 5 at Heathrow
- the use of air travel as an alternative to road or rail journeys, e.g. journeys to Spain or France.

Train travel
A big development has been the construction of the Channel Tunnel Rail Link (CTRL). This was a Public Private Partnership and cost over £5bn.

Markets: housing

The housing market is important because a booming housing market gives people confidence and encourages spending. If homeowners see the value of their house increasing they are more likely to spend. Also if people are moving or buying homes they often need more consumer durables (e.g. washing machines, carpets, wardrobes).

There is no single market for housing; it depends on which region you are considering as market conditions can vary considerably. It also depends on which sector is being considered, e.g. private housing or council housing. The market for family accommodation in the South East is very different from the market for flats in the North, for example.

Types of tenure
- *Owner occupation.* Individuals own their own houses; this accounts for around 70% of the housing stock in the UK since 1980 when it became possible for people to buy their council houses.
- *Private rented.* Individuals rent from other individuals.
- *Social (or public) rented.* Individuals rent from the state or local council; this sector has fallen in importance in the UK since the 1980s.
- *Housing associations.* This is a relatively new sector. Housing associations are in effect a mix between the private sector and the public sector. Combined private sector finance and Government funding ensure the provision of subsidized accommodation for tenants who pay rent. Recent legislation has encouraged the establishment of such associations.

House prices
In the free market house prices are determined by supply and demand. With an increase in demand prices will rise. With a fall in demand prices will fall.

Demand and supply conditions can be very different between regions, causing major differences in house prices. Also over time conditions can change (e.g in a boom demand is likely to rise) and this leads to fluctuations. Because houses are the major item of expenditure for most people in their lives and their main assets such changes are very significant in terms of their impact of their income and wealth.

After several years of growth, house prices fell in the UK in 2008. Worries about the economy, slower economic growth and tougher lending terms reduced demand, bringing down prices.

Demand for owner-occupied housing will be influenced by:
- Income. Demand for housing is likely to be income elastic. With more income people trade up to better houses.
- Population trends. Increases in the population will increase demand; however it is not just the absolute number of people that matters, it also depends on social trends. For example, in the UK more households have been created as people choose to live on their own, as more divorces have occurred because people are living longer and people leave home at earlier age.
- Price and availability of substitutes. Demand for houses will increase if the price of rented accommodation rises or it becomes more difficult to find.
- Mortgages. The ability of people to buy a house will depend on how easy and expensive it is to get a mortgage. A mortgage is a form of borrowing in which the property is used as collateral. The greater the ease of getting a mortgage and the lower the cost of borrowing, the higher demand for houses will be.
- Social attitudes. Owner-occupied homes are much more popular in the UK than in other European countries such as Germany.
- Speculation. People may demand houses because they think there is going to be a property boom and that prices will increase more in the future.
- Government policy. The Government may encourage the ownership of houses by giving tax relief on the interest paid on mortgages. This makes it cheaper to repay. Also the way in which financial institutions are regulated can affect their ability to lend for housing. In the 1980s the UK Government significantly deregulated the financial institutions, making it easier to borrow money and thus increasing demand for owner-occupied housing. Also in 1980 the Housing Act encouraged people in council houses to buy their own houses.

The supply of owner-occupied housing will be influenced by:
- Price. If price is rising, this will encourage individuals to sell their own house and more building will be encouraged. Also landlords of rented accommodation may become tempted to sell their houses. As a result the supply of owner-occupied housing will increase.
- Prices of the factors of production. A rise in wages or in the price of land may make it less viable to build more houses and sell at a profit.
- Government policy. Subsidies to building firms would increase the supply of houses. Also, the ability to build houses will depend on how easy it is to get permission to build in a particular area.
- Technology. This will affect the speed with which houses can be built and the cost of building, e.g. some firms are now producing house parts in a factory and then assembling them on site.

Negative equity
This occurs when house prices fall and individuals find that their house is now worth less than the loan they originally took to buy it. This happened in the early 1990s and 2008 in the UK when the recession brought house prices down. People who had borrowed in the boom to buy their houses (which were usually increasing in price at that time) found they now had negative equity. If people cannot repay their mortgage their property may be repossessed by the bank. Falling house prices and negative equity reduce consumer confidence and are likely to reduce demand throughout the economy.

Markets: housing continued

Rent controls

The Government may try to limit rents by imposing a maximum price. The aim would be to make housing more affordable. The consequences of rent controls can be shown below:

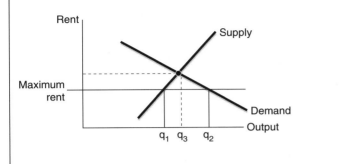

Given the maximum rent, the quantity supplied falls compared to equilibrium (q_3 to q_1) whilst quantity demanded increases (q_3 to q_2). The result is *excess demand*. Those who are in rented accommodation (q_1) benefit from lower rents but note how fewer people are in such accommodation compared to the free market (q_1 compared to q_3).

The extent of the excess demand depends on:

(a) how much the maximum rent is below equilibrium
(b) the price elasticity of demand and supply.

Publicly rented accommodation

The supply of this type of accommodation depends on the Government's willingness to invest in and maintain council houses. The importance of this type of housing has been decreasing in recent years. It is now less than one fifth of the housing stock.

Local authorities are obliged by law to provide housing for those declaring themselves to be homeless. Those meeting various criteria (e.g. pregnant women, people with children, old people) may also need to be housed by the local authority if no other form of housing exists. Demand from these groups exceeds supply and so demand has to be rationed by using a waiting list.

An increase in demand increases prices

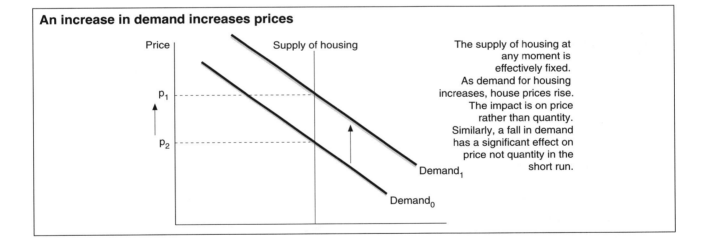

The supply of housing at any moment is effectively fixed. As demand for housing increases, house prices rise. The impact is on price rather than quantity. Similarly, a fall in demand has a significant effect on price not quantity in the short run.

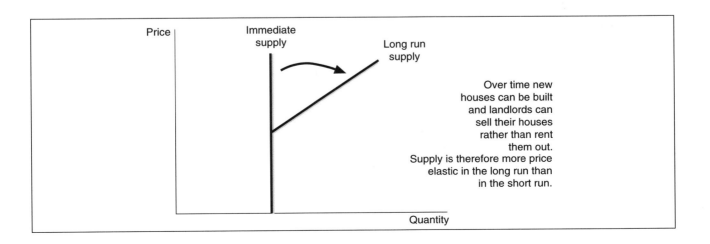

Over time new houses can be built and landlords can sell their houses rather than rent them out. Supply is therefore more price elastic in the long run than in the short run.

Markets: sport and leisure

Sport and leisure are fast-growing sectors in the UK. They are both income elastic so as economies grow, demand for these services grows more than proportionately.

Time spent on sport and leisure activities depends on:
- how many hours people work
- how many hours are spent on 'maintenance', e.g. washing, cooking and eating; with more appliances and easier access to e.g. takeaway foods. In recent years people have been spending less time on maintenance, leaving more time for sport and leisure.

Choosing between work and leisure

The choice between work and leisure will depend on the opportunity cost of staying at home. This depends on:
- benefits available to the unemployed
- earnings in work
- the tax rate when working
- the threshold at which tax begins to be paid.

The greater the earnings at work, the greater the opportunity cost of leisure. However, if earnings keep increasing, employees can work fewer hours and still earn enough money.

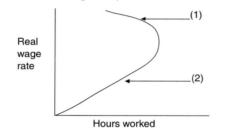

1 At high wage rates people may work less because they can still achieve a target income level
2 As wage rates begin to increase, people work more hours

Use of leisure time

The most popular home based activity in the UK is watching television! Other popular activities include:
- visiting/entertaining
- listening to the radio
- listening to CDs
- reading books
- DIY
- gardening

The most common leisure activity outside the home is going to the pub! Some leisure activities are more popular with some social groups than others, e.g. a visit to the library is more popular with higher socio-economic groups.

Watching/listening to sport

The numbers of adults watching sports is much higher than the number participating. They may watch it live or on television or listen to the radio.

The supply of seats and tickets at sporting events is fixed at any moment, e.g. the number of tickets to a football ground. This means there will be shortages if demand is too high. This can lead to a black market developing where ticket touts are selling tickets for more than their face value. The same is obviously true for many leisure events such as pop concerts.

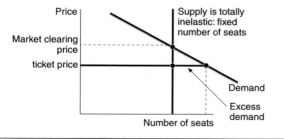

The pricing at sports events is likely to vary according to where people sit and what facilities they get access to or even what match is being played. The price should depend on the expected level of demand and the price elasticity of demand. Prices should be higher if there are higher levels of demand and/or demand is price inelastic.

Revenue for sporting providers is generated not just from the tickets but also the merchandising, e.g. football clubs sell replica football kits and videos of games.

How do we spend our leisure time in the UK?
- Men in the UK are more likely than women to watch TV or listen to the radio and take part in 'other leisure' activities including sport, entertainment, hobbies and using the computer (224 minutes per day compared with 180 minutes per day for women in 2005). Women were more likely than men to spend time reading or socializing with other people (113 minutes per day compared with 100 minutes per day). Computers are increasingly used at home for a range of activities, such as contact with friends, helping the children with homework and listening to music. On average, men spent 28 minutes per day using a computer and women 13 minutes.
- Women spend more time than men cooking and washing up, cleaning and tidying, washing clothes and shopping (159 minutes per day compared with 71 minutes per day for men). Men spend more time performing DIY repairs and gardening (23 minutes per day compared with 11 minutes per day for women). (Office for Natonal Statistics.)

Hosting sports or leisure events, e.g. a pop concert
- Brings revenue to the area; can help regenerate an area.
- Generates jobs both in terms of jobs directly connected with staging the event and secondary industries, e.g. supplying the food, security.
- May raise status/awareness of an area, bringing in tourists/visitors.

But
- May have environmental impact, e.g. noise and litter at a concert.
- May not be profit making, e.g. the Millennium Dome had financial difficulties as it did not attract as many people as expected.

Spectator sports

The main spectator sport is the UK is football. Other popular ones include rugby and cricket. Interestingly the product is non-homogeneous, i.e. one rugby match is different from another. Demand conditions will vary for each match.

Barriers to entry into the spectator market include:
- There is brand loyalty to particular clubs which can make it difficult for new clubs to start up.
- The cost of running clubs also makes it difficult for newcomers to set up.
- Location, since people in a particular area tend to support their local club (although not exclusively!); this again makes it difficult for new firms to set up.

Major clubs have some monopoly power and can exploit this by charging higher prices for tickets, e.g. demand for Premier League matches is price-inelastic so revenue can be increased by raising the price. Clubs also **price discriminate**, i.e. charge different prices for different matches, different types of customers (e.g. corporate customers).

Markets: sport and leisure continued

Participation in sports, games and physical activities

- Approximately 60% of adults play sport regularly (i.e. take part in at least one activity a month). The most popular activity is swimming, followed by keep-fit.
- More men take part than women, and younger people take part more than older people. Socio-economic grouping also plays an important part – nearly three-quarters of ABs, but only a third of Es, take part regularly.
- Nearly half of those who take part in sports and exercise do so at a local authority sports centre, and around a third at a private gym.
- The main reason for taking part in sport is to keep fit, followed by relaxation and the social aspects of sport.
- Men tend to take part in team and competitive sports more than women.

Factors affecting sports participation

- Income levels: taking part in sport often involves purchases of clothing and equipment which can be relatively expensive. Also the prices of using local authority centres is increasing.
- More interest in health: there is increasing awareness of health and fitness issues and the value of sport; participants may also be trying to lose weight.
- The population: the age structure of a population influences participation, with younger people participating more than older people.
- The government: e.g. provision of sports facilities in the community, raising the status of sports by hosting major events (e.g. the Olympics 2012).

Playing sport is good for people's health and therefore affects the level of illness, days missed from work and absenteeism.

Tourism

- Tourism is income-elastic: demand for tourism in general grows faster in percentage terms than income. (However, the income elasticity varies from one type of holiday to another.)
- Tourism represents a growth sector for the UK.
- Tourism is often international, so e.g. demand for holidays in the UK does not just depend on UK income and demand; it also depends on income and demand from other countries.
- International tourism is affected by exchange rate movements; if the pound is strong (i.e. it has appreciated) this gives it more purchasing power abroad and this may encourage increased visits abroad.
- Tourism is likely to be sensitive to interest rates; many holidays are bought on credit (e.g. with a credit card); higher interest rates reduce households' disposable income (e.g. due to higher mortgage repayments) and increase cost of borrowing, and this may reduce holidays.

It is important to appreciate there are many markets within the overall 'tourist' market: e.g. demand for holidays within a country as well as going abroad; demand for short breaks; demand for tourist attractions such as theme parks. The market for each of these segments and the determinants may differ, e.g. the exchange rate may have a relatively large influence on UK holidays overseas *but* less impact on short breaks within the country.

Package holidays are high volume and low profit margin; companies need to sell large numbers of holidays to generate sufficient returns. By comparison cruise holidays are lower volume but much higher profit margin.

Benefits and costs of tourism to an area

Tourism can bring income and jobs to an area. This can have a positive multiplier effect. However, it may also bring pollution, e.g. traffic and noise. This can create a negative externality.

Also there is a need to consider how much of the income stays within the country. Are the holidays provided by local firms or foreign firms? Do the holiday companies employ local staff? Are the profits invested into the area?

Focus now is on: ethical and sustainable tourism, i.e. trying to ensure the area's culture, traditions and environment are not destroyed by the tourist industry.

UK holiday industry

This is dominated by a few large firms.
In 1998 the Competition Commission investigated the package holiday industry; the Commission was concerned about the lack of consumer power relative to the providers. At times there may be an illusion of choice, e.g. you think there are many different companies but in reality these are in fact owned by the major companies.

Demand for holidays depends on:

- real income (in general demand for holidays likely to be income elastic)
- exchange rate (affecting the purchasing power of the pound)
- consumer confidence, e.g. expectations about employment in the future.

Supply: tends to be fixed in the short run and therefore price inelastic. Over time firms will find/build more hotels, organize more flights etc, i.e. more price elastic.

Tourism facts and figures

- The number of visits by overseas residents to the UK, in the year ending June 2008, was 32.5 million. Visits from European residents numbered 23.6 million. Visits from North America decreased (4.3 million), and visits from other parts of the world totalled 4.6 million. The number of visits abroad by UK residents was 70.6 million. Visits to Europe increased to 55.7 million. Visits to North America numbered 4.7 million, and visits to other parts of the world 10.2 million.
- London continues to be one of the most popular cities for overseas tourists, with over 11 million visitors. The most popular attractions in London are the National Gallery, the British Museum, the London Eye and Tate Modern.

The market mechanism: failures and imperfections

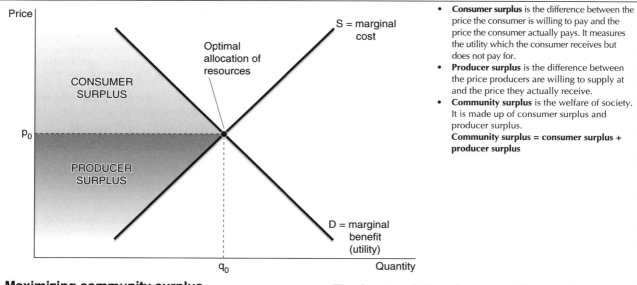

Consumer surplus is the difference between the price the consumer is willing to pay and the price the consumer actually pays. It measures the utility which the consumer receives but does not pay for.

Producer surplus is the difference between the price producers are willing to supply at and the price they actually receive.

Community surplus is the welfare of society. It is made up of consumer surplus and producer surplus.

Community surplus = consumer surplus + producer surplus

Maximizing community surplus
Community surplus is maximized at $p_0 q_0$. This is the price and quantity combination which maximizes the area of consumer surplus plus producer surplus. Any other combination of price and quantity would give less overall community surplus.

The free market and community surplus
In a free market the price mechanism will bring about equilibrium at $p_0 q_0$ and this is the combination of price and quantity which maximizes community surplus. This is why the free market is desirable and provides the optimal allocation of resources.

Market failures and imperfections
These are features of the free market which prevent it producing an optimal allocation of resources. **A market failure** occurs where the free market does not result in allocative (or productive) efficiency. **Complete market failure** results in a missing market. **Partial market failure** occurs when a market exists but contributes to resource misallocation. Eight different failures and imperfections are examined here (pages 26–28).

1 Market power
In a free market firms may come to dominate and have monopoly power. This can lead to higher prices and lower levels of output and cause a loss in welfare.

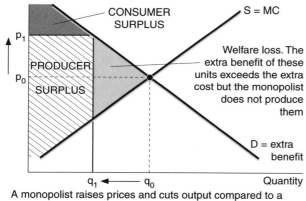

A monopolist raises prices and cuts output compared to a perfectly competitive industry which would produce at $p_0 q_0$. Consumer surplus decreases; producer surplus increases; community surplus decreases (welfare loss)

2 Factor immobility
In a perfect market factors of production are able to move easily between markets. An increase in the demand for one product will lead to higher prices which will attract resources out of another industry. In reality there is often factor immobility. Resources cannot always move between industries. For example, if one industry declines and another is in a boom, individuals cannot easily leave one and work in another because they may lack the necessary skills; they may not even know the job exists (see occupational and geographical immobility).

3 Inequality
The free market may lead to significant differences in the income and wealth of different groups. Society may feel this is unfair and want to reallocate income to make it more equal. To achieve this the Government can tax higher income groups at a higher rate and pay subsidies to low income groups, e.g. in the form of benefits.

4 Merit goods
These are goods which are socially desirable, e.g. museums, libraries, education. (Note: this means our view of what is and what is not a merit good may change over time.) They can be provided by the market mechanism but to make them more available the Government provides them, subsidizes them or legislates to make consumption compulsory. **Merit goods** are underprovided by the market mechanism (i.e. a product that society thinks should be provided in greater quantities). Underprovision may be due to lack of information (e.g. individuals do not appreciate the benefits that would occur) and/or positive externalities. **Demerit goods** are goods which society feels are undesirable, e.g. certain drugs. They are overprovided by the market mechanism, e.g. due to a lack of information or negative externalities. The Government legislates against demerit goods.

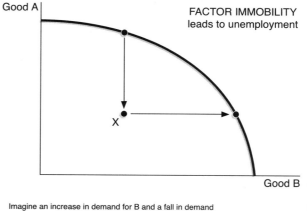

Imagine an increase in demand for B and a fall in demand for A. Individuals come out of industry A but lack the skills to accept a job in industry B or do not know the job exists. Unemployment occurs at point X. This causes inefficiency

The market mechanism: failures and imperfections /cont.

5 Externalities

An externality occurs when there is a divergence between social and private costs and benefits.

With a **negative** externality, such as pollution, the social cost is greater than the private cost.

Social cost = private cost + external cost

- **Private costs** are costs faced by the decision makers themselves/ someone who is directly involved in the transaction/production/ consumption decision. These costs are internal to the market.
- **External costs** are costs imposed on society (spillover effects) as a result of a firm's activities that are not directly paid for by the firm.

With a **positive** externality, the social benefit is bigger than the private benefit.

Social benefit = private benefit + external benefit

- **Consumption externalities** occur when the social costs or benefits of consumption are different from the private costs or benefits of consumption.
- **Production externalities** occur when the social costs or benefits of production differ from the private costs or benefits of production.

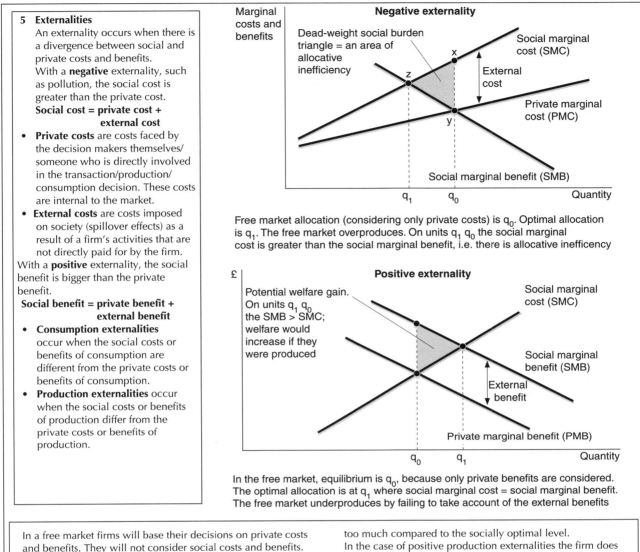

Free market allocation (considering only private costs) is q_0. Optimal allocation is q_1. The free market overproduces. On units $q_1 q_0$ the social marginal cost is greater than the social marginal benefit, i.e. there is allocative inefficency

In the free market, equilibrium is q_0, because only private benefits are considered. The optimal allocation is at q_1 where social marginal cost = social marginal benefit. The free market underproduces by failing to take account of the external benefits

In a free market firms will base their decisions on private costs and benefits. They will not consider social costs and benefits. In the case of negative production externalities they will overproduce; because firms do not take account of the negative external effect of their actions, they produce too much compared to the socially optimal level.

In the case of positive production externalities the firm does not take account of the positive external effect of its action and so undervalues the output and produces too little compared to the socially optimal level.

Common property rights

The problem of externalities exists because of a lack of clear property rights. In the case of air, for example, you do not have private property rights – it does not belong to you. Instead there are common property rights – air belongs to everyone. Because no one in particular owns it people are not so concerned about what happens to it and so noise and air pollution occurs.

Voluntary agreements

One way of overcoming externalities is for all those involved to agree on particular forms of behaviour, e.g. you agree with your neighbours that you will not make too much noise; alternatively they agree not to plant trees in their garden which block out your sunlight! In some cases these agreements may involve payment: you want to make a noise; they don't want you to, so they pay you to reduce your volume!

For such agreements to occur there must be low transaction costs (i.e. they must be cheap and easy to set up relative to the potential gains). Also it must be possible to bring together all those involved: neighbours coming together to sort out their disagreements is feasible, but getting everyone in the country together to agree on pollution is not realistic.

Coase theorem

If the creators of externalities do deals with the sufferers of externalities (i.e. by bribing them to accept the externality or by being charged for it) the externality will be internalized and the socially efficient output can be achieved.

Tradeable permits

In a system of tradeable permits, polluters are granted permission to create a certain amount of pollution. Polluters can sell or buy permits from each other depending on the amount of pollution they want to create. The aim is to fix the total amount of pollution – within that firms can bargain among themselves to buy the permits they need. Firms which really need/want more permits will bid up the price and buy them from organizations which do not need them so much.

The market mechanism: failures and imperfections /cont.

Government intervention to improve the environment

The government can:

- provision information so that producers and consumers know the impact of their actions, e.g. are aware of the external effect of their activities
- use taxes and subsidies, e.g. impose taxes on producers to make them take account of the external costs, subsidize activities and products which are environmentally friendly
- establish property rights, e.g. establish individuals' rights to clean water so that any polluter must pay those affected. This may be difficult to enforce and organize.
- legislate, e.g. prevent certain products and methods of production.
- introduce tradeable permits.

Types of externality: production and consumption externalitites

- External costs of production:
  A firm dumps waste into a river or pollutes the atmosphere.
- External benefits of production:
  A firm trains its employees; these leave and go to work for someone else and, because they are already trained, it reduces the costs of the second firm.
- External costs of consumption:
  By driving a car consumers increase the amount of pollution.
- External benefits of consumption:
  By listening to music, you not only give pleasure to yourself, but can also provide enjoyment for others.

6 Instability

The free market leads to instability in many markets. In agriculture, for example, shifts in supply due to natural occurrences such as the weather can lead to major movements in the price. To avoid this the Government might intervene using a buffer stock system (see page 17).

On a macroeconomic level, the economy often goes through cycles of booms, recessions, slumps, and recoveries. To avoid this instability the Government may intervene with fiscal or monetary policy (see pages 74 and 78).

Government intervention to solve externalities

- Negative externalities: the Government can legislate to reduce output, e.g. to reduce noise levels, to limit pollution; the Government can tax firms to try to make their private costs equal the social costs (e.g. by taxing leaded petrol more than unleaded) – this is known as 'internalizing externalities'.
- Positive externalities: the Government can legislate, e.g. all children must go to school until the age of 16; or it can subsidize to reduce the costs and encourage more production.

8 Public goods

These are goods that are non excludable and non diminishable. Consumers cannot be prevented from consuming them once they are provided and additional consumers do not reduce the amount left for other people, e.g. national defence. Once a country is defended all of its inhabitants benefit automatically. Many public goods such as lighthouses could in theory be provided by the market mechanism but are not; these are called 'quasi public goods', rather than 'pure public goods'. Public goods suffer from the free rider problem. If asked whether they would pay for them, households would lie and say no because, once provided, they could benefit for free anyway. Because no-one is willing to pay for these goods (because they hope someone else will) they will not be provided in a free market. Therefore, the Government must provide them. (Note: for a 'private good', if one unit is consumed by one person it cannot be consumed by another.) (This is not the case for public goods.) Public goods are also non-rejectable. Once provided, people will have them whether they want them or not.

7 Information problems

Consumers and producers do not always have perfect information. For example, restaurant and cinema owners do not know in advance what demand will be on a particular evening and so cannot change the price accordingly. This is why on some nights there may be empty seats; on other evenings there are queues. Producers in this situation have to estimate demand over a period and set an average price; on some occasions this will prove higher than the equilibrium price; on other occasions it will be too low.

- **Information failure**
  This occurs when individual consumers fail to take into account full costs and/or benefits when making a decision, e.g. consumers do not see how good/bad a product is for them because they lack the relevant information (or have the wrong information) and so over- or under-consume. Imperfect information results in allocative inefficiency.

- **Asymmetric information**
  In an efficient market, buyers and sellers have excellent knowledge of the product and market conditions. However, at times information may not be perfect, e.g the consumer may not know all of the options when looking for a new car.

  Nobel Prize winner George Akerlof highlighted that buyers of second-hand cars are never sure if they will be buying a lemon (the name he gave to a poor-quality second-hand car) and so are only willing to offer average prices for what might actually be better-than-average second-hand cars. This then means that people with better-than-average second-hand cars decide not to sell them; the average price thus becomes too high for what is actually on the market and the price falls. This could potentially lead to the collapse of the market entirely.

  Asymmetric information occurs in many markets, e.g. a garage may recommend that certain parts are changed without the customer knowing whether it is actually needed. In the private health care market doctors know more than patients about health care so may be tempted to diagnose treatments that are not needed.

- **Adverse selection:** where people taking out insurance are those who have the highest risk. Imagine that an insurance company offers medical cover. It calculates that the average person requires £500 of treatment a year so charges a premium of £600 to make a profit. However, those most likely to take out insurance are those most likely to become ill. To identify these, the insurance company has to select carefully from those who apply.

- **Moral hazard:** having an insurance policy may make you more careless – you will be less likely to look after your possessions because you are covered by insurance. To reduce carelessness, insurance companies often have an excess policy so that even if you claim you pay something towards the claim.

The market mechanism: failures and imperfections /cont.

Type of failure/imperfection	Consequence of failure/imperfection in free market	Examples of intervention
market power (1)	high prices, low output	legislation, e.g. competition policy
factor immobility (2)	inefficient allocation of resources	training; improved information flows
inequality (3)	unequal income distribution, felt to be unfair	redistribution, e.g. taxes and subsidies
merit goods (4a)	underprovided	Government subsidizes or legislates, e.g. education
demerit goods (4b)	overprovided	Government taxes or legislates, e.g. alcohol
negative externalities (5a)	overproduction	taxes, legislation
positive externalities (5b)	underproduction	subsidies, legislation
instability (6)	price fluctuations	buffer stocks
information problems (7)	inappropriate pricing	attempts to improve information flow
public goods (8)	not provided	Government provides, e.g. defence

Government intervention in the free market

The Government can:
- directly provide goods and services, e.g. with public goods
- legislate, e.g. with merit goods such as education or demerit goods such as some drugs
- provide incentives or disincentives through taxation and subsidies, e.g. by taxing activities with negative externalities and subsidizing the provision of merit goods

Examples of interventions include price controls, buffer stocks, pollution permits and state provisions.

Public private partnerships (PPPs) are arrangements that typically involve collaboration and joint working between the public and private sector. PPPs can cover all types of collaboration between the public and private sectors to deliver policies, services and infrastructure. Where delivery of public services involves private sector investment in infrastructure, the most common form of PPP is the Private Finance Initiative (PFI).

PFI occurs when a private company is contracted by the Government to finance and build a new project such as a bridge or new road. The Government pays the company to maintain and / or to run this and then rents the assets from the private business. The Government is therefore buying these services rather than directly providing them.

Government failure

This occurs when the Government intervenes but this intervention reduces economic welfare rather than increases it (i.e. intervention makes it worse not better).

Reasons for this include:
- Inadequate information, e.g. about the state of the economy, the impact of legislation and the social benefits or costs of an action.
- Conflicting objectives, e.g. the Government may take action that is politically popular even if it is economically inefficient. Investing money into an inefficient business may save jobs and gain votes but is not necessarily the right economic decision (not least because the money has to be raised from somewhere and the consequences of this must be considered, e.g. higher taxes might reduce the incentive of some firms to invest).

- Administrative costs. Coming up with a policy and implementing it costs money; these funds have to be raised from somewhere and could be used elsewhere. The opportunity cost must be considered.
- Market distortion. Intervention may create distortions, e.g. the effects of higher taxes needed to raise money to subsidize merit goods may have a disincentive effect in other markets.

Public choice theory: this analyses how and why government spending and taxation decisions are made. A key element in this is, of course, the voters. Voters typically want large quantities of goods and services without much tax. This would maximize their welfare. Politicians want to maximize votes (and possibly other objectives such as their earnings). To get votes they will appeal to the bulk of voters (the centre ground) and take decisions that may not necessarily make the best economic sense in order to keep votes, e.g. keeping jobs in key voting areas (even if this means subsidizing inefficient firms), favouring key individuals or business leaders who can convince others to vote for a political party or focusing on decisions that bring quick results (long-term investments are dangerous because you may not be in power when they come into effect).

Using taxes to remedy market failure

- Indirect taxes are inherently inflationary
- Taxes can increase costs and so damage the international competitiveness of the UK
- Problems deciding on the level of tax, e.g. assessing the monetary value of external costs
- Costs of enforcing the taxes
- Impact on income distribution, e.g. VAT is regressive

Problems of regulating to remedy market failures

- What is the right level of regulation?
- What are the costs of introducing and regulating?
- Opportunity costs
- Is there a danger of evasion?
- For some issues, such as tackling pollution, regulation would need to be worldwide, not just in the UK, to have a real effect
- Will it just drive producers abroad?

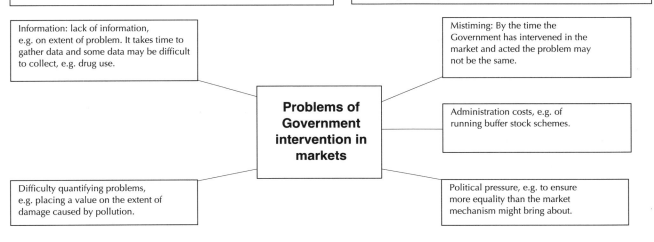

Information: lack of information, e.g. on extent of problem. It takes time to gather data and some data may be difficult to collect, e.g. drug use.

Mistiming: By the time the Government has intervened in the market and acted the problem may not be the same.

Problems of Government intervention in markets

Administration costs, e.g. of running buffer stock schemes.

Difficulty quantifying problems, e.g. placing a value on the extent of damage caused by pollution.

Political pressure, e.g. to ensure more equality than the market mechanism might bring about.

Environmental issues

Problems of markets and the environment

Markets sometimes fail because consumers and producers fail to take account of the negative external costs of their actions. These negative externalities may involve damage to the environment, e.g. land, air and noise pollution. This means that there is over-production and consumption of such products.

A misallocation of resources can also occur due to:

- ignorance: many individuals do not appreciate the environmental damage they do by their actions
- inter-generational problems: many actions will be harmful over time; consumers often focus on the short term and do not take into account the long-term effects of their actions.

How can the government intervene to make the market take account of environmental issues?

- Define property rights. Property rights are the power of control, including the right to be compensated for externalities. If people or firms are given the right to no pollution then they can charge those who want to pollute; this creates a market for pollution and leads to a socially efficient output. This is the Coase Theorem. Polluters would consider the extra benefit to them of producing more and how much they are prepared for this right; others would consider the payment offered relative to the extra costs of pollution. The market should adjust until a price is offered at which the extra benefit = extra cost.
- Charging for the use of the environment, e.g. emissions charges for firms producing waste or user charges to consumers (e.g. for rubbish collections). By increasing charges to firms and individuals it makes them aware of the full social costs of their actions.
- Permits. These can be used to limit production, e.g. permits could be issued to allow firms to pollute. The total number of permits issued will determine the total pollution output. The allocation of permits may be based on previous levels of pollution or linked to some other criteria. Permits can be traded between firms, enabling a price to be put on pollution or emissions. In a simple regulation there is no incentive for firms to cut their pollution if they do not need to do so; in the permit system it may be worth their while because they can sell the rights to the 'unused pollution' to another business. Firm A may be able to reduce its emissions by 100 tonnes for £10m and sell this to firm B; it might have cost B £15m to achieve the same reduction and so society is saving £5m overall to get pollution down.

Legislating to protect the environment

Air pollution

Under the Clean Air Act 1956, the UK Government has created clean air zones in which certain pollutants are illegal. The Government has also reduced the quantity of lead allowed in petrol.

Water pollution

Since 1951 the UK Government has imposed controls on discharges into inland waters.

UK landfill tax

This was introduced in 1996. It was aimed at a market failure – households and firms were disposing of waste in landfill sites and not taking account of the full social costs of their rubbish (e.g. leakage from landfill sites, noise and impact on the neighbourhood, throwing away recyclable materials). Landfill tax for disposing of certain products at landfill sites is aimed at increasing costs to households and firms and thereby internalizing the externality.

Pollution as a negative externality

The social marginal cost is greater than the private marginal cost due to pollution. In a free market there would be overproduction so the government may intervene to reduce production, e.g. via taxes or legislation. (See the negative externality graph on page 27.)

1997 Kyoto Protocol

The UK Government agreed to reduce greenhouse gas emissions to 12.5% less than 1990 levels by 2010. In 2004 it agreed to reduce emissions to 20% of their 1990 levels by 2010.

Problems meeting this include:

- The end of the useful life of existing nuclear power stations; they can be replaced (given that they are better in terms of emission levels) but politically nuclear energy is unpopular.
- Although renewable energy may be an option, there has been considerable resistance to the methods available, e.g. wind turbines spoiling the countryside.
- Increased road travel causing pollution.
- Increased air travel causing pollution.

Emissions trading, as set out in Article 17 of the Kyoto Protocol, allows countries that have emission units to spare – emissions permitted to them but not 'used' – to sell this excess capacity to countries that are over their targets.

Thus, a new commodity was created in the form of emission reductions or removals. Since carbon dioxide is the principal greenhouse gas, people speak simply of trading in carbon. Carbon is now tracked and traded like any other commodity. This is known as the 'carbon market'.

Sustainability

Economists are increasingly aware of the importance of sustainability, i.e. the need to consider future generations when making decisions about how to use resources. Awareness has been raised through studies such as the Brundtland Report 1997.

Marginals, averages and totals

Marginal

Marginal means extra, e.g. the marginal cost is the extra cost of producing another unit; the marginal revenue is the extra revenue from selling another unit.

Marginals and totals

The marginal shows what has happened to the total, e.g. if the marginal cost of making another unit is £4, the total cost will increase by £4.

Number of units	Total cost (£)	Marginal cost (£)
0	10 (fixed costs)	0
1	14	4
2	20	6
3	30	10
4	50	20
5	75	25
6	105	30
7	145	40

If the marginal is positive the total will increase. If the marginal is negative the total will fall.

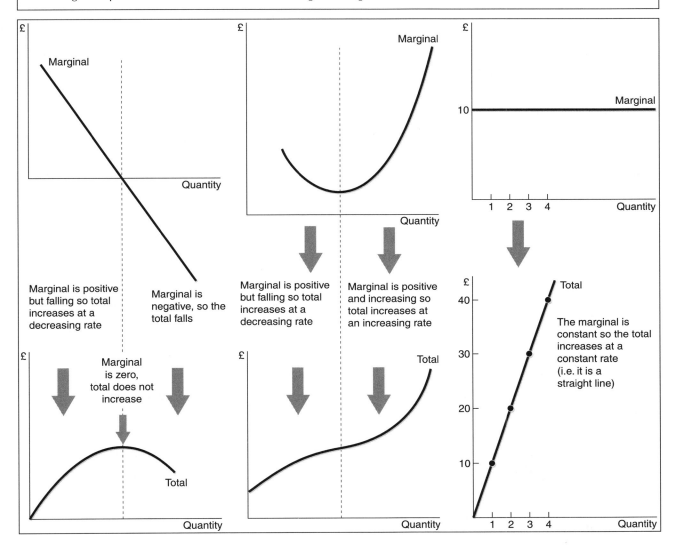

Averages and totals

To calculate the average, take the total and divide by the number of units, e.g. the average cost is the total cost divided by the number of units. If the total cost of making 3 units is £9, on average they cost £3 each. If the total revenue from selling 4 units is £20, then on average the revenue from each one is £5.

Averages and marginals

If a marginal is above an average, the average will increase. Imagine that a team has scored 3 goals per game on average and in the next game scores 10. This will pull up their average. If marginal > average, then average increases.
If a marginal is less than an average, the average will fall. If a team has scored 3 goals per game on average and in the next game scores 1, this will pull down the average. If marginal < average, then average decreases.

Marginals, averages and totals continued

Output and costs

The short run is the period of time when at least one factor of production is fixed.
The long run is when all factors are variable.

The law of diminishing returns (or the law of variable proportions)

As additional units of a variable factor (such as labour) are added to a fixed factor (such as capital), the extra output (or marginal product) of the variable factor will *eventually* diminish. (Note: the total output is still increasing, but at a diminishing rate.)

Assumptions of the law of diminishing returns
* at least one factor is fixed
* each unit of the variable factor is the same (e.g. each worker is equally trained)
* the level of technology is held constant

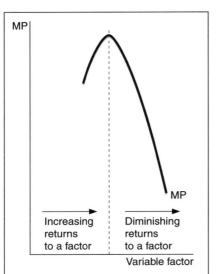

Number of Employees	Total output (Product)	Marginal product (MP)	Average product (AP)
0	0	-	-
1	10	10	10
2	26	16	13
3	39	13	13
4	48	9	12
5	55	7	11
6	60	5	10

In the table above we have assumed labour is the variable factor. At first there are increasing returns to labour, but with the third worker, marginal product falls and diminishing returns to a factor set in.

The marginal and average product

The marginal product (MP) is the extra output from hiring an additional unit of the variable factor. The average product (AP) is the average output per unit of the variable factor (also called the productivity of the factor). Imagine the variable factor is labour. If the extra worker makes more units than the employees were making on average before he or she joined, the average output per worker will rise, e.g. if three workers make 9 units in total and the fourth adds another 11, the average will rise from 3 units each to 5 units each. If the extra worker makes fewer extra units the average will fall, e.g. three workers make 9 units in total (on average 3 each); if the fourth adds only 1 unit, the average is 10 divided by 4, i.e. 2.5 units each.

If MP > AP, then average product increases.
If MP < AP, then average product decreases.

This means the marginal product crosses the average product at the maximum point of the average product.

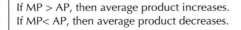

Output

Term	Explanation
Total product (TP)	total output produced by factors of production
Average product (AP)	the output per unit of the variable factor, e.g. output per worker; also called labour productivity
Marginal product (MP)	the extra output from employing another unit of a variable factor, e.g. the extra output from employing an additional worker

Productivity = output per factor, e.g. output per worker. Employees' productivity can increase with more training, more capital equipment, better management, improved technology.

Costs

Costs

- Costs are expenses of the business. They represent the value of inputs used up. They include materials, labour, depreciation of equipment, the cost of capital and the opportunity cost of capital.
- **Fixed costs (FC)** are costs which do not change with output, e.g. the rent of a building is not related to output.
- **Variable costs (VC)** are costs which do vary with output, e.g. materials costs will increase if more units are produced.
- **Total costs (TC)** = fixed costs + variable costs

$$TC = FC + VC$$

- **Marginal cost (MC)** is the extra cost of producing another unit. The marginal cost curve in the short run is inversely related to the marginal product – when the marginal product increases, the marginal cost falls and vice versa. Imagine the variable factor is labour. When each extra worker is more productive, less of their time is needed to make an extra unit. Assuming wages are constant, this means the extra cost of a unit will fall. When each extra worker is less productive, more of their time will be needed to make an extra unit and so the marginal cost of the unit will rise.

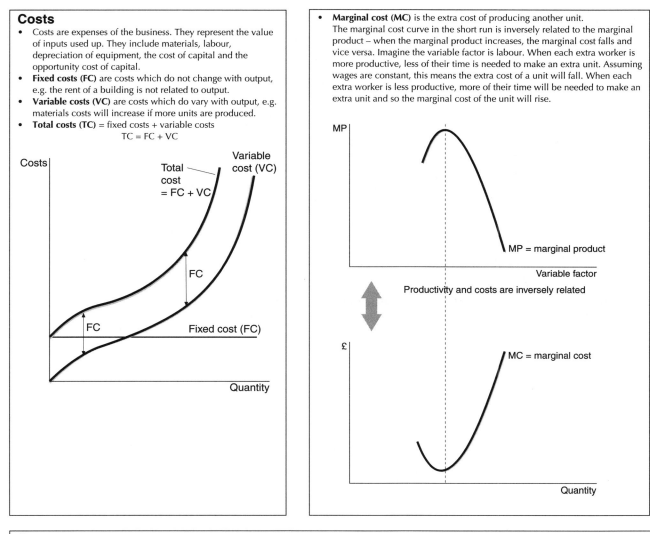

Costs

Total costs:	fixed costs + variable costs	FC + VC
Average cost:	total costs / output	$\dfrac{TC}{Q}$
Average variable cost:	variable cost / output	$\dfrac{VC}{Q}$
Average fixed cost:	fixed cost / output	$\dfrac{FC}{Q}$
Marginal cost:	change in total cost / change in output	$\dfrac{\Delta \text{ in TC}}{\Delta \text{ in Q}}$

Productivity and unit costs are inversely related

Output (units)	Number of employees	Output per worker (labour productivity); units	Wage costs (if workers are paid £100 / week each) £	Wage cost per unit £
100	1	100	100	100/100 = 1
300	2	150	200	200/300 = 0.66
600	3	200	300	300/600 = 0.5
1000	4	250	400	400/1000 = 0.4
1300	5	260	500	500/1300 = 0.38
1440	6	240	600	600/1440 = 0.42
1400	7	200	700	700/1400 = 0.5

Costs continued

Average costs

- **Average fixed cost (AFC)** falls as more units are made; fixed costs are spread over more and more units.
- **Average cost** = the cost per unit = $\frac{\text{total cost}}{\text{output}}$ = AC (also called ATC)
- **Average cost** (or ATC) = average fixed cost + average variable cost

$$AC = AFC + AVC$$

Output	Fixed costs	Average fixed costs
0	£20,000	infinite
100	£20,000	£200
200	£20,000	£100
300	£20,000	£66.66
400	£20,000	£50

Average variable cost (AVC)
Generally 'U'shaped. On average the variable factor becomes more productive at first and then becomes less productive (see the average product curve). The average cost of the variable factor per unit of output falls when the factor is more productive and rises when the factor is less productive.

Average cost (AC) (also called average total cost (ATC))
Summation of the average fixed cost and the average variable cost. As more units are produced, the average fixed cost declines and so the average total cost is increasingly made up of the average variable cost (i.e. the ATC and the AVC converge).

Average costs, average variable costs and average fixed costs

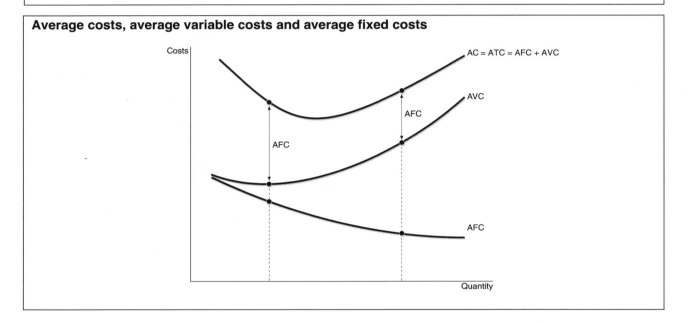

Marginal costs and average costs

If the extra cost of making a unit (the marginal cost) is greater than the cost of a unit on average, this will increase the average cost, e.g. if each unit costs £5 to make and the next one costs £20, the average cost will rise.
If the extra cost of making a unit (the MC) is less than the cost per unit, the average cost will fall, e.g. if the average cost of a unit is £5 and the firm produces an extra one for £1 this will bring down the average cost.

So if   **MC > AC, then AC rises**
If   **MC < AC, then AC falls**

This means that the marginal cost crosses the average cost at its minimum point.

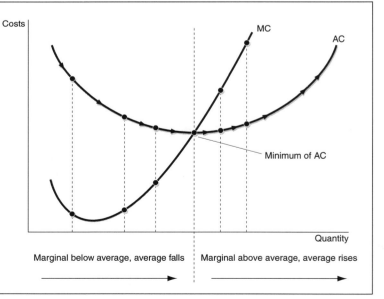

Long run cost curves

Long run cost curves
In the long run all factors of production are variable.

From short run cost curves to long run cost curves
A short run average cost (SRAC) shows the minimum cost per unit for different levels of output given a fixed factor, e.g. given 10 machines. There will be an infinite number of short run curves depending on the constraint, e.g. one SRAC for 11 machines, one for 12 machines, one for 13 machines and so on. As the firm changes its fixed factor over time, e.g. buys another machine, this is shown by a new short run average cost curve.

- If when the firm expands it moves on to a new lower short run average cost curve, it is experiencing internal economies of scale
- If when the firm expands it moves on to a long run average cost at the same level, it is experiencing constant returns to scale
- If when the firm expands it moves onto a higher short run average cost curve, it is experiencing internal diseconomies of scale.

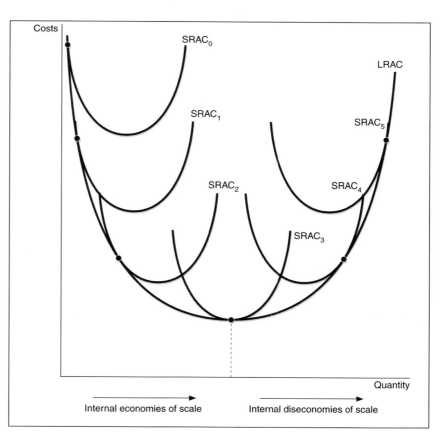

Internal economies of scale
Purchasing (or bulk buying). Larger firms tend to buy larger quantities of inputs and so are in a stronger position to negotiate discounts.

Managerial. The number of managers needed by a firm does not normally increase at the same rate as output, e.g. if the firm's output doubles, this does not mean it needs twice as many managers. This lowers the cost of management per unit. Also, as a firm grows, it will usually develop specialist management jobs, i.e. managers begin to specialize in different areas. This can lead to better decision-making and more efficiency.

Technical. Some production processes are very expensive to run on a small scale. Imagine a car production line only producing two cars a week. By using the line to its capacity and making far more cars, the cost of the equipment can be spread over more units, lowering the cost per unit. Technical economies include:

a   specialization – employees can be given specialist tasks to undertake; this should lead to higher productivity through repetition

b   indivisibilies – some pieces of equipment cannot be split up easily; they are indivisible, e.g. a production line. If the line is only used to produce a few units, the cost per unit will be high; if it is used on a large scale to its full capacity the cost per unit will fall.

c   increased dimensions – if a container is doubled in size, the volume will more than double, making the storage costs cheaper per unit.

d   linked processes – most production consists of interlinked stages; the capacity of the machines at each stage may vary, e.g. machine A may be able to make 40 units a day; machine B may only be able to make 10. If only one machine A and one B is bought, A will be under utilized. If 4 B machines are bought the firm can produce 40 units and not have excess capacity.

Financial economies. Larger firms are often able to borrow money at a cheaper rate; this is because they have more assets and so it is less risky to lend to them.

Risk-bearing economies. By diversifying into several regions or countries, the firm is likely to have more stable demand patterns. Sudden falls in demand for the product in one area are likely to be offset by increases in demand elsewhere. As a result, demand is more predictable and the firm does not need to hold as much stock just in case. This reduces stockholding costs.

Marketing economies. The costs of advertising and promotion can be spread over more units as a business grows, so the cost per unit falls.

Internal diseconomies of scale
Occur when the unit (or average) cost per unit rises with more output.
This may be because of:
- poor communications
- low morale; employees may feel alienated as the company grows and the gap between 'top' and 'bottom' grows
- lack of control

These are essentially problems of management. They may be overcome by decentralizing so that people lower down in the organization are involved in decisions and by ensuring that communication is good.

Long run cost curves continued

Minimum efficient scale (MES) This is the first level of output at which the cost per unit is minimized.

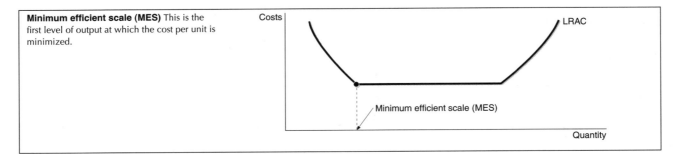

Returns to scale

These occur in the long run when all factors of production can be altered.

- Increasing returns to scale mean that a proportionate increase in all factors of production leads to a more than proportionate increase in output. For example, if the amount of land, labour and capital the firm uses is doubled, this will lead to an increase in output which is more than double. As a result, the cost per unit falls.
- Decreasing returns to scale occur when a proportionate increase in all factors of production leads to a less than proportionate increase in output. This leads to an increase in the average cost.

- Constant returns to scale occur when a proportionate increase in all factors of production leads to a proportionate increase in output, e.g. if all factors of production are doubled, output doubles. The cost per unit stays constant.

Increasing returns to scale v. economies of scale

Economies of scale refer to a fall in the <u>cost</u> per unit. Increasing returns to scale refer to changes in <u>output</u>. Increasing returns to scale contribute to economies of scale but one measures costs, the other output.

Cost minimization: least cost combination of factors

To minimize costs, firms hire resources where

$$\frac{MP\ labour}{price\ of\ labour} = \frac{MP\ capital}{price\ of\ capital} = \frac{MP\ land}{price\ of\ land}$$

i.e. the extra output per pound of each factor of production is equal. If the last unit of labour was more productive per pound than, say, capital, the firm will hire more labour and less capital.

External economies of scale

Occur when the cost per unit at every level of output is reduced because of factors within the industry but outside of the firm, such as

- economies of agglomeration, e.g. if a firm is based in a particular area with other firms in the same industry, they can share resources (e.g. research or distribution) and specialist supplier firms may set up, supplying goods more cheaply.
- if the suppliers grow larger, they may benefit from internal economies of scale. This will lead to cheaper inputs for a firm and reduce costs. This may be caused by growth in the industry as a whole, which leads to more orders for suppliers so they can expand.

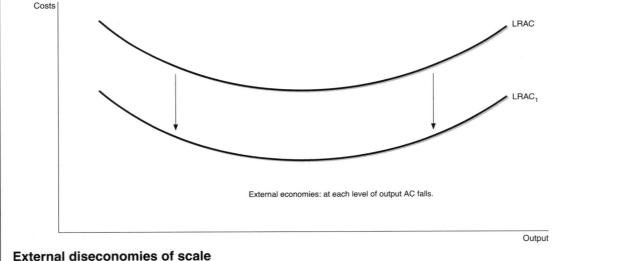

External economies: at each level of output AC falls.

External diseconomies of scale

Occur when the cost per unit increases at every level of output because of factors outside of the firm, e.g. growth of the industry bids up prices of inputs, making it more expensive for all firms.

Technology

Technology involves the use of science and engineering to innovate and develop tools, equipment and processes to undertake work more effectively or more efficiently. Technological developments can add value to products affecting demand and/or reduce costs (e.g. reducing the average cost of production) affecting supply.

Technology can lead to the development of new and better products and processes. This can lead to innovative products and provide more choice for customers. Innovation can help firms to gain control of a market. New inventions can be legally protected via **patents**. If a business registers a patent, competitors cannot use this idea unless it is licensed to them for a

fee, which gives providers monopoly power for a given period of time. This may encourage other firms to innovate to gain their own control over a market.

Technology can make it easier to enter markets, e.g. a firm can set up a website and trade globally fairly cheaply. If firms are able to reduce costs, they may also be able to reduce their prices. Technology can create markets, e.g. computer games; it can also threaten industries, e.g. with more people booking their holidays directly, travel agents are less profitable. It can also upset markets, e.g. the market for CDs has changed following the growth of MP3 players and downloading.

Price and output decisions

The marginal condition

This shows firms where to produce, i.e. what level of output to produce.

- If the extra revenue from selling a unit (the marginal revenue) is greater than the extra cost (the marginal cost) the firm will make extra profit by selling the unit. It should always make units where extra profit can be made (assuming it is aiming to profit maximize).
- When the extra revenue from selling a unit equals the extra cost from producing it (i.e. MR = MC) the firm must be making the maximum profit possible because no extra profit can be made.
- If the extra revenue is less than the extra cost the firm should cut back because a loss is being made on this extra unit.

To maximize their profits, firms should produce where marginal revenue = marginal cost

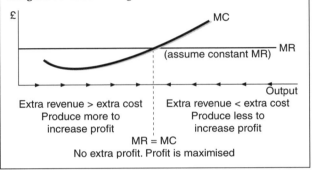

The average condition

This shows the firm how much profit (or loss) it is making at a given level of output.

To calculate a firm's profits look at the average revenue per unit (or price) and the average cost. The difference between these is the profit per unit. If we multiply this by the number of units we get the total profit (or loss).

- If the average revenue is greater than the average cost the firm is making an abnormal profit on each unit.
- If the average revenue is less than the average cost the firm is making a loss on each unit.
- If the average revenue is equal to average cost the firm is breaking even on each unit and just making normal profit.

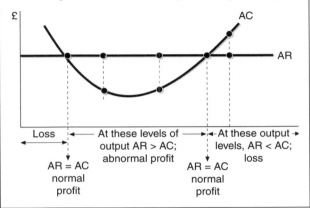

Profits

Normal profits

This is the amount of profit which is needed to keep resources in their present use in the long run. If the firms in an industry are making normal profit there is no incentive for them to leave or for other firms to join. Normal profit occurs when revenue equals cost. This is because the costs in economics include a reward to the entrepreneurs for being in that industry to cover the risk of being there.

Economic and accounting profit

There is a difference between an accountant's definition of profits, and an economist's view of profits. The economist includes a figure in the costs to cover the risk of the firm being in that industry and give a reward to the entrepreneur. If the firm were not making this amount, it would leave and join another industry in the long run. On paper, for example, a firm may make £200,000 accounting profit. An economist, however, may look at the firm's resources and the nature of the industry and claim that this amount must be made to stay in the industry. In this case, £200,000 is simply normal profit – the firm is just covering its costs (including opportunity cost).

Abnormal profit (or super normal profit)

This is profit in excess of normal profit. If firms in an industry are making abnormal profit, there is an incentive for other firms to join the industry if they can. Abnormal profit occurs when the revenue is greater than the costs.

Losses occur when the revenue is less than the cost.

Producing in the short run and long run

In the short run firms may stay in the industry even if they are making a loss.

This is because of fixed costs. In the short run, fixed costs must be paid, even if the firm is closed down, e.g. even if output is zero, the firm may be committed to paying rent. Therefore, if the firm stops production, it will make a loss equal to its fixed costs. If it produces, it starts to incur variable costs. Provided the revenue can pay for these variable costs, it is worth producing. If the revenue more than covers the variable costs, the firm is gaining a contribution to fixed costs, i.e. the loss by producing would be smaller than by closing down.

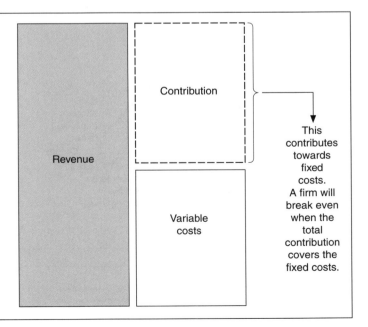

Price and output decisions continued

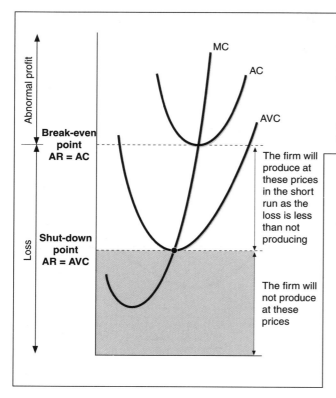

Break-even point
AR = AC

Shut-down point
AR = AVC

The firm will produce at these prices in the short run as the loss is less than not producing

The firm will not produce at these prices

Short run production decision

In the short run a firm will produce provided revenue is greater than or equal to variable costs. In terms of each unit, this means it will produce provided
average revenue (which is price) is greater than or equal to average variable cost

Long run production decision

In the long run the firm will only produce if revenue is greater than or equal to cost (i.e. at least normal profits). Per unit this means that
average revenue must be greater than or equal to average cost

Efficiency

Pareto optimality includes:

- **Productive efficiency** – when it is not possible to make more of one good without making less of another, i.e. the economy is operating on its production possibility frontier.
- **Allocative efficiency** – no-one can be made better off without someone else being made worse off.
  If all markets were perfectly competitive without any failures or imperfections, the free market would lead to a Pareto optimal allocation of resources, i.e. the free market would achieve productive and allocative efficiency.
- **Static efficiency** – occurs at a point in time.
- **Dynamic efficiency** – results from improvements in technical or productive efficiency which occur over time, e.g. new products, new methods of producing, new methods of management. Dynamic efficiency can increase with innovation, invention and research and development, investment in human capital.

Efficiency at firm level

- **Allocative efficiency**

This occurs at the output where the social marginal benefit equals the social marginal cost (SMB = SMC).

If the social marginal benefit is greater than the social marginal cost, society would gain by producing an extra unit. The firm should keep producing until the two are equal, i.e. the extra benefit just equals the extra cost.

If the social marginal cost is greater than the social marginal benefit, society would gain by producing less of this good.

If the price reflects the social marginal benefit of a unit, then allocative efficiency occurs when the firm produces where
Price = social marginal cost

If P > MC then the benefit from an extra unit exceeds the extra cost
If P < MC then the extra benefit is less than the extra cost

- **Productive efficiency (technical efficiency)**

Firms are productively efficient when they produce at the lowest cost per unit, i.e. at the minimum point of the average cost curve.

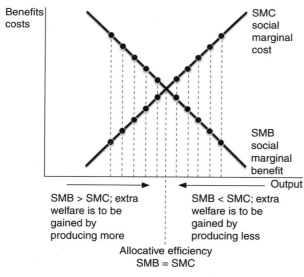

SMB > SMC; extra welfare is to be gained by producing more

SMB < SMC; extra welfare is to be gained by producing less

Allocative efficiency
SMB = SMC

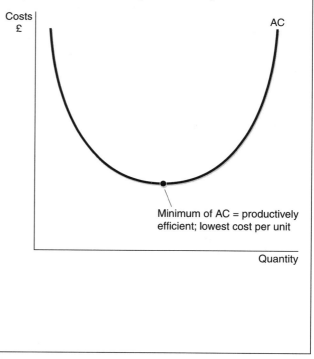

Minimum of AC = productively efficient; lowest cost per unit

Theory of second best

If a distortion or inefficiency exists in one market it is inefficient to treat other markets as if that distortion did not exist, e.g. if distortions exist, the Government may improve the overall welfare of society by introducing distortions in other markets.

Markets: health

Problems of the health care market
- Consumers do not have perfect information. They do not necessarily know what is good for them and so cannot necessarily act rationally.
- There is *asymmetrical information*. The doctor or consultant knows more than the patient. The doctors take decisions which affect supply and demand; they determine what you need and whether you get it. Potentially this could create problems, e.g. they might decide you need more health care or dental treatments than you actually do if this benefits them financially.

Why does the market system not provide the efficient amount of health care?
- Due to the income distribution some people cannot afford health care; on the grounds of equity it may be argued that medical care should be available on the basis of need.
- Difficulty in estimating your likely future health care needs and planning accordingly; due to uncertainty individuals may not budget enough for their health care needs.
- Health care generates positive external benefits (e.g. a healthy workforce produces more and earns more for the economy; also a healthy person does not spread disease); in the free market individuals will not take account of this and so they underconsume.

Excess demand for health
The supply of services in the Health Service is fixed at any time. Given a level of demand, a price P_1 should be charged. However, given that the service is free, there is excess demand ($Q_1 - Q_0$). This leads to waiting lists as a means of rationing demand.

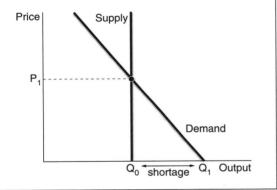

Why does a shortage exist in the National Health Service?
a Limited supply: the Government can only provide a certain amount of finance for health services as it has a limited budget and other responsibilities.

b Zero price so the price mechanism cannot act as rationing or signalling device.

c Increasing levels of demand: with advances in technology and higher living standards our view of what should or can be treated is always increasing. Also the average age of the population is increasing which leads to greater demands.

Health care insurance
In other countries private or public health care insurance schemes are common. In the UK health care insurance schemes are increasing but still not very common.

In this type of scheme individuals pay an insurance premium to cover themselves in case they should need health care.

Problems of running such schemes include:
- Asymmetric information, i.e. you know more about your health than your insurance company. You might not tell them everything they need to know.
- Adverse selection, i.e. you may be able to hide from the insurance company that you are high risk
- Moral hazard, i.e. it is in your interests to lie about your health if it is poor
- If you are insured there is less incentive to avoid accidents or become ill because someone else will pay for your treatment. This may mean you use the doctors for 'unnecessary' advice/treatment. Also the doctors know you are not paying directly so may prescribe treatment more generously/easily than if you or they were paying directly, e.g. let you stay in hospital for longer after an operation rather than get you out quickly

'Good' health as a positive externality
Health care will be underconsumed in the free market because individuals do not realize how beneficial health care is – they do not take account of the full social benefits.

Individuals do not fully appreciate the benefits of health care, e.g. if you are healthy:
a this helps you be more productive for your firm and the economy
b you are less likely to make others ill.

As a result the marginal social benefit of health care is greater than the marginal private benefit. Therefore health care is underconsumed by individuals. Consumption will be at Q_0. In an efficient market in which individuals appreciated the full social benefits of health care consumption would be at Q_1.

On the units $Q_0 Q_1$ the extra social benefit is greater than the extra social cost, therefore there is a benefit for society if they are produced. If they are not produced, there is allocative inefficiency and a welfare loss to society.

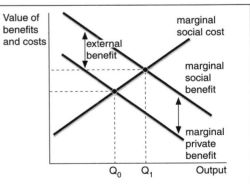

Management of the National Health Service
Internal markets can occur with health care systems. This means that providers of health care treatments can compete for patients whilst still receiving funding from the Government rather than charging patients directly for it. Hospitals, for example, could compete for patients to be referred by General Practitioners (doctors) and earn more from the Government as a result. GPS could be delegated their own budgets based on the number of patients, their age and their health profiles. GPs could then purchase medicines direct from suppliers and decide which hospital to send patients to (for which they would be charged out of their budget). Some think this approach leads to greater efficiencies as GPs look for better deals and hospitals try to provide a better service. Others feel it leads to more bureaucracy and administration.

Preventative medicine aims to prevent illnesses occurring rather than treating them when they do occur. A preventative approach raises questions such as:
- To what extent should the Government use taxes to discourage smoking and drinking?
- Should the Government legislate more to ensure that customers are fully informed about the health care issues related to any food?
- Should the Government take action to increase personal fitness?

Perfect competition

The **assumptions** of a perfectly competitive market are that:
- there are many buyers and sellers
- there is perfect information so buyers know what products are on offer and at what price

- the product is similar (homogeneous) so firms cannot differentiate their product
- there are no barriers to entry so firms can enter and leave the industry in the long run

- producers have similar technology and there are perfectly mobile resources (so one firm cannot maintain an advantage over another)

The firm as price taker

Each firm in perfect competition is a price taker. This means that changes in output by one firm do not shift the industry supply curve sufficiently to alter the price. If the whole industry makes more or less output the supply will shift and the price will change, but not if one firm increases or decreases output. This means each firm can sell all it wants at the given market price. This also means that marginal revenue equals price.

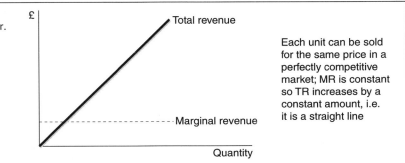

Each unit can be sold for the same price in a perfectly competitive market; MR is constant so TR increases by a constant amount, i.e. it is a straight line

The short run and long run in perfect competition

In the short run, firms in perfectly competitive markets can make abnormal profits or losses. In the long run they can only make normal profits.
- If firms are making abnormal profits, other firms will enter the market in the long run. This will shift supply to the right and lead to a fall in price. This will continue until only normal profits are earned, e.g. price falls from p_0 to p_1.

- If firms are making losses, they will leave the industry, shifting the industry supply to the left. This will cause the price to increase. This will continue until the firms left in the industry are making normal profit, e.g. the price increases from p_2 to p_1.

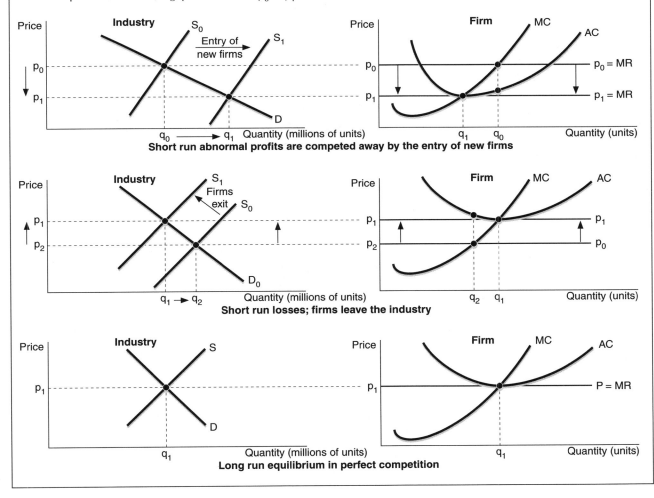

Short run abnormal profits are competed away by the entry of new firms

Short run losses; firms leave the industry

Long run equilibrium in perfect competition

Perfect competition continued

The supply curve

A profit maximizing firm will produce where marginal revenue = marginal cost. At this level of output there is no extra profit to be gained so the firm is profit maximizing.

In perfect competition the price is equal to the marginal revenue because each unit is sold for the same price.

So, **P = MR**
and to profit maximize, **MR = MC**
This means: **P = MC**

i.e. the firm will produce where the price equals the marginal cost. This means that given a particular price, the MC curve shows how much is to be supplied: it is the supply curve.

Short run supply

In the short run the price must cover average variable cost to produce (otherwise its loss would be bigger than if it shut down) so the supply is the marginal cost above the average variable cost.

Long run supply

In the long run the firm must cover the average cost to produce (otherwise it will not break even) so the supply curve is the marginal cost above the average cost.

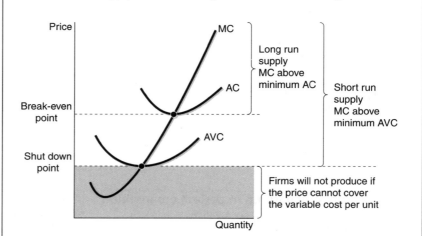

Long run industry supply curves

- **Constant cost industries**
  Long run supply curve is horizontal. Demand increases, price rises, and existing firms make abnormal profit; this is an incentive for other firms to enter, shifting supply to the right until the price returns to its old level.
- **Decreasing cost industries**
  When firms enter they bring with them new technology; or the increase in the size of the industry allows suppliers to gain economies of scale, reducing costs. The new equilibrium price is below the old level. The long run supply is downward sloping.
- **Increasing cost industries**
  When firms enter input prices are bid up; the new equilibrium price is above the old equilibrium price; the long run supply is upward sloping.

Note: there is no supply curve in monopoly; there are no unique price and output combinations; firms can produce different quantities at the same price or the same quantity at different prices, depending on cost and demand conditions.

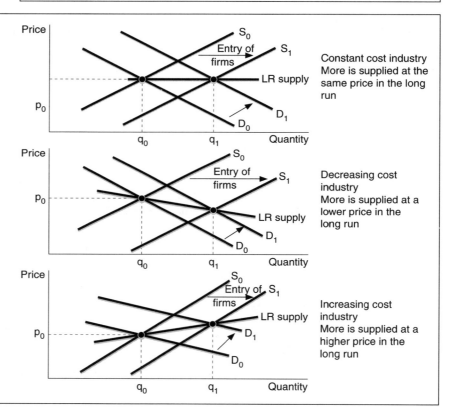

Constant cost industry
More is supplied at the same price in the long run

Decreasing cost industry
More is supplied at a lower price in the long run

Increasing cost industry
More is supplied at a higher price in the long run

Why are perfectly competitive markets desirable?

- in the long run firms only make normal profits
- firms are allocatively efficient because they produce where the extra benefit of a unit (represented by the price consumers are willing to pay for it) equals the extra cost, e.g. P = MC

- productively efficient, i.e. firms produce at the minimum of the average cost curve; this is the lowest possible cost per unit
- if a firm becomes more efficient than the others it can earn abnormal profit in the short run; there is an incentive for firms to innovate and become more efficient

But
- firms may not be able to afford research and development because they do not earn abnormal profits in the long run
- there is a lack of variety for consumers because the products are not differentiated

Monopoly

Monopoly

A monopoly exists where there is a single seller in a market.

A monopolist is a price taker. The monopolist faces a downward sloping demand and can set the price or the output but not both. If the monopolist sets the price it must accept the quantity that is demanded at this price; if it sets the output it must accept the price it can get for this quantity.

In a monopoly situation we assume that the firm is faced with a downward sloping demand curve and must lower the price to sell an additional unit.

In the situation of a single price monopolist, only one price can be charged for all the goods, so if the price is lowered on the last unit it must also be lowered on the ones before.

Imagine the firm was selling one unit for £10. To sell another unit, the price must be lowered to, for example £9. The firm's revenue for two units is £18 (9 × 2) compared to £10 for one. Its marginal revenue is therefore £8 (£18 – £10). The firm gained £9 on the second unit which was not sold before but lost £1 on the first unit which was previously sold for £10.

Similarly, if the price of two units is £9 each, the firm may have to lower the price to £8 to sell three units. The revenue is now 3 × £8 = £24 compared to 2 × £9 = £18, i.e. the marginal revenue is £6. The firm has gained £8 on the third unit but lowered the price of the two units before by £1 each, meaning it loses £2.

In each case the firm is gaining revenue from the sale of the extra unit but losing revenue on the ones before, where the price has been lowered.

Quantity demanded	Price (£)	Total revenue = price × quantity (£)	Marginal revenue (£)
1	10	10	–
2	9	18	8
3	8	24	6
4	7	28	4
5	6	30	2
6	5	30	0
7	4	28	–2
8	3	24	–4

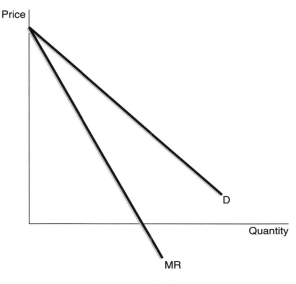

The marginal revenue is below the average revenue (or price) line and gets further away from it as more units are sold. This is because the price is continually being reduced on all the units before.

Marginal revenue and total revenue

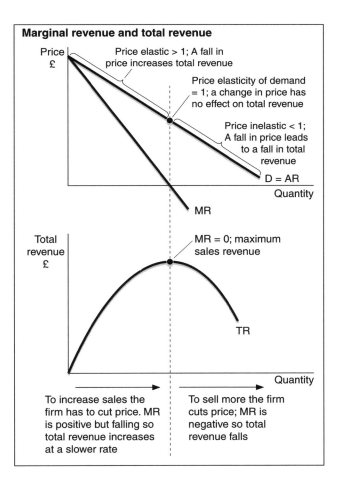

To increase sales the firm has to cut price. MR is positive but falling so total revenue increases at a slower rate

To sell more the firm cuts price; MR is negative so total revenue falls

Short-run abnormal profits

Monopolies can earn abnormal profits in the short run and in the long run. This is because of barriers to entry which prevent abnormal profits being competed away.

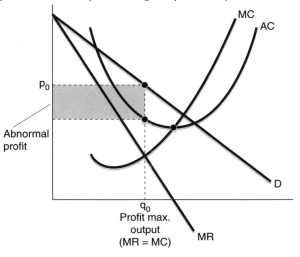

Monopoly continued

A monopoly can earn abnormal profits in the long run, due to barriers to entry.

- legislation, e.g. the Government may restrict the ability of firms to compete in a market. For example, for many years British Gas and British Telecom were Government owned and had monopoly positions.

- patents and trademarks – these provide firms with legal protection for their ideas or designs, which prevent other firms imitating them.

- product differentiation – by making their product seem very different from the competition through their marketing and branding, a firm can establish a monopoly position.

Barriers to entry
These prevent firms entering an industry in the long run.

- control over supplies – if a firm has a monopoly control of the supplies in an industry, other firms will not be able to enter.

- control over outlets so competitors cannot get their products to the market.

- a cost advantage – if a firm has a major cost advantage, e.g. because of economies of scale, other firms will not be able to compete.

- fear of reaction of existing firms, i.e. other firms may not enter if they think this will trigger a price war.

Monopoly and efficiency

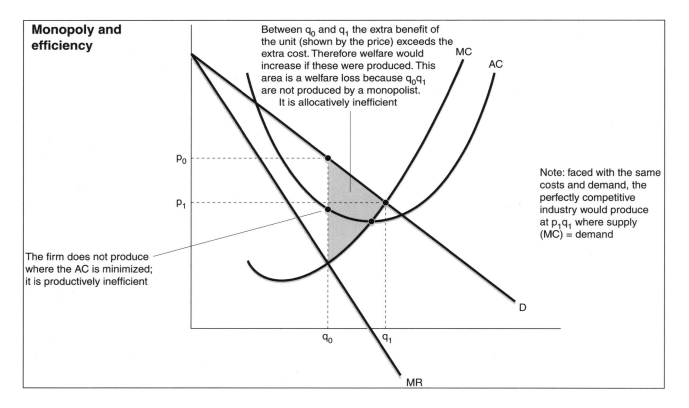

Between q_0 and q_1 the extra benefit of the unit (shown by the price) exceeds the extra cost. Therefore welfare would increase if these were produced. This area is a welfare loss because $q_0 q_1$ are not produced by a monopolist. It is allocatively inefficient

Note: faced with the same costs and demand, the perfectly competitive industry would produce at $p_1 q_1$ where supply (MC) = demand

The firm does not produce where the AC is minimized; it is productively inefficient

Monopoly continued

Natural monopoly

A natural monopoly occurs when there are large economies of scale; the minimum efficient scale is at an output which is higher than the total demand in the industry.

One firm will keep expanding to gain economies of scale; other firms cannot compete due to cost disadvantages of operating at a smaller scale. If both expanded, the increase in output would lead to a major fall in price. Only one would survive in the long run.

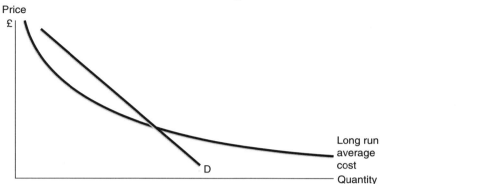

Control of natural monopolies

The Government may take over natural monopolies to control them. It may introduce marginal cost pricing to achieve allocative efficiency. If MC is below AC, the firm makes a loss (equal to the shaded area) and needs to be subsidized.

Alternatively, a firm sets prices where price = average cost, so it does not make a loss.

Another option is to have a fixed fee, e.g. monthly rental to cover the loss and set the price equal to marginal cost for allocative efficiency. This is called a 'two-part tariff'.

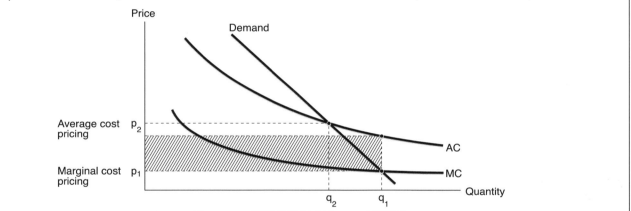

Arguments in favour of monopolies

- The monopolist produces more than any single firm would in a perfectly competitive market. This may lead to economies of scale and, therefore, lower costs than in a perfectly competitive market. This in turn might lead to lower prices and higher output than perfect competition.

- The abnormal profits may be used to invest in research and development which may lead to cost saving innovations. Joseph Schumpeter argued that monopolists are a positive force in the economy – to gain a monopoly position firms often have to innovate; they then gain abnormal profits which encourage other firms to innovate in other areas to gain similar rewards and take away the first firm's market. This may be true in some markets but certainly not all monopoly situations.

- Competitive markets may over-produce, e.g. in the case of a negative externality – by restricting output the monopolist may actually improve resource allocation.

Arguments against monopolies

- The monopolist can earn abnormal profits even in the long run due to barriers to entry.

- The monopolist is allocatively inefficient, i.e. the price charged is greater than the marginal cost. This causes a welfare loss.

- The monopolist may be productively inefficient, i.e. it may not produce at the minimum of the average cost curve.

- Compared to a perfectly competitive industry with the same cost and demand conditions, the monopolist will charge a higher price for less output.

- X inefficiency – because a monopolist dominates a market, it may have less incentive to be efficient and keep costs down. Over time costs may rise because of inefficiency and complacency. This idea was put forward by Liebenstein.

Monopolistic competition and contestable markets

Monopolistic competition involves many sellers with differentiated products, e.g. shoe producers or restaurants.

In the short run firms can make abnormal profit because they have some control over the market as their products are different in some way, e.g. better location, better design or new technology. In the long run other firms will be attracted by the abnormal profits; demand for any one firm will fall until only normal profits are made.

In the long run the firm is:

* allocatively inefficient because the price the consumer is willing to pay is greater than the extra cost of production (P > MC).
* productively inefficient because the firm is not producing at the lowest cost per unit, i.e. not at the minimum of the average cost.

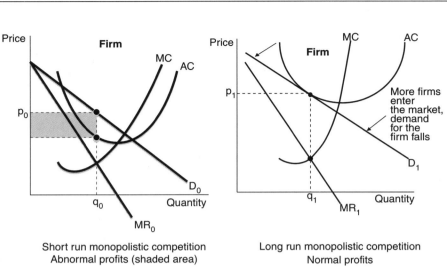

Short run monopolistic competition
Abnormal profits (shaded area)

Long run monopolistic competition
Normal profits

Contestable markets

Most markets in the UK are dominated by a few firms. This is known as oligarchy. In the traditional model of oligopoly it is assumed that there are barriers to entry; in reality it is likely that other firms can enter the market. These are contestable markets, i.e. it is possible for competition to increase within them and this puts pressure on existing firms to behave efficiently.

According to the theory of contestable markets: if entry to a market is easy then even though there may be only a few producers they may act in a competitive manner. The existence of high profits would act as a signal for others to enter and this therefore forces existing firms to be competitive.

The assumptions of theory of the contestable markets include:
* there is freedom of entry and exit
* the number of firms competing will vary, e.g. it may be a monopoly at one time and then there may be many other firms competing at other times
* firms compete (rather than collude).

According to the theory of contestable markets, abnormal profits are earned in the short term; this attracts others firms into the market and in the long term only normal profits are earned.

A market will be more contestable if:
* profits are high – so there is an incentive to enter
* barriers to entry and exit are low so it is relatively easy to join a market and leave if needed. With low entry and exit barriers the industry may suffer from hit and run competition whereby firms enter when profits are high and then leave when profits fall.

A perfectly contestable market is one in which the costs of entry and exit are zero. In this situation there is a high degree of pressure on firms to act competitively; abnormal profits will act as an incentive to bring in more firms. Entry is likely to lead to lower prices, better quality service, more choice and higher output.

Markets such as banking have become more contestable as it has become easier to enter them due to changes in technology, e.g. internet banking.

Sunk costs are costs already invested in an industry which cannot be recovered; when considering whether to continue in an industry a firm should ignore sunk costs. If the sunk costs in an industry are high, e.g. high initial expenditure on specialist equipment is required, this will deter entry into the market and make it less contestable. If sunk costs are low, e.g. if any initial investment can be easily recovered, the market is likely to be highly contestable.

Barriers to entry include:
* sunk costs; these are low if it is cheap to set up (e.g. no specialized equipment needed, no major investment in land or IT is required)
* marketing costs: how expensive will it be to promote the product and get distribution? Do established products have strong brand loyalty?
* threats and previous actions; if a business has cut prices in the past in response to new entrants this sends a signal that it is prepared to fight for its market share. This may frighten off new potential entrants. Similarly, if established firms hold excess capacity this is a signal that they can quickly increase output and drive the price down.

Price discrimination

Price discrimination involves charging different prices for the same good or service which have the same costs of production, e.g. charging a pensioner and student different amounts to use the same train.
To price discriminate a firm must

- be able to keep the markets separate, i.e. prevent individuals in one market buying at the lower price in the other market; it must also be able to prevent the people buying at the lower price from reselling at the higher price

- have some control over the price, i.e. it must be a price maker
- there must be different price elasticities of demand in the different markets

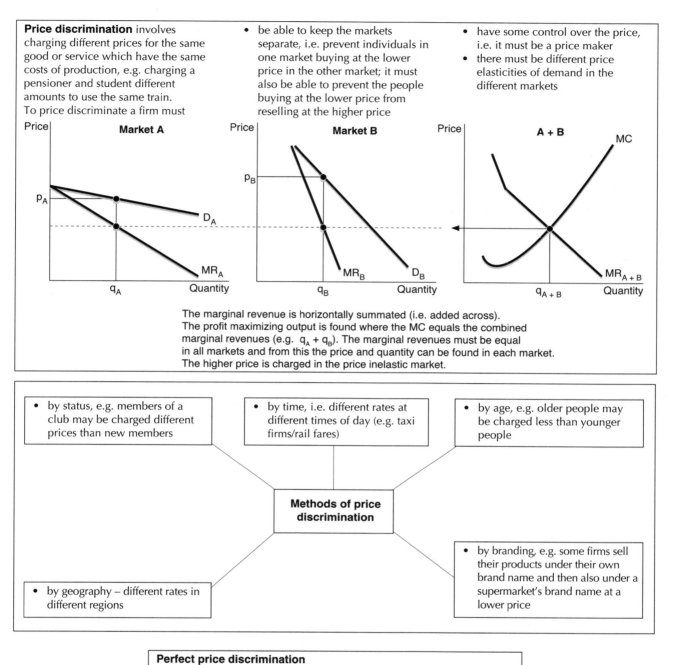

The marginal revenue is horizontally summated (i.e. added across).
The profit maximizing output is found where the MC equals the combined marginal revenues (e.g. $q_A + q_B$). The marginal revenues must be equal in all markets and from this the price and quantity can be found in each market.
The higher price is charged in the price inelastic market.

- by status, e.g. members of a club may be charged different prices than new members

- by time, i.e. different rates at different times of day (e.g. taxi firms/rail fares)

- by age, e.g. older people may be charged less than younger people

Methods of price discrimination

- by geography – different rates in different regions

- by branding, e.g. some firms sell their products under their own brand name and then also under a supermarket's brand name at a lower price

Perfect price discrimination
The consumer is charged the maximum he/she is willing to pay for each unit.
The price is different for *every* single unit. This removes all consumer surplus.

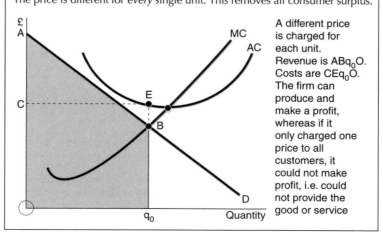

A different price is charged for each unit. Revenue is ABq_0O. Costs are CEq_0O. The firm can produce and make a profit, whereas if it only charged one price to all customers, it could not make profit, i.e. could not provide the good or service

Oligopoly

An **oligopoly** occurs when a few firms dominate a market, e.g. the newspaper industry, supermarkets, airlines. (A duopoly occurs when two firms dominate.) Because there are only a few firms, the actions of one of them can have a significant effect on the behaviour of the others. There is no one price and output outcome in oligopoly. Firms are interdependent and a firm's behaviour will depend on what it thinks the others are going to do. Economists build different models with different assumptions; each will have its own price and output solution.

Competition and collusion

Oligopoly firms have two conflicting aims:
- to collude with other firms to maximize their combined profits
- to compete with other firms to take business away from them and make more profit independently

Tacit collusion occurs when firms collude without any formal agreement being reached or even without any communication between them.

Kinked demand curve: non-co-operative model of oligopoly

We assume:
- if the firm increases its price other firms do not follow so demand is price elastic
- if the firm decreases its price the other firms do follow so demand is price inelastic

This model explains price rigidity in oligopoly, i.e. why prices do not change very much and firms tends to compete via non price competition, e.g. advertising, sales promotions. This can be explained in two ways:
- if the price is increased, demand is price elastic and revenue falls; if the price is cut, demand is price inelastic and revenue falls, i.e. any price change leads to a fall in revenue, and so the firm leaves price unchanged.
- the kinked demand causes a discontinuity in the marginal revenue curve; changes in marginal cost between MC_1 and MC_3 do not change the profit maximizing price and output, i.e. prices are likely to be relatively fixed despite cost changes.

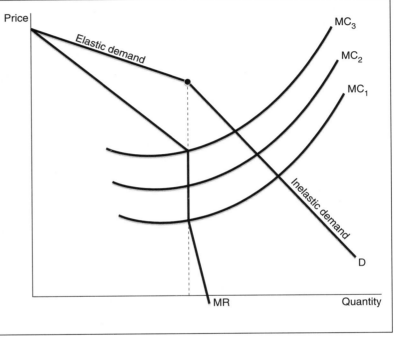

Collusive model of oligopoly (cartel)

Firms collude, i.e. work together and act like a profit maximizing monopolist. They fix a profit maximizing price and output for the industry, e.g. p_0 q_0 and give each other quotas. This maximizes the industry's profits, but there is an incentive for individual producers to cut their price and exceed their quotas to increase their own profits at the expense of the industry, i.e. cartels tend to break down as there is an incentive to cheat unless there is an effective policing mechanism (an effective means of ensuring that firms are not producing too much or undercutting the agreed price).

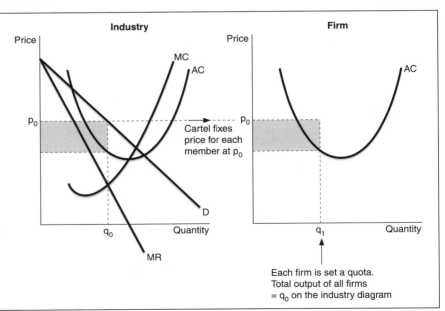

What makes collusion more likely?

- if there are only a few firms, it is easier to check on each other and share information
- effective communication and monitoring systems mean that any cheating can be identified early on
- stable cost and demand conditions mean that quotas are easy to allocate and measure and the policy is easy to administer
- similar production costs so they make similar profits

Oligopoly continued

Game theory

The decision that a firm makes in oligopoly depends on its assumptions about other firms. This means firms will try to calculate the best course of action depending on how others behave. Economists try to build models of this behaviour; this is known as 'game theory', e.g. the prisoner's dilemma.

An example of game theory
Payoff matrix for pricing strategies of firm A and firm B

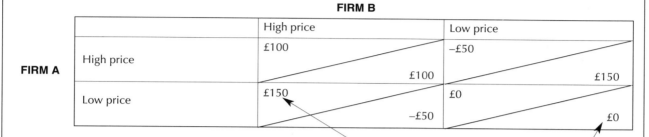

In the diagram above, the top left in each box shows the payoff for firm A, the bottom right shows the payoff for firm B.
If both firms co-operate and raise price they can both earn an extra £100; this is the most profitable outcome for both firms combined. However, if one firm agrees to raise price it is in the interests of the other firm to cut price. If firm A has a low price and firm B has a high price, for example, A earns £150 and B loses £50. B wins customers off A. If both firms fail to trust each other they will cut price because they want to win at the expense of the other and fear the other one might cut price as well. The end result will be that they both earn £0 because they have both cut price. The actual outcome depends on whether they can trust each other.

A Nash equilibrium occurs in game theory when no firm can improve its position given the strategy of the other firms; it is an equilibrium because no firm has an incentive to change.

Pricing and non-pricing strategies

- Cost plus pricing. Firms add a percentage profit on to their costs. This is a relatively straightforward strategy to implement (e.g. just add 10% to costs) and is often used by retailers. However it ignores demand conditions.
- Predatory pricing. Occurs when firms deliberately undercut their competitors to force them out of the market; it is anti-competitive.
- Limit pricing. Selecting the highest price possible without encouraging entry. If competitors entered the extra supply would drive the price down to a level at which they could not survive, therefore they do not enter.
- Price wars. These occur when firms in an oligopoly try to undercut each other. The aim is to gain sales from the competition. It often happens when there is overcapacity in an industry, e.g. cars and PCs.
- Price leadership. Sometimes in an oligopoly there is an obvious price leader, i.e. all firms follow the pricing decisions of one of the other firms. This may be because the price leader is the dominant firm in the industry and so the other firms do not want to challenge it by making different decisions. The decision to follow may be clearly agreed between the firms or it may occur without any formal agreement (this is known as 'tacit collusion').

Non-price competition

This is quite common in oligopoly. Rather than using price changes which can easily be followed, firms look for other means to compete, for example

- advertising
- branding, i.e. developing a well known brand name and brand loyalty
- sales promotions, i.e. offers (such as buy one get one free) and competitions
- distribution, i.e. controlling distribution to retail outlets

In industries such as confectionery, cigarettes, cleaning products and jeans, spending on promotional campaigns is very high.

Firms may try to develop a USP (Unique Selling Proposition) to differentiate their products, e.g. locally made, natural ingredients or 24-hour service.

Role of advertising

Advertising is a paid form of communication. It is part of the promotional mix, which also includes sales promotions, sponsorships, special offers and the sales force. Advertising aims to generate Awareness, generate Interest, generate Desire and generate Action. This is the AIDA model.

Advertising:

- can persuade
- can inform
- can increase demand

But

- can mislead
- can create barriers to entry by making demand more inelastic, by shifting demand for other firms' products inwards, and by making the costs of entry higher

Competition policy

Competition policy

Competition policy by the government may aim to
- encourage business start-ups
- encourage entry into markets by removing barriers to entry
- take actions against anti-competitive practices
- prevent firms from abusing monopoly power

Competition policy can
- fine firms
- force firms to remove barriers to entry
- make firms sell off their assets / break up dominant firms
- introduce price controls
- stop collusion
- block mergers/takeovers

The **Office of Fair Trading** (OFT), led by the Director General of Fair Trading (DGFT), is an independent body funded by the Government for making sure that markets work in the interests of customers, e.g. preventing and stopping firms from abusing their market positions. It can impose sanctions or refer to the Competition Commission for investigation. The OFT can fine firms up to 10% of their turnover if they are found guilty.

The Competition Commission investigates potential monopoly situations. A firm or group of firms is defined as having a dominant position if it has a market share of 40%; it has a monopoly if it has a market share of 25%: these definitions refer to local as well as national markets. Privatized monopolies such as British Telecom are regulated by regulatory bodies such as OFCOM.

The **European Commission** investigates and punishes firms guilty of breaking EU competition law. Firms can appeal to the European Court of Justice.

EU restrictive practices policy
Article 81 covers agreements between firms and practices that prevent, restrict or distort competition. It aims to restrict collusive behaviour. Practices that are considered anti-competitive include collusion to
- fix the price
- limit production, markets or investment
- share out the market

European monopoly power: Article 82 relates to the abuse of market power and has been extended to cover mergers.

EU mergers: 1990 legislation covers mergers where the combined worldwide annual sales exceed €5 billion; where EU sales of at least two of the companies exceed €250 million; and where at least one of the companies conducts no more than two thirds of its EU-wide business in a single member state.

UK competition laws
1948 Monopolies and Restrictive Practices Act
Monopolies are to be investigated on an individual basis. It is not assumed that they are always acting either for or against the public interest.

1956 Restrictive Trade Practices Act
Firms are obliged to register any restrictive practice agreements; these are assumed to be against the public interest unless those involved can justify them to the Restrictive Practices Court

1964 Resale Prices Act
Minimum resale prices are prohibited

1965 Monopolies and Mergers Act
Mergers can now be investigated

1973 Fair Trading Act
Created the Office of Director General of Fair Trading, who advises the Secretary of State. Monopolies can now be referred if they have 25% of the market (it used to be 33%). Nationalized industries can be investigated. Local and not just national monopolies can be investigated

1980 Competition Act
Aims to deal with anti-competitive practices by firms, for example
- predatory pricing – which involves selling products at a loss to drive out a competitor
- full line forcing – which involves making retailers buy the whole product range even if they only want one product
- exclusive supply, i.e. selling to only one outlet in an area

1998 Competition Act
This Act:
- prohibited anti-competitive agreements, cartels and concerted practices based on Article 85 of the EU treaty
- prohibited abuse of dominant market position based on Article 80 of the EU treaty
- established that a Director General of Fair Trading (DGFT) would be appointed by the Government. The DGFT is responsible for overseeing competition policy and consumer protection. He/she has the right along with Secretary of State for Industry to refer a monopoly to the Competition Commission for investigation
- established the Competition Commission (formerly the Monopolies and Mergers Commission). The Competition Commission investigates potential monopoly situations. A firm or group of firms with over 40% of the market has a 'dominant position'. A firm with a market share of over 25% of the market is a 'monopoly'. (These market shares can relate to both national and local markets.) After an investigation the Commission produces a report; this is given to the Secretary of State who may or may not accept its findings. If found guilty a firm may be fined up to 10% of its turnover.

2002 Enterprise Act
The Competition Commission must determine whether the merger will impact adversely on competition, in other words if it 'prevents, restricts or distorts competition'; if so, then the merger is likely to be blocked.

UK competition policy is generally pragmatic, e.g. it appreciates the potential gains as well as costs of monopoly power, and investigates each case on its own merits.

Cartels
The Enterprise Act identifies certain situations which would result in prosecutions for unlawful behaviour if the actions of at least two firms:
- directly or indirectly fix a price for the supply in the UK of a product or service by those firms
- limit or prevent supply in the UK of a product or service by the firms
- limit or prevent production in the UK of a product or service by the firms
- divide between firms the supply in the UK of a product or service to a customer or customers
- fix the terms of a bid in such a way that prevents the normal operation of the bidding process.

The punishment can include imprisonment for up to a maximum of five years and/or a fine.

Other anti-competitive practices include:
- resale price maintenance: this occurs when firms fix the prices (or the minimum prices) at which shops sell their goods
- refusing to supply: a firm may refuse to sell to some companies, e.g. if the business will not sell at the price it wants or if it will not take competitors' goods off its shelves
- predatory pricing: this occurs when a firm sells at a loss to drive out competitors; once they are removed prices will increase again
- tie-ins: a business may only agree to sell one of its products if others are also bought at the same time

Types of business

- Sole trader – an individual runs his or her own business; the owner is personally liable for any debts and has unlimited liability
- Partnerships – individuals work together and share joint responsibility for any decisions; unlimited liability
- Companies – a company has a separate legal existence from its owners; the owners have limited liability; companies are owned by shareholders
- **a** private companies: have 'ltd' after their name; shares cannot be advertised
- **b** public limited companies: have 'plc' after their names; shares can be advertised and traded on the Stock Exchange.

- Public corporations or nationalized industries are in the public sector

Shares

Shareholders are part owners of a company. Usually they have one vote per share. More shares = more votes. Shareholders vote on the amount of dividends (rewards) to be paid out and how much should be retained in the business. Shareholders may also gain by selling their shares for a higher price than they paid for them originally (although the price can also fall).

Multinationals (or transnationals)

Firms which have production facilities in more than one country, e.g. Shell, BP

Why become multinational?

- To exploit resources in different countries, e.g. cheap labour
- To reduce risk of stoppages and reduce union power, e.g if there is a strike in one country the firm can carry on producing elsewhere
- To enter markets; some governments (e.g. China) are reluctant to let in foreign firms unless they are based in the country
- To be closer to the market; reduced distribution costs
- To benefit from fewer regulations, e.g. on health and safety

Benefits to countries of having multinationals locate there

Foreign direct investment by multinationals may:

- Bring jobs; this creates more income and generates tax revenue for the Government through the multiplier effects

- Bring knowledge
- Bring methods that lead to higher productivity and lower unit costs
- Invest capital, boosting demand
- Pay corporation tax
- Provide more choice for customers
- Stimulate economic growth
- Improve balance of payments on the current account by boosting exports

Why might governments be suspicious of multinationals?

- May not use local employees or only for unskilled jobs
- May not re-invest profits
- May damage the environment
- May exert power over the government

Growth of firms

Internal (organic) growth and external

- **Internal (or organic) growth** occurs when firms sell more of their products. External growth occurs when a firm joins with another business. This may be through a takeover (which occurs when one business takes control of another; this is also called an acquisition) or a merger (which occurs when one firm joins together with another one to form a new business).
- **External growth** tends to be quicker. It can lead to rapid changes in the size of a business. This may be good in terms of, e.g., shared resources, market power, purchasing power and the ability to produce on a large scale (i.e. internal economies of scale). However, it can bring problems with managing a much bigger business (e.g. problems of coordination, communication, motivation and control leading to higher unit costs, i.e. diseconomies of scale).

Why takeover or merge with another business?

- Access to new markets; it may be a way of overcoming protectionist measures
- Fast growth
- Share resources and expertise; this can create synergy (2 + 2 = 5)
- Share strengths in different areas, e.g. different regions of the world
- Cut costs, e.g. will not necessarily need two research and development teams or two marketing directors, so can make redundancies

Reasons for growth

- Safer from takeover
- Economies of scale
- More market power
- Status
- Personal motives, e.g. desire of managers for more control

Types of growth

- Horizontal: one firms joins with another at the same stage of the same production process, e.g. two car manufacturers. Can lead to internal economies of scale.

- Vertical: one firm joins with another at a different stage of the same production process. Forward vertical: firms buys up a firm nearer the customer, e.g. a distributor. Backward vertical: a firm buys up a supplier. Can guarantee supplies or access to the market.
- Conglomerate: a firm buys up another firm in a different industry, e.g. a cigarette company buys up a chocolate company. Can spread risks.

Share prices are determined by supply and demand. An increase in demand for shares should lead to higher prices: it may be because investors expect the company to perform well in the future, increasing the share price and/or the dividends paid. Confidence in the future performance of the business is therefore a major determinant of demand. Buyers may also be speculating about the price increasing in the future.

Franchising: a franchise occurs when an individual or firm buys the right to use another firm's name, sell its product and use its systems. The franchisor sells these rights to the franchisee. e.g. McDonald's franchises some of its outlets.

Benefits of franchising to the franchisor:

- Can grow fast because the franchisee provides the investment
- The franchisee should be quite motivated because they share the rewards
- Can share overheads such as marketing between the franchisees

Benefits of buying a franchise

- Can buy an established business with proven track record
- Have access to the experience and systems of the franchisee; can learn from other franchisees
- Can share costs such as marketing between all franchisees
- Part of a bigger organization, e.g. benefiting from a national or international

Objectives of firms

Profit maximization

The classical model of economics assumes firms want to maximize profits, i.e. produce

where MR = MC (marginal revenue = marginal cost). However other models suggest firms may have different objectives.

Managerial models
Managerial utility maximization (Williamson)

The owners of companies are shareholders. The people who control the company day to day are managers. In large companies, in particular, there is a divorce between ownership and control, i.e. the people who run the business are not the owners. This can lead to conflicting objectives. What the managers want to do is not necessarily what the owners want them to do. Given the fact that shareholders do not usually keep themselves well informed (or are not kept well informed), managers often have considerable freedom in their decision taking. They may then pursue their own objectives and try to maximize their own utility rather than profit. Managerial objectives may include:

- increasing their salary – this may or may not be linked to profit (it is often linked to sales rather than profit)
- increasing the number of employees – this makes managers feel more powerful and important
- investing – this again makes managers feel more powerful
- getting additional benefits, e.g. a big office, first class travel, a bigger car

Sales revenue maximization (Baumol), (produce where MR = 0)

Assumes managers want to maximize revenue rather than profit. *Why?*

- consumers value companies with increasing sales and are more likely to buy from them; consumers rarely know about the profits of companies
- financial institutions may be more willing to lend to a company with increasing sales
- salaries may be linked to sales

Growth maximization (Marris), (i.e. produce at the highest output where AR = AC)

Managers may seek to increase the size of their firm. *Why?*

- large firms are less vulnerable to takeover
- salary may be linked to size of the firm
- big firms are perceived as more successful than smaller ones

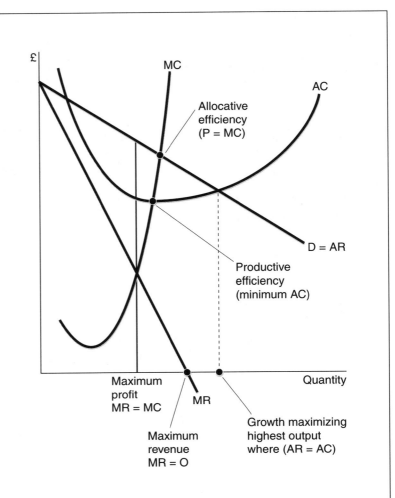

Satisficing (Simon)

A firm involves or deals with many interest groups all with their own objectives, e.g. different departments, (e.g. marketing, production and finance), the unions, suppliers, consumers, the local community.
The overall objectives of an organization will be the result of discussion, negotiation and bargaining with all these groups. The end result is likely to be a compromise which reaches a satisfactory conclusion but which does not maximize anything. The firm aims to SATISFICE these different groups and still function.

Labour

Demand for labour
The demand for labour is derived from the marginal revenue product of labour.

People are employed because of the value of their output. This depends on the extra output they produce (their marginal product) and the extra revenue this generates when it is sold (the marginal revenue).

The value of the output produced by an extra employee is called the marginal revenue product (MRP).

MRP = MP x MR

The MRP is downward sloping; MP slopes downwards because of the law of diminishing returns; MR also slopes downwards in an imperfect goods market or is constant in a perfectly competitive goods market.

- **Derived demand:** the demand for labour is a derived demand. Firms only demand employees because of the demand for the actual goods and services.
- **Marginal product of labour:** the extra output produced by an additional worker. As additional units of labour are added the marginal product will eventually fall to a fixed factor because of the law of diminishing returns
- **Marginal cost of labour:** extra cost of hiring another employee

The demand for labour will shift outwards:
- with more training, capital or better management, labour can become more productive
- if demand for the final product increases (i.e. MR increases)
- if the price of a substitute factor of production increases

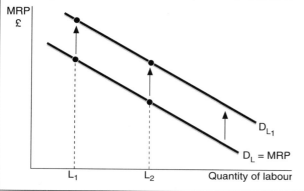

The elasticity of demand for labour Depends on —
- labour costs as a percentage of the total cost – the higher the percentage, the greater the impact of any wage increase and the more likely it is that the quantity demanded of labour will fall, i.e. the more elastic demand for labour will be.
- the time period – in the short run the firm may find it difficult to replace labour with other factors, e.g. capital equipment; over time it may prove easier and so demand will be more price elastic.
- the price elasticity of demand of the final good or service – a wage increase will increase costs and may increase price. If the effect of the price increase of the good is relatively small, the effect on the quantity demanded of labour is also likely to be relatively small, i.e. a price inelastic demand for the product is likely to lead to a wage inelastic demand for the labour.

An individual's supply of labour
An individual can choose between leisure and work. If he/she decides to work more, then leisure time falls and vice versa. The decision whether to work or not depends on an income and substitution effect. For example, if the wage increases
- it is more expensive to have leisure time (because every hour you do not work you are giving up more money). The employee will therefore substitute towards work and away from leisure.
- at the same time more money is earned for every hour that is being worked, and so an employee might feel that he or she can work fewer hours and still have enough total income (the income effect).

Usually the substitution effect is greater than the income effect and people will want to work more hours when the wage increases. However, at some wages the income effect outweighs the substitution effect and people will decide to work less when the wage increases. This causes a backward sloping supply curve for labour.

Wage rate

An individual's supply of labour

Income effect outweighs substitution effect: individuals work less as the wage rate increases

Substitution effect outweighs income effect: individuals want to work longer as the wage increases

Hours worked

The supply of labour to an industry depends on
- the working population, e.g. population size, working age, and retirement age
- the non-monetary aspects of the job, e.g. job security, better working conditions
- the number of people who know about the job
- wages in other industries
- attitudes to work, e.g. attitudes towards women working in certain jobs

Hiring employees
Employees will be hired up to the point where the extra cost of hiring an employee is equal to the addition to sales revenue from hiring them (their MRP).

i.e. employees will be hired up to the point where MRP = MC labour

Labour continued

A perfectly competitive labour market

There are many firms and many employees; each firm is a wage taker, i.e. it can hire as many employees as it wishes at the given wage rate; a decision by one firm to employ more people will not shift the industry demand enough to increase the wage rate; although if all firms decided to hire more people, wages would increase.
In a perfectly competitive labour market, wages will be determined by market forces of demand and supply.

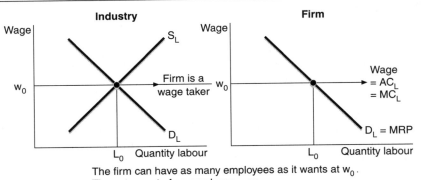

The firm can have as many employees as it wants at w_0.
The extra cost of an employee = w_0.
so wage = average cost of labour = marginal cost of labour = w_0

Wage differences

In theory all wages will be equal because high wage rates in one industry will attract workers from another industry; this increases supply until the wage rates are equal.
However, wage differences would still exist due to:
- quasi-pecuniary benefits (such as pension rights and subsidized healthcare); non-pecuniary benefits (e.g. long holidays); non-pecuniary disadvantages (e.g. risk of boredom).
- labour immobility, e.g. geographical or occupational; this immobility prevents labour moving from one industry to another
- lack of perfect information, so employees do not know the jobs exist or what the wage rate is

Imperfections in the labour market

- imperfect knowledge – workers do not know what jobs are available
- immobility – workers cannot move from one job to another due to geographical or occupational immobility
- employers may not be profit maximizers – they may pay more than they need to; employees may not be rational economic maximizers, i.e. they may stay with a company out of loyalty even if they are 'underpaid'
- there may be monopoly buyers (monopsony) or sellers (unions)
- exploitation – this occurs when employees are paid less than their value. This happens when the employer is in a strong bargaining position, e.g. if the employer is a monopsonist (i.e. the major employer in the area)

Geographical immobility occurs

because people may have difficulty moving from one job to another in a different part of the country, e.g. because:
- they have children in education and do not want to move them
- they have family and friends in the area
- it is too expensive to move (e.g. removal costs and house prices)

Occupational immobility occurs

when people cannot move from one type of job to another. This may be because:
- they do not have the right skills
- they do not know the job exists

Problems with marginal productivity theory of wages

- difficult to apply in some labour markets - how is the productivity of a receptionist measured?
- in some markets, e.g. in the public sector, wages are set by the Government and not market forces
- the theory is circular – wages depend on the demand for labour, which depends on the demand for the good, which depends on wages!

Wage determination in imperfect markets
Monopsony

This is a situation where the firm:
- is a major buyer of labour and has power over the market
- is a wage maker not a wage taker
- faces upward sloping supply curves – they need to increase wages to attract more workers. They must increase the wage for the last worker and all the ones before; this means the marginal cost of labour is higher than the average wage rate (the average cost)

For example
3 workers are paid £200 a week each. Average cost of labour is £200.
To attract a fourth worker the wage must be increased to £300. The average cost is now £300. But the marginal cost is £600 – the new worker is paid £300 and each of the other three are paid £100 extra each. Looking at it another way: total cost was 3 x £200 = £600. It now is 4 x £300 = £1200, so the marginal cost of labour is £600.

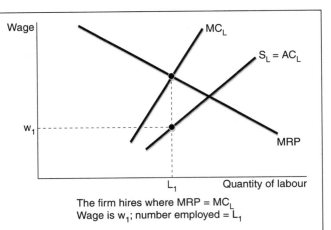

The firm hires where MRP = MC_L
Wage is w_1; number employed = L_1

*The marginal cost of labour is above and diverging from the average cost of labour; to hire more the firm must increase wages for the last worker **and** all the workers before.*

Labour continued

Trade unions

Trade unions are organizations which represent employees. Unions are established to protect employee interests and to bargain on their behalf. By joining a union, employees gain more strength in their bargaining.

Unions will typically bargain over issues such as pay, working conditions, and training.

Collective bargaining occurs when unions represent a group of employees. This gives the employees more bargaining strength with management.

Trade unions can affect the wage rate by:
- improving productivity – by negotiating for better conditions and protecting the workforce, the unions may improve workers' output
- using industrial power (e.g. the threat of strikes) to force employers to pay more
- by restricting supply – in the past there have been closed shops in various industries and firms; this means that only union members are allowed to work there, which reduces the possible supply of labour and increases the wage rate.

The power of trade unions depends on
- the number of members
- the legal environment – in the 1980s the Conservative Government considerably reduced the powers of trade unions; it made them more liable for the consequence of their actions and prevented industrial action without a secret ballot
- the demand for the product; e.g. if demand is inelastic the firm will be more likely to pay higher wages because it will be easier to pass on the higher costs to the consumer in the form of higher prices
- if labour costs are a small percentage of total costs – the effect of a wage increase will be smaller if labour is only a relatively small percentage of total costs
- if the firm is profitable – this means it may be more likely to pay more to employees compared to a situation where it was making a loss

Bilateral monopoly

This occurs when a monopoly buyer of labour faces a monopoly seller, e.g. a monopsonist v. a union. The outcome here depends on the bargaining strength of each side.

Power over labour supply

Unions can use their power to push up the price of labour. This causes a surplus and reduces the number employed. Unions must decide whether to maximize the total wage bill, maximize the wages of those employed, or to maximize the number employed.

To try to increase pay and employment, unions must aim to increase productivity so that the demand for labour shifts outwards. This could be achieved through better working practices.

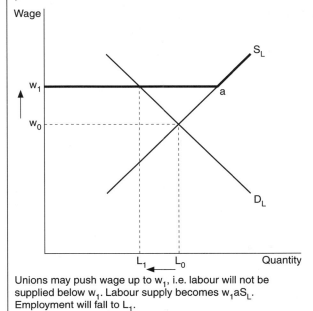

Unions may push wage up to w_1, i.e. labour will not be supplied below w_1. Labour supply becomes w_1aS_L.
Employment will fall to L_1.
Those in employment earn more but fewer are employed.

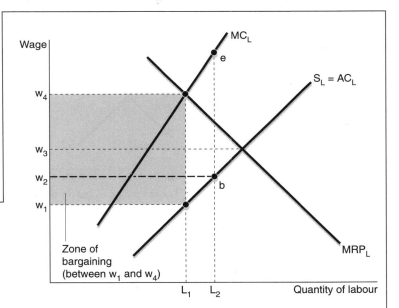

Monopsonist would hire L_1 workers at w_1. If union imposes minimum wage of, e.g. w_2, supply becomes w_2bS_L. Firm can hire as many workers as it wants up to L_2 at a wage of w_2; after this point it would have to increase wages for extra workers and all the ones before. The MC curve is W_2beMC_L. The Firm will hire up to the point where $MRP = MC_L$, i.e. L_2 workers at w_2, i.e. the union has increased wages and employment. The union can keep doing this up to w_3. After w_3 (up to w_4) it can increase wages but employment begins to fall back towards L_1.

Labour continued

Differences in individuals' earnings

Depend on:

- ability and skills – the greater an individual's skill, the more he or she is likely to earn, e.g. if they are more trained or have achieved higher qualifications
- non-monetary characteristics of a job, e.g. people may have to be paid more to do a dangerous job

- age – earnings tend to increase with age up to a point and then decline
- gender and race: women and non whites tend to earn less; this could be because of discrimination
- location: wages vary across the country and between countries
- demand for the individual, e.g. a well-known personality might earn more

---

Minimum wage A minimum wage above equilibrium creates excess supply.

The impact of a minimum wage is greater when demand for and supply of labour are elastic

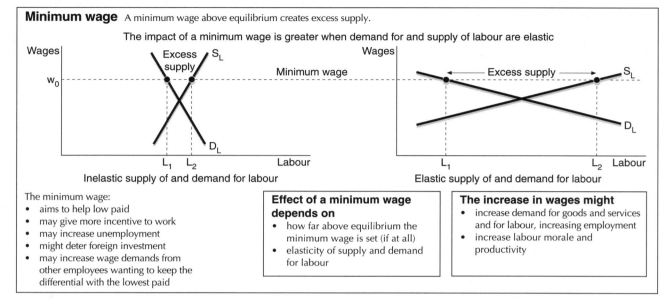

Inelastic supply of and demand for labour

Elastic supply of and demand for labour

The minimum wage:

- aims to help low paid
- may give more incentive to work
- may increase unemployment
- might deter foreign investment
- may increase wage demands from other employees wanting to keep the differential with the lowest paid

Effect of a minimum wage depends on

- how far above equilibrium the minimum wage is set (if at all)
- elasticity of supply and demand for labour

The increase in wages might

- increase demand for goods and services and for labour, increasing employment
- increase labour morale and productivity

Government intervention in labour markets

Legislation exists to protect employees, e.g. they are entitled to notice and redundancy pay if they have been with the firm for over a year, have the right to join a trade union,

have the right not to be 'unfairly' dismissed, have the right not to be discriminated against (e.g. on the grounds of gender or ethnic origin).

Also the Health and Safety at Work Act puts obligations on the employer to protect staff.

Other regulations include **National Minimum Wage**: limit to how low wages can go. Introduced in the UK in 1999.

Transfer earnings

This is the amount that a factor of production must earn to keep it in its present usage in the long run.

Economic rent is payment over and above transfer earnings.

Quasi rent

Imagine a machine with only one use is purchased. Once bought, all its earnings are economic rent, assuming it has no alternative use. Over time it will depreciate and will not be replaced unless it earns a satisfactory return; some of its earnings are now transfer earnings – if it does not make enough, a new machine will not be bought.

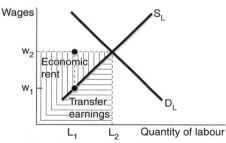

Worker L_1 would work for w_1 but receives w_2. w_1w_2 is 'economic rent'

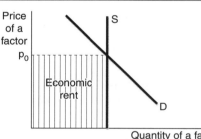

Supply of the factor is completely inelastic; it has no alternative use; all of its earnings are 'economic rent'

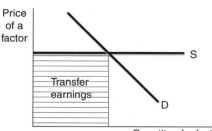

With a perfectly elastic supply all earnings are transfer earnings. There is no economic rent

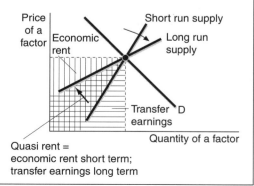

Quasi rent = economic rent short term; transfer earnings long term

Income and wealth

Income v wealth

Income is a flow, e.g. the money an individual earns in a year.

Wealth is a stock, i.e. the total value of an individual's assets at a moment in time. The two can be linked: with more income more wealth can be acquired which can then generate more income.

Flow per year

Stock at a particular moment

Income

Wealth

Sources of income

Individuals may earn income from different sources, including:
- earned income, i.e. from employment
- unearned income (i.e. income earned from wealth, e.g. dividends from shares, interest from savings)
- transfer payments, e.g. pensions from the Government

Why do incomes differ?

Incomes depend on:
- demand – this will depend on the marginal revenue product of an individual. This in turn will depend on the individual's skills, his or her training, the level of technology, the amount of capital and an individual's experience.
- supply conditions in the labour market.
- bargaining power (e.g. trade unions).
- government policy (e.g. wages in the public sector; minimum wage legislation).
- direct taxation and benefits policy.
- wealth, e.g. if an individual owns various properties these will generate income through rent.
- discrimination, e.g. on gender or ethnic origin or age.

2007 Annual Survey of Hours and Earnings (ASHE) show median earnings of full-time male employees was £498 per week in April 2007; for women the median was £394. The top 10% of the earnings distribution earned more than £906 per week, while the bottom 10% earned less than £252.

The occupations with the highest earnings in 2007 were 'Health professionals' followed by 'Corporate managers' and 'Science and technology professionals'. The lowest paid of all full-time employees were 'Sales occupations'.

Wealth

- may be inherited
- may be acquired with earnings

Wealth in the UK is unevenly distributed.

Personal wealth: can be held in many forms of assets, e.g. cars, savings, household items. Most significant form of personal wealth is ownership of housing.

Marketable wealth: assets which can be bought and sold, e.g. housing

Non-marketable wealth: cannot be transferred, e.g. pension rights – these belong to an individual and cannot be sold on

Taxes to reduce wealth inequality include:
- inheritance tax
- capital transfer tax
- wealth tax.

Equality and equity (fairness)

In a market economy individuals receive different incomes: given different supply and demand conditions, rewards will vary. If employees have rare skills that are limited in supply and highly demanded, their earnings will be higher than someone who is pursuing a career with a high supply and low demand. Similarly individuals own assets: cars, houses, land and so on. The value of these depends on supply and demand as well.

As a result of supply and demand the economy will contain rich and poor people, i.e. there will be inequality.

The degree of income inequality can be measured by the Lorenz curve and the Gini coefficient (see page 57).

People may think this inequality is unfair (i.e. there is a lack of equity); this does not mean it is necessarily inefficient. A 'fair' distribution (which involves a normative decision about what is fair) may lead to inefficiency, e.g. taxing high income earners to make incomes more equal may remove the incentive to compete or succeed.

- **Horizontal equity:** occurs when there is identical treatment of people who are in the same situation. e.g. no discrimination against people on the basis on race or gender. Horizontal equity may be measured by considering e.g. the earnings of women compared to men, or earnings in one region compared to another.

- **Vertical equity:** the different treatment of people with different characteristics to promote greater equity, e.g. redistributing from rich to poor. In the case of taxation this means taxing the rich more in proportion to their earnings.

Equity v efficiency

The free market leads to an uneven distribution of income. Governments intervene because society regards this distribution as unacceptable. However, while subsidies to the poor and higher taxes on the rich may be regarded as socially desirable, they are interfering with the market mechanism and so are actually creating inefficiency.

On the other hand given that inefficiencies exist already within the market (e.g. monopolies or externalities) intervention may actually improve efficiency overall (one inefficiency offsetting another– this is the Theory of Second Best).

Poverty

- Absolute poverty: occurs when human beings cannot consume sufficient necessities to maintain life: e.g. people are malnourished and homeless. Absolute poverty is rare in the UK
- Relative poverty: means that some people are poor in relation to others. This does not necessarily mean they are poor in absolute terms.

Desirability of income distribution in the UK

The present distribution of income may be regarded by some as undesirable because:
- absolute poverty exists; some people are sleeping on the streets
- relative poverty exists; e.g. the gap between rich and poor may be viewed as too wide
- horizontal inequality exists; e.g. differences between the earning of men and women

Government and the redistribution of income

The Government redistributes income via:
- spending, e.g. on social security benefits and pensions; on the provision of goods and services, e.g education, health and housing
- taxation, e.g. progressive income taxes
- legislation, e.g. minimum wage legislation and equal pay legislation
- training; this may improve wages in the long term.

National income accounting

Calculating national income

Three methods of calculating national income:
- expenditure method
- income method
- output method

If £100 worth of goods has been produced (output) this has generated £100 of income for the various factors of production (income) and will lead to £100 of spending (expenditure). *Note*: if no-one else buys the goods, the firm will end up with stocks, and we count this as if it bought them itself. Therefore:

OUTPUT = INCOME = EXPENDITURE

The expenditure method adds up spending in the economy.

C   consumers' expenditure
+ I   investment spending by firms; this includes planned investment in capital and unplanned increases in stock (listed as gross fixed capital formation and the value of physical increases in stock)
+ G   Government spending (usually listed as general Government consumption)
+ X   export spending
− M   import spending

Import spending must be deducted because it is spending on goods and services from outside the UK, i.e. this spending leaves the economy.
Adding up C + I + G + X − M gives Gross Domestic Product (GDP) at market prices

The income method involves adding up:

wages & salaries
+ self-employed income
+ trading profits
+ rent (includes 'imputed rent', e.g. the rental value of owne-occupied housing is estimated and included)
+ interest
= total domestic income − stock appreciation (if stocks increase in value over the year this exaggerates their value)
= GDP

Note: transfer payments should be excluded; these are payments for which no corresponding good or service is produced, e.g. social security payments.

The expenditure method: market prices to factor cost

If the spending of different groups in the economy is added up, this will show the spending at current or market prices. This does not reflect the income earned by the factors of production because:
- the market price is too high because of indirect taxes
- the market price is too low because of subsidies

Market price − indirect taxes + subsidies = factor cost

The output method

i) Adds up the added value of every firm's output (i.e. the value of the output minus the value of the input); this avoids double counting, e.g. counting the value of the steel and the value of the car which also includes the value of the steel.
<u>Or</u>
ii) adds up the output of <u>final</u> goods and services.

Measures of actual income

Gross Domestic Product (GDP) shows the value of final goods and services produced by factors of production within a country.

Gross National Product (GNP) shows the value of final goods and services produced by factors of production owned by a country's citizens, regardless of where in the world this is earned.
GNP = GDP plus net property income from abroad

Gross National Product to Net National Product (NNP)
Out of the income earned in the economy some will be spent replacing equipment that has depreciated. To measure the additional (or new or net) income earned, we deduct the amount spent simply on replacement of items.
Gross National Product − Depreciation *(also called 'capital consumption')* = Net National Product (NNP) *(also called 'net income')*

GDP deflator

Real national income is calculated by adjusting national income figures for inflation. The Retail Price Index is not used as it only considers consumer prices; a more complex measure of inflation is used, called the GDP deflator.

Summary

GDP market prices + net property income from abroad	=	GNP market prices
GNP market prices − indirect taxes + subsidies	=	GNP factor cost
GNP factor cost − depreciation	=	NNP

National income accounting continued

Problems comparing national income figures between countries

- the income figures of each country have to be converted into a common currency. It can be difficult deciding what value to use, because the value of the exchange rate is often changing all the time
- accounting techniques vary between countries, which can alter the way in which income is calculated
- it is important to take the price level into account, as well as the nominal income figure – a country may have less average income but also lower prices
- you should consider factors such as climate – one country may have to produce heat; another may get it for free
- the composition of output may vary considerably – one country may be spending on defence, another may be producing consumer goods
- the distribution of income is likely to vary
- some economies have much more barter and a greater black economy (illegal) than others

Standard of living

Often measured by real GDP per capita.

$$\text{real GDP per capita} = \frac{\text{real GDP (which is the GDP adjusted for inflation)}}{\text{population}}$$

But

- this ignores the value of goods and services which are not traded, e.g. goods which are swapped in a barter economy; housework; the black economy (work which is not declared to the Government); DIY.
- it ignores the distribution of income – although the average real GDP per person may be quite high, there could be a few extremely rich people and many poor.
- it does not take account of what is produced – one economy might be producing capital goods, which involves less consumption now but should lead to more future growth; another might be producing consumption goods which involves high levels of consumption today but less in the future.
- there are problems comparing over time, e.g. the price of videos and personal computers has gone down over the years. This might reduce the value of national income, even though the quality of the goods and the number of features has improved.
- economic 'bads' can increase the figure even though the 'quality of life' has fallen, e.g. a traffic jam causes more consumption of petrol and increases the output and income of the country but makes people worse off.
- valuation problems, e.g. some output such as defence or the health service does not have a market price; the value of these services is assumed to be the cost of providing them, which may over or under-value them.
- the quality of life – if we take longer holidays or work fewer hours, output and income may fall but we may enjoy life more; similarly, tougher restrictions on pollution might reduce output but increase the quality of our lives.

The Easterlin paradox suggests that increases in GDP do not increase happiness. Simply having more income to buy more products does not seem to 'buy' happiness, which seems to depend on many different factors such as the quality of our relationships, our experience of work, health, trust in the Government, and relative income (e.g. income relative to other countries rather than absolute income).

Other indicators of standard of living

Given the problems using national income figures to compare standards of living between countries or over time, some commentators use other indicators, such as:

- number of doctors per 1000 population
- adult literacy
- life expectancy.

Net Economic Welfare (Tobin and Nordhaus)

This is a measure of economic welfare; it adjusts GNP by deducting economic 'bads' (e.g. pollution) and adding the value of non-marketed activities (such as barter) and the value of leisure.

Similarly the **Index of Sustainable Economic Welfare** considers not just income levels but also factors such as income distribution and cost associated with pollution and other economically unsustainable costs. It uses this formula:

ISEW = personal consumption
+ non-defensive public expenditures
– defensive private expenditures
+ capital formation
+ services from domestic labour
– costs of environmental degradation
– depreciation of natural capital

Lorenz curve

This illustrates the distribution of incomes in an economy, e.g. in the diagram 30% of the households in the country have only 15% of the income.

The **Gini coefficient** measures the income equality by measuring the area between the line of absolute equality and the line of actual distribution of income (see shaded area). The bigger this area, the more unequal the distribution.

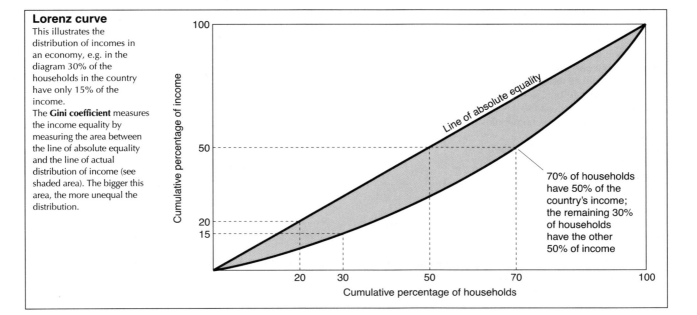

70% of households have 50% of the country's income; the remaining 30% of households have the other 50% of income

Aggregate demand, injections and withdrawals

Aggregate demand is the total planned expenditure on final goods and services in an economy.
It is made up of:

  C   consumption spending by households
+I   investment spending by firms
+G   Government spending by the Government
+X   exports spending from overseas
−M   imports spending on foreign goods and services

Note: Imports spending has to be deducted, because some of the spending in C + I + G is on foreign goods and services and so does not stay within the economy.

Aggregate demand will increase with:
- an increase in consumption (e.g. due to lower income tax)
- an increase in investment (e.g. due to lower interest rates)
- an increase in Government spending (e.g. a budget deficit)
- an increase in exports (e.g. due to a lower exchange rate)
- a fall in imports (e.g. due to quotas)

Injections (J) represent spending on final goods and services in addition to consumers' spending. Injections increase aggregate demand.
Planned injections represent spending in addition to that of the households in the economy, e.g. spending by other groups such as the Government firms, and overseas buyers, i.e. injections = investment + Government spending + exports

$$J = I + G + X$$

Withdrawals (W) represent a leakage from the economy. They represent income which is earned by households but which is not spent on final goods and services. Withdrawals reduce aggregate demand.
Planned withdrawals represent income which the households have earned which they do not want to spend within the economy. This could be because they want to save it (S), they have to pay it in tax (T) or they want to spend it overseas (on imports M),
i.e. $$W = S + T + M$$

Simple circular flow

Imagine the income in the economy is £100. This means £100 of output is produced and in a simple circular model this is all bought by households who earn £100 and spend £100.

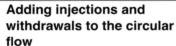

Adding injections and withdrawals to the circular flow

In reality, households may not want to spend all of the £100 in the economy; they may withdraw £40 and only want to spend £60. In this case the level of demand in the economy is too low; £100 is produced but only £60 is demanded. Equilibrium will be restored provided the other groups (firms, Government and overseas buyers) want to buy up the £40 of output that the households do not want.
i.e. provided the planned injections = the planned withdrawals, there will be equilibrium.

If the other groups only want to buy £30 of goods, there will still be £10 left over. Aggregate demand is too low. Because the planned injections did not compensate for the planned withdrawals, demand is too low, i.e. **if planned injections are less than planned withdrawals, then aggregate demand is too low.**
If the other groups had wanted to buy £50, demand would have been too high because there was only £40 of goods left over, i.e. **if planned injections are greater than planned withdrawals, then aggregate demand is too high.**

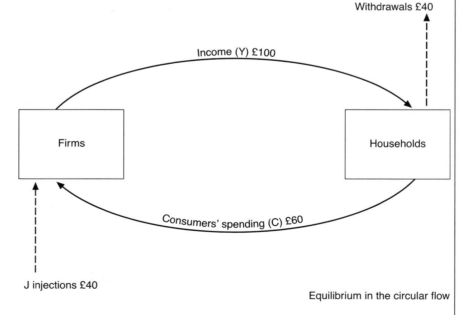

Equilibrium in the circular flow

Aggregate demand, injections and withdrawals /cont.

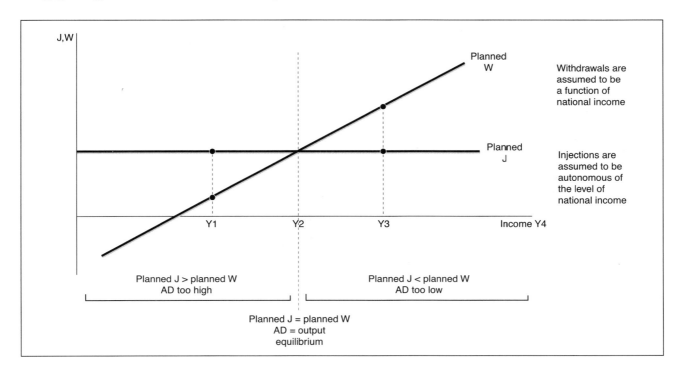

Withdrawals are assumed to be a function of national income

Injections are assumed to be autonomous of the level of national income

Planned J > planned W
AD too high

Planned J < planned W
AD too low

Planned J = planned W
AD = output
equilibrium

Types of economy
- Two sector: households and firms
- Three sector: households firms, and Government
- Four sector: households, firms Government and trade
- Open economy: has trade
- Closed economy: no trade

The paradox of thrift

If households try to save more of their income, they may end up saving exactly the same amount of money as before! This is because if they save more of their money, this reduces the level of demand in the economy, which leads to a downward multiplier and a fall in the level of income. Although they may save a greater *proportion* of their income, because income has fallen their total savings in a <u>two sector</u> economy will be the same total amount as before (because for equilibrium, planned savings must still equal planned investment, which is unchanged).

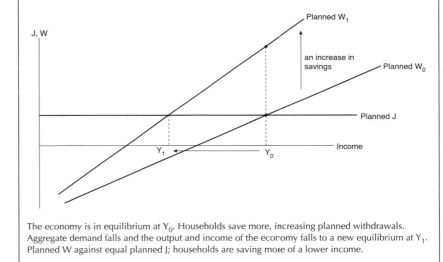

The economy is in equilibrium at Y_0. Households save more, increasing planned withdrawals. Aggregate demand falls and the output and income of the economy falls to a new equilibrium at Y_1. Planned W against equal planned J; households are saving more of a lower income.

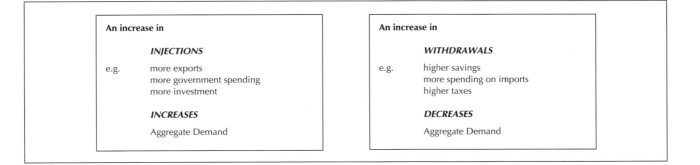

An increase in

INJECTIONS

e.g.   more exports
         more government spending
         more investment

INCREASES

Aggregate Demand

An increase in

WITHDRAWALS

e.g.   higher savings
         more spending on imports
         higher taxes

DECREASES

Aggregate Demand

Consumption

Consumption
The level of consumption in the economy is the planned level of spending on final goods and services by households. It is a major element of aggregate demand.

Keynesian consumption function
According to Keynes, the level of national income is a major determinant of consumer spending.

$C = a + bY$

where C = the level of consumption

    a = autonomous spending. This represents spending which the household would do even if income was zero.

    b = the marginal propensity to consume. This is the extra spending out of each extra pound and is given by the equation: $\dfrac{\text{change in consumption}}{\text{change in income}} = \dfrac{\Delta C}{\Delta Y}$

    Y = current income

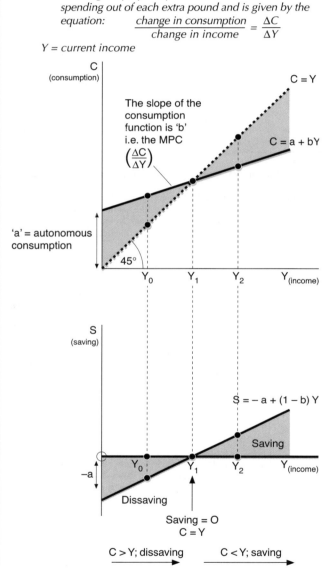

At income level Y_0, the level of consumption is greater than the level of income; consumers are spending more than they earn; this means they are dissaving.

At income level Y_1, the level of consumption = the level of income; consumers are spending all that they are earning; there are no savings.

At income level Y_2, the level of consumption is less than the level of income; consumers are saving.

The size of the marginal propensity to consume depends on:
- a consumer's level of income – usually we assume the mpc is constant, i.e. the consumer consumes the same amount out of each pound; therefore the consumption function is a straight line. In reality, as consumers earn more they are likely to save more out of each pound and spend less.

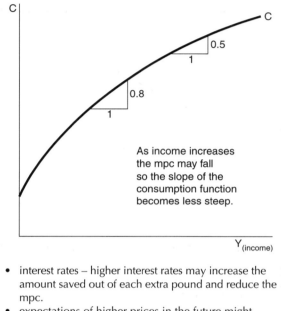

As income increases the mpc may fall so the slope of the consumption function becomes less steep.

- interest rates – higher interest rates may increase the amount saved out of each extra pound and reduce the mpc.
- expectations of higher prices in the future might increase the mpc *now*.
- taxation – with higher tax rates, less will be spent out of each pound.

Savings
Savings are related to consumption. If we are spending more of our income, we are saving less.

Levels of saving will depend on:
- interest rates – if interest rates increase, there is a greater incentive to save.
- income levels – higher income groups are more likely to save out of each extra pound (they have a higher marginal propensity to save).
- inflation – with inflation, the purchasing powers of people's savings may be reduced. To maintain the same real level of savings they may have to save more.
- expectations – if people are worried about the future state of the economy and whether they will have a job, they may save more.

Discretionary and contractual savings
- With contractual savings, an individual agrees to save a certain amount each month, e.g. as part of a pension plan.
- With discretionary saving an individual may or may not save; they are not contractually obliged to – but they may voluntarily decide to save money.

Consumption continued

The average propensity to consume

The average propensity to consume shows the amount consumed on average out of each pound earned.

$$APC = \frac{C}{Y}$$

On a diagram, the APC is shown by the gradient of rays from the origin to each point on the consumption function. The APC falls with higher levels of income. This is because when income is low the level of consumption is relatively high because of the autonomous element of consumption. As income levels increase, the autonomous level of consumption becomes less significant.

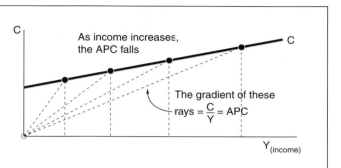

Income (Y) (£)	Consumption (C), assume C = 10 + 0.8Y (£)	Average propensity to consume (APC)
0	10	Infinite
10	18	1.8
20	26	1.3
30	34	1.13
50	50	1
100	90	0.9
500	410	0.82
1000	810	0.81

If there is no autonomous element of consumption, the APC = MPC.

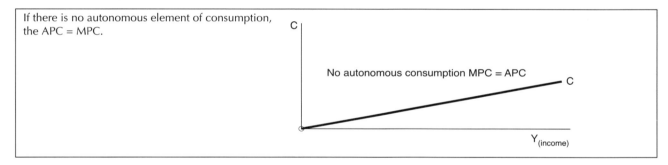

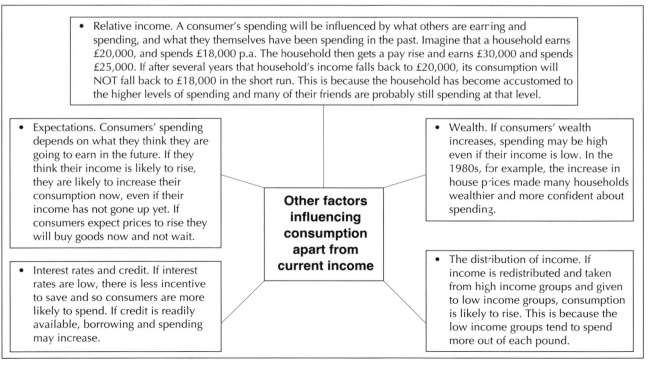

- Relative income. A consumer's spending will be influenced by what others are earning and spending, and what they themselves have been spending in the past. Imagine that a household earns £20,000, and spends £18,000 p.a. The household then gets a pay rise and earns £30,000 and spends £25,000. If after several years that household's income falls back to £20,000, its consumption will NOT fall back to £18,000 in the short run. This is because the household has become accustomed to the higher levels of spending and many of their friends are probably still spending at that level.

- Expectations. Consumers' spending depends on what they think they are going to earn in the future. If they think their income is likely to rise, they are likely to increase their consumption now, even if their income has not gone up yet. If consumers expect prices to rise they will buy goods now and not wait.

- Wealth. If consumers' wealth increases, spending may be high even if their income is low. In the 1980s, for example, the increase in house prices made many households wealthier and more confident about spending.

Other factors influencing consumption apart from current income

- Interest rates and credit. If interest rates are low, there is less incentive to save and so consumers are more likely to spend. If credit is readily available, borrowing and spending may increase.

- The distribution of income. If income is redistributed and taken from high income groups and given to low income groups, consumption is likely to rise. This is because the low income groups tend to spend more out of each pound.

Consumption continued

Other theories of consumption

Permanent income hypothesis (Friedman) Households estimate their expected future earnings and divide these up over the remaining time periods to calculate their permanent income. Consumers then consume a proportion of their permanent income rather than their current income. At any moment a consumer may be earning more or less than their permanent income because of unexpected gains or losses (called positive or negative transitory income). Imagine you are given a one off bonus of £1000 – this is transitory income. Because you know it is a one off, it will have little impact on your overall earnings throughout your life and therefore your permanent income, and so consumption is unlikely to change much. If, however, you knew you were going to inherit a significant sum of money in the future, you may take this into account and increase your estimate of your permanent income. This would increase consumption now, even though current income has not increased.

Life cycle hypothesis (Modigliani)

Households plan their expenditure over their life spans and aim to have fairly steady consumption. In your early years, for example, you will dissave because you have a low current income; during your mid-life you will save; and during retirement you will dissave. Consumption is related to your stage in the life cycle, not just current income.

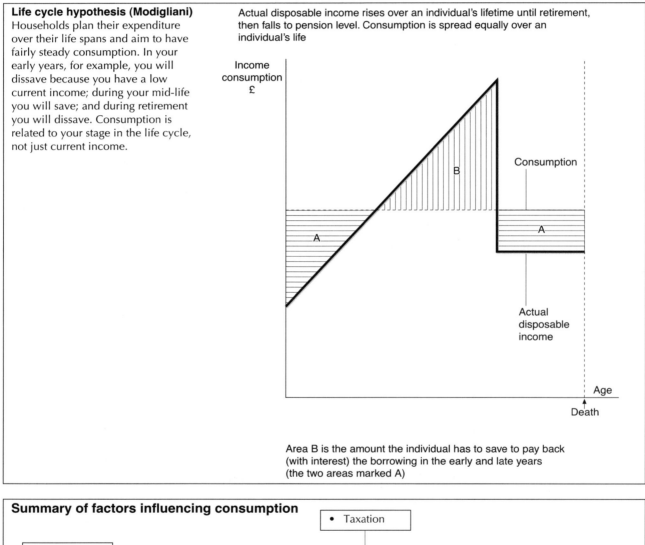

Actual disposable income rises over an individual's lifetime until retirement, then falls to pension level. Consumption is spread equally over an individual's life

Area B is the amount the individual has to save to pay back (with interest) the borrowing in the early and late years (the two areas marked A)

Summary of factors influencing consumption

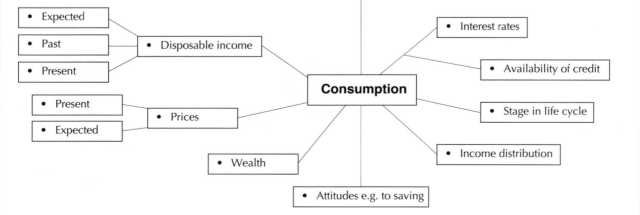

Investment

Investment refers to spending by firms. It has two elements:
- the purchase of new capital, such as equipment and factories
- an increase in stock levels

Gross and net investment

Gross investment is the total level of investment
Net investment is the increase in the capital stock – some investment simply replaces capital which has worn out (i.e. depreciation)
Net Investment = Gross Investment – depreciation

Planned v actual

Planned investment is the level of investment which firms intend to undertake at the beginning of the period. Actual investment is the level which has occurred at the end of the period. If firms fail to sell as much as they want to, they will be left with stocks which they had not planned for, i.e. actual investment will be greater than planned investment.

Autonomous and induced investment

- Autonomous investment is unrelated to the level of national income
- Induced investment is investment which is related to changes in the level of national income (see the accelerator)

Real v Money investment

- 'Real' investment is investment in capital goods, e.g. factories, equipment, machinery
- Money investment is investment (savings) in 'paper', e.g. shares, bonds

The level of investment depends on
a) availability of finance
b) interest rates
c) the expected rates of return from the investment

The expected return from investment depends on, for example
- the initial cost of capital goods
- expected costs
- expected revenues
- expected productivity

If the expected rate of return is greater than the cost of borrowing (i.e. interest rates) the firm will invest.
If the expected rate of return is less than the cost of borrowing, the firm will not invest.

Marginal efficiency of capital (MEC) shows the rate of return on each additional unit of capital
(Note: technically the MEC shows the discount rate which equates the present value of a stream of expected inflows to its initial cost)

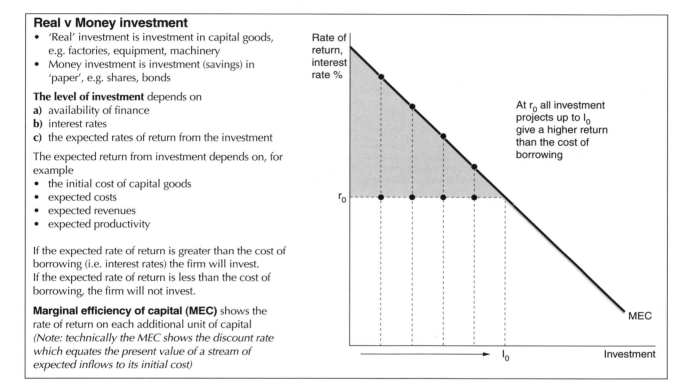

At r_0 all investment projects up to I_0 give a higher return than the cost of borrowing

Shifts in the investment schedule

Expectations are a key element of investment. Firms estimate costs and benefits for the future to determine the expected rate of return.

If expectations become more positive, e.g. the firm is more confident about the state of the economy and the level of demand for their product, then each project will be expected to have a higher rate of return; the MEC schedule will shift outwards.
The investment schedule can also shift because of
- a change in technology – this can increase productivity and make the projects more profitable
- lower taxation by the Government, increasing expected profits
- a fall in the purchase price of capital goods – this would increase the expected rate of return

With an outword shift in the MEC more investment occurs at any given interest rate.

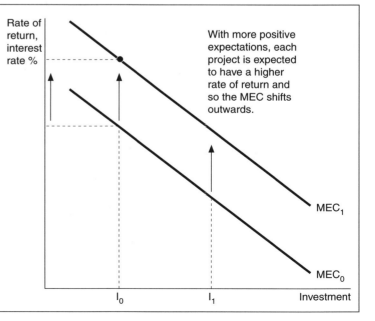

With more positive expectations, each project is expected to have a higher rate of return and so the MEC shifts outwards.

Investment continued

An increase in investment
- increases aggregate demand (and sets off the multiplier)
- can increase the growth of the economy (by increasing aggregate supply)
- increases capacity

The precise effect depends on the type of investment, e.g. whether it is in people, products or processes

Movements along the investment schedule: changes in the interest rate
- with an increase in interest rates, investment is likely to fall. This is because it is more expensive to borrow and there are now fewer projects which have a higher rate of return than the cost of borrowing.
- with a fall in interest rates there are more projects which have a higher return than the cost of borrowing and investment should increase.

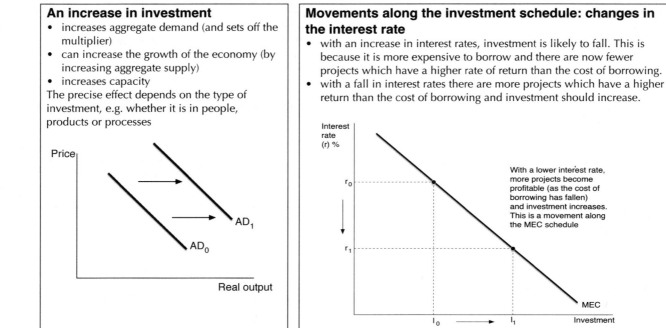

With a lower interest rate, more projects become profitable (as the cost of borrowing has fallen) and investment increases. This is a movement along the MEC schedule

The accelerator shows the relationship between net investment and the rate of change of national output.
The accelerator assumes a constant capital to output ratio, e.g. £2 of capital has to be purchased to be able to increase output by £1.

Desired output level (£)	Desired capital level (£)	Change in output (£)	Level of net investment (£)
200	400	–	–
220	440	+20	40
250	500	+30	60
300	600	+50	100
400	800	+100	200
600	1200	+200	400
700	1400	+100	200

Assume capital: output ratio of 2:1
- If output increases by an increasing (accelerating) amount firms will have to buy more machines each period, i.e. net investment will increase.
- If output increases by a constant amount each period, firms will have to buy the same number of machines and factories; net investment will be constant.
- If output increases but by less than the year before, firms will not need to buy as many machines and factories; net investment will actually fall.

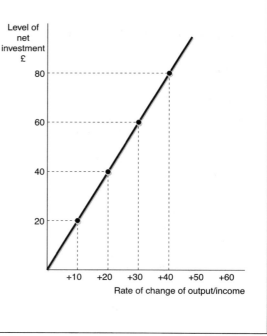

Limitations of the accelerator model
- firms often have stocks, so if output increases they can meet this without having to produce more; they may not need net investment
- the capital goods industry, which produces the capital goods, may not be able to increase supply, e.g. even if firms want to buy more machines they may not be able to
- with changes in technology, the accelerator coefficient may change and firms may not need to invest as much as before
- firms will have to be convinced the increase in demand is long term; otherwise they will be reluctant to invest – they may try to meet demand by using overtime

Investment continued

Rate of interest and aggregate demand

Higher interest rates increase the cost of borrowing. This affects:

- households' mortgages; with more money to repay there will be less left over for buying other goods and services
- the cost of borrowing on credit cards
- the cost of overdrafts
- the cost of loans

As a result higher interest rates mean aggregate demand is likely to fall.

Note: Demand for some products is likely to be hit more than others, e.g. people tend to borrow to buy a house or a car so demand for these products is very sensitive to interest rate changes. Demand for salt is less likely to be affected by interest rates.

Interest rate

This is the return generated on capital and the cost of borrowing money.

The interest paid for borrowing will depend on

- how long the loan is for – generally if you borrow for a longer time you are charged more
- risk – the riskier the project, the more the lender will usually charge
- the cost of setting up the loan, i.e. it is cheaper to arrange one loan for £1m than 100 loans cf £10,000

What determines the interest rate?

a The demand and supply of loanable funds.

Supply of loanable funds depends on

- people's willingness to save (and therefore provide funds which can be lent out)
- the ability of the banks to lend

Demand for loanable funds:

- from households to buy consumer durables and non-durables
- from firms for investment
- from the Government to finance their deficit

The demand is downward sloping because at higher rates of interest, households, firms, and the Government want to borrow less because it is more expensive to repay. Firms will find there are fewer projects which have a higher return than the cost of borrowing

b The demand and supply of money *(see later)*

Real interest rates means that they have been adjusted for inflation, e.g. if the nominal rate is 10% but inflation is 4% then in real terms the cost of borrowing is 6%.

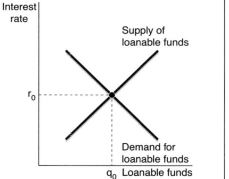

The rate of interest and the exchange rate

If the UK interest rate increases this is likely to lead to a stronger pound. High UK rates attract 'hot money' in from abroad seeking higher returns holding pounds in UK banks than are available elsewhere. This increases demand for pounds and pulls up the exchange rate.

Investment appraisal and present value

Discounted cash flow: technique of assessing investments

Firms estimate future expected revenues and costs and discount these to get their present value. £100 in 5 years' time is not equal to £100 now – this is because money tends to grow over time due to interest rates. £60 now might become £100 in five years'

time, due to interest rates; and so the present value of £100 in five years' time is £60 now. £100 has been discounted to £60. The higher the interest rate, the faster money grows over time and the lower the present value of any future income.

Firms compare the present value of their expected earnings from a project with the supply price. If in today's terms the project is worth

more than the initial cost, the firm will invest, i.e. if present value > supply price, invest. If the project in today's terms is worth less than the initial cost, do not invest, i.e. if the present value < supply price, do not invest. With a lower interest rate, the present value of future expected inflows increases and so more investment is likely to occur.

CBA (cost benefit analysis)

This is a technique used by governments to decide on whether to go ahead with investment such as roads, schools and defence projects. Unlike private sector investment projects, CBA looks at social benefits and costs (not just private benefits and costs), i.e. it takes account of externalities. If the social marginal cost is greater than the social marginal benefit the project should not go ahead. If the social marginal benefit is greater than the social marginal cost the project should go ahead. A project such as the London Olympics 2012 may go ahead because of the external benefits.

All costs and benefits are estimated and monetary values are assigned to them. In practice, estimating these may be difficult and controversial because the assessment is a normative judgement.

When undertaking a CBA for building a road:

- **Social costs** may include damage to the environment, destruction of habitats of animals, adverse effects on the landscape, damage to a site of special scientific interest (SSSI), damage to an area of outstanding natural beauty, increased pollution and problems of global warming.
- **Social benefits** may include, e.g. increased speed of traffic, increased traffic flow, fewer accidents.

The **Hicks Kaldor** criterion suggests that a project is desirable if those that win if it goes ahead could in theory compensate those who lose. This theory lies behind CBA; if the benefits outweigh the costs then in theory those who suffer could be compensated (although this does not mean they are).

Problems of CBA

- What factors should be included/measured?
- Difficult to quantify and attach values to external costs; if the wrong values are used the wrong decisions may be made.
- Setting monetary values involves a degree of subjectivity; some people will value certain factors more highly than others, i.e. it involves value judgements and possible bias.

Government policy and objectives and the multiplier

Objectives
- Stable prices, i.e. to keep inflation under control. This is important to keep UK firms competitive abroad and to help firms and households plan.
- Full employment, i.e. when all those willing and able to work at the given real wage are working. Unemployment is a waste of resources and means the economy is underproducing.
- Economic growth – this increases the standard of living.
- A balance of the balance of payments on the current account – a deficit means that there is more spending on imported goods and services than is earned by exported goods and services; a surplus means another country has a deficit. A 'balance' may be desirable.

Priorities
These objectives cannot necessarily be achieved at the same time. Policies taken to achieve one might disrupt others. More spending to increase employment levels, for example, may lead to higher inflation.

In the 1950s and 1960s the priority was usually full employment.

From the late 1970s the priority was to control inflation.

Types of Government policy
- **Demand side policies:** attempts to influence aggregate demand
- **Supply side policies:** attempts to influence aggregate supply
- **Reflationary policies:** increasing aggregate demand, e.g. lower tax rates, higher Government spending, lower interest rates
- **Deflationary policies:** decreasing aggregate demand, e.g. higher tax rates, lower Government spending, higher interest rates

Instruments of Government Policy
- Fiscal policy: government spending and taxation rates
- Monetary policy: controlling the money supply and interest rates
- Incomes policy: controlling growth in wages and salaries
- Regulations, e.g. changes in the law

Regional policies
Aim to reduce unemployment and increase the income of depressed regions or areas.

Interventionist policies:
- subsidies and tax concessions – these can be used to encourage firms into an area and to encourage firms to hire more people
- provision of facilities in depressed areas, e.g. better infrastructure (roads, communications, etc.)
- taxation can be used to tax companies more in richer areas
- regulation – the Government can make it difficult for firms to expand in richer areas and easier to expand in poorer regions, e.g. in terms of giving planning permission

Funds
- Regional Selective Assistance involves discretionary grants for projects in assisted areas. To be given the grants, firms must prove they will create jobs.
- European Regional Development Fund – provides grants for job creating projects which develop the infrastructure.
- Regional Enterprise Grants – consist of innovation and investment grants.

Urban policy includes
- Enterprise zones – very small districts in urban areas. Major incentives are given to the firms setting up here, e.g. less bureaucracy, exemption from rates

Multiplier
If aggregate demand increases and aggregate supply is elastic, there will be an increase in national income which is bigger than the initial increase in aggregate demand. This is because of the multiplier effect.

When demand first increases firms produce more, and this generates extra income for suppliers and employees. The suppliers and employees will then spend a proportion of this extra income buying more goods and services. The producers of these products will have extra income and once again a proportion of this will be spent on more goods. The multiplier is based on the principle that 'one person's spending is another person's income'; an initial boost in demand leads to rounds of spending and a bigger overall increase in income in the economy.

Example: The government spends £200m on roads. The road building companies, their employees and their suppliers earn £200m. Of this let us say £100m is spent on other goods and services. The producers of these goods earn £100m; of this say, £50m is spent and so on. This means the initial spending of £200m generated income of £200m + £100m+ £50m + ... there is a multiplier effect.

The size of the multiplier will depend on what proportion of income is spent at each stage within the economy. This depends on the marginal propensity to consume (MPC) which is calculated from the equation:

$$MPC = \frac{\text{change in consumption}}{\text{change in income}}$$

For example, if the mpc is 0.8 this means 80% of income is spent at each stage. In the example above the MPC was assumed to be 0.5. The bigger the MPC the more is spent at each stage and the bigger the multiplier.

For more details on how to calculate the multiplier see pages 72–73.

However the multiplier process does not go on forever because:

a as people's income increases they tend to move into higher tax brackets and spend more on imported goods; this reduces the proportion spent within the economy.

b as the economy approaches full employment, aggregate supply becomes more inelastic and so prices increase rather than output, i.e. nominal national income may increase but real national income will not increase as much. At full employment output cannot increase.

Privatization

Privatization
This involves transferring assets from the public sector to the private sector, e.g.

- contracting out – this is when activities undertaken by the public sector are sold off to the private sector, e.g. providing school meals, cleaning the roads
- deregulation – this is where regulations are changed or removed to allow more competition, e.g. bus services
- sale of assets, e.g. organizations such as British Gas have been sold to shareholders and are now privately owned

Examples of privatization
British Aerospace 1981, British Gas 1986, British Airways 1987, British Steel 1989.

Why not privatize?
- may create private monopolies
- often sold very cheaply to make sure the shares are sold
- may lead to job losses (politically unpopular)
- may lead to a focus on profits at the expense of, e.g. safety or social objectives
- may lead to a natural monopoly

Regulation of privatized industries
Each of the public sector utilities that has been privatized has been monitored by a regulatory body, e.g. Office of Gas and Electricity Markets (Ofgem), the Office of Communications (Ofcom) and the Office of Rail Regulation (ORR).

These bodies aim to protect the consumer and ensure the privatized companies do not abuse their monopoly power. This can be done via:

- price restrictions: price controls have been placed on the utilities using an equation based on inflation. Targets are set for 'RPI – X' whereby the firms must achieve efficiency gains to make sure their prices actually fall.
- prohibiting anti-competitive behaviour, e.g. preventing price rigging
- increasing competition, e.g. making it easier to enter a market. For example, British Gas no longer has a monopoly on the provision of gas and as a result many other firms have moved into this market.
- fixing minimum investment levels to ensure standards of service are high enough.

Evaluating **the regulation of privatized industries**
- If the percentage X is set too low, and firms can make big cost savings through technology or re-organization, they might make very high profits.
- There is a danger that firms will take short-term actions such as cost-cutting on research and development.
- Danger of 'regulatory capture' – as the regulators become more involved in the industry they are increasingly likely to see the managers' point of view and may not be tough enough. Alternatively they might serve the political interests of Government rather than make decisions on economic grounds.

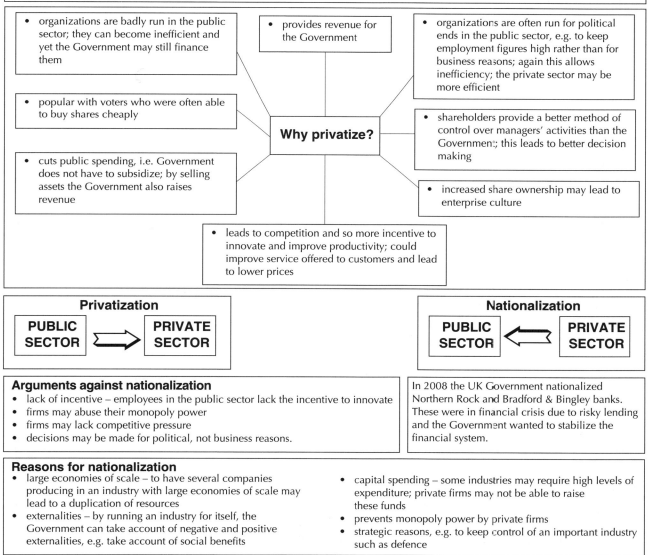

Arguments against nationalization
- lack of incentive – employees in the public sector lack the incentive to innovate
- firms may abuse their monopoly power
- firms may lack competitive pressure
- decisions may be made for political, not business reasons.

In 2008 the UK Government nationalized Northern Rock and Bradford & Bingley banks. These were in financial crisis due to risky lending and the Government wanted to stabilize the financial system.

Reasons for nationalization
- large economies of scale – to have several companies producing in an industry with large economies of scale may lead to a duplication of resources
- externalities – by running an industry for itself, the Government can take account of negative and positive externalities, e.g. take account of social benefits
- capital spending – some industries may require high levels of expenditure; private firms may not be able to raise these funds
- prevents monopoly power by private firms
- strategic reasons, e.g. to keep control of an important industry such as defence

Aggregate demand and supply

Aggregate demand

This aggregate demand schedule shows the total level of planned expenditure on final goods and services at different prices, i.e. it shows the relationship between price and real national output.

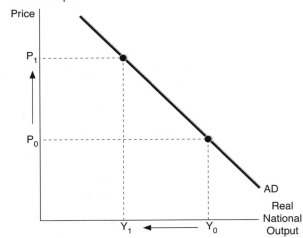

Why does aggregate demand slope downwards?

- interest rate effect – with higher prices in the economy, nominal interest rates tend to increase. This reduces demand for goods which are sensitive to interest rates such as TVs, cars, or houses, which are usually bought on credit or with a loan.
- wealth effect – higher prices reduce the purchasing power of any cash balances. Individuals, therefore, tend to spend less.
- purchase of foreign goods and services – if UK prices increase, consumers and firms tend to switch to imports which are relatively cheaper. Also there will be less demand for UK goods from overseas.

Shifts in the aggregate demand

Caused by a change in factors other than price. An outward shift could be caused by:

- an increase in consumer or business confidence
- expansionist fiscal or monetary policy, e.g. lower tax rates, higher Government spending, higher exports, lower rates of interest, less spending on imports

Aggregate supply

Aggregate supply shows the level of real income (and output) in an economy in relation to the price.

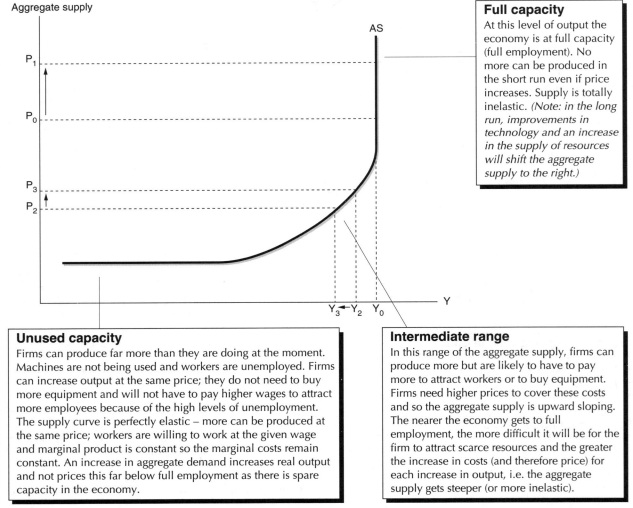

Full capacity

At this level of output the economy is at full capacity (full employment). No more can be produced in the short run even if price increases. Supply is totally inelastic. (*Note: in the long run, improvements in technology and an increase in the supply of resources will shift the aggregate supply to the right.*)

Unused capacity

Firms can produce far more than they are doing at the moment. Machines are not being used and workers are unemployed. Firms can increase output at the same price; they do not need to buy more equipment and will not have to pay higher wages to attract more employees because of the high levels of unemployment. The supply curve is perfectly elastic – more can be produced at the same price; workers are willing to work at the given wage and marginal product is constant so the marginal costs remain constant. An increase in aggregate demand increases real output and not prices this far below full employment as there is spare capacity in the economy.

Intermediate range

In this range of the aggregate supply, firms can produce more but are likely to have to pay more to attract workers or to buy equipment. Firms need higher prices to cover these costs and so the aggregate supply is upward sloping. The nearer the economy gets to full employment, the more difficult it will be for the firm to attract scarce resources and the greater the increase in costs (and therefore price) for each increase in output, i.e. the aggregate supply gets steeper (or more inelastic).

Aggregate demand and supply continued

Aggregate supply

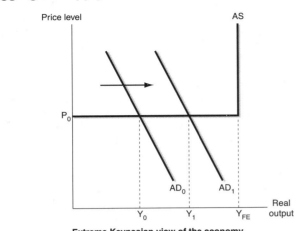

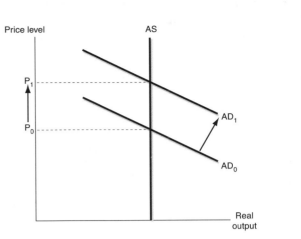

Extreme Keynesian view of the economy
Up to full employment aggregate supply is horizontal, perfectly elastic. An increase in aggregate demand increases output and *not* prices. Only when full employment is reached will prices increase. The Government should control aggregate demand to ensure equilibrium occurs at full employment.

Extreme monetarist view of the economy
(new classical)
Aggregate supply is vertical - any increase in aggregate demand increases the price level but *not* output and employment. To increase output and employment supply side policies are needed to shift aggregate supply to the right.

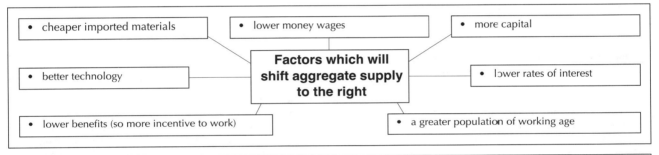

- cheaper imported materials
- lower money wages
- more capital
- better technology
- **Factors which will shift aggregate supply to the right**
- lower rates of interest
- lower benefits (so more incentive to work)
- a greater population of working age

Supply-side policies: increasing aggregate supply

Policies for the labour market
- Reducing welfare benefits may encourage people to take work rather rely on the state for funding
- Increasing minimum wages may increase the rewards for some jobs and thereby encourage more people to work
- Changing marginal tax rates; the government needs to ensure that people are not worse off by working, e.g. because they now pay tax and lose benefits (enable them to get out of the poverty trap)
- More information on jobs available so people know what their options are
- Education and training opportunities to provide employees with greater flexibility and the skills to find better jobs
- Reducing the power of trade unions may lead to greater competition between workers for jobs (by removing restrictions on supply) and enable management to achieve greater flexibility in terms of hours and duties

Policies for the capital goods market
The government can help improve aggregate supply by:
- providing a stable business environment that encourages investment and enables firms to generate a profit (which will fund further investment)
- encouraging the financial system to provide the funds for investment, e.g. contributing to generating an entrepreneurial culture and removing administrative barriers.

Policies for the goods market
- Encourage free trade
- Encourage small business start-ups
- Privatization
- Deregulation

All of these promote competition, which can encourage innovation and improved productivity.

Supply side and taxation
Keynesians focus on the demand side effects of changes in taxation and Government spending, e.g. a tax cut may increase aggregate demand. Supply side economics, by comparison, focuses on the micro effects, e.g. the effect of a tax cut on the incentive to invest or work. Tax cuts can shift supply to the right by encouraging employees to work and firms to invest.

Laffer curve
Higher tax rates will eventually lead to a decline in taxation revenue. The higher tax rates act as a disincentive for firms and employees – although the rate is higher, fewer people are working and so the revenue is lower. In this case, tax cuts can lead to more revenue for the Government (as more people want to work and firms want to expand).

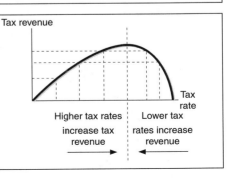

Aggregate demand and supply continued

From short run aggregate supply (SRAS) to long run aggregate supply (LRAS)

Each short run aggregate supply is drawn for a given money wage. If money wages increase, firms will want to hire less and produce less at every price level. The short run aggregate supply shifts up. If costs fall, e.g. due to a fall in money wages, the aggregate supply shifts down.

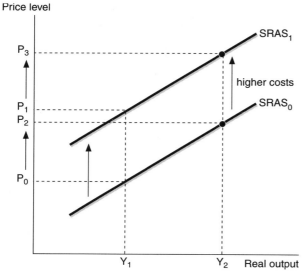

• the effect of an increase in aggregate demand

In the diagram below long run equilibrium is at E; the economy is at full employment. An increase in aggregate demand pulls up the price level. The higher price reduces real wages, firms hire more and supply increases, as shown on the aggregate supply (point F). Firms are now producing beyond their normal capacity output, so there is excess demand for labour, pulling up money wages and shifting aggregate supply upwards (point G). If real wages return to the old level, equilibrium is restored at the full employment level; prices and money wages have both increased but the economy is back at full employment. The long run aggregate supply is vertical.

Keynesians think the move from short run to long run aggregate supply is slow, as money wages are slow to adjust. Monetarists think the adjustment is quick, as money wages are quick to adjust.

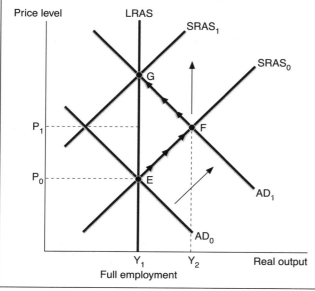

• the effect of a decrease in aggregate demand

Long run equilibrium is at E; the economy is at full employment. A decrease in aggregate demand leads to a fall in the price level and a new equilibrium at B. With the old money wages and a lower price, real wages have increased. Less is being produced and there is an excess supply of labour. The economy is below full employment. In the long run, money wages will fall, shifting aggregate supply downwards. With lower money wages and lower prices, the real wage returns to the long run equilibrium rate and the economy is back at full employment. Monetarists think this process is quick; Keynesians think money wages are slow to fall and so the economy can remain at B below full employment.

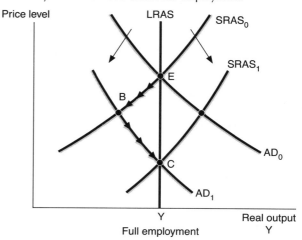

• the effect of an increase in costs

In the short run, an increase in costs shifts the aggregate supply upwards (to SRAS$_1$) as costs of production have risen. Price rises to P$_1$; output falls to Y$_1$. This illustrates 'stagflation', i.e. higher prices and lower output and employment. If the Government does nothing, then according to monetarist economists, the economy will return to the long run equilibrium – unemployment will put downward pressure on money wages, which reduces costs and the short run aggregate supply shifts back to SRAS$_0$. Keynesians argue this adjustment is likely to take a long time, because money wages are slow to fall. Alternatively, the Government could intervene by increasing the money supply and boosting demand, because output has fallen to Y$_0$. This reflationary action will shift aggregate demand outwards to AD$_1$; output returns to full employment level; and prices rise to P$_2$. The economy ends up back at full employment, with the natural rate of unemployment but higher prices.

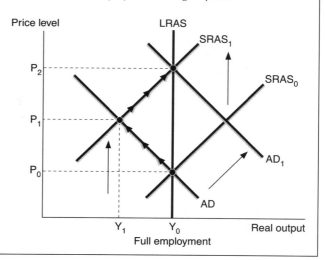

Keynesian cross diagrams (45° diagrams)

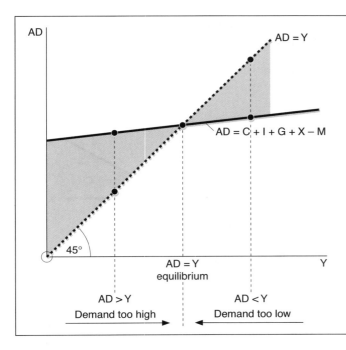

The 45 degree line shows all the combinations of points where the values of two axes are equal.

In this case the 45 degree line shows all the points at which the level of aggregate demand (AD) equals the level of output and income (Y), i.e. all the possible points of equilibrium where AD = Y, i.e. aggregate demand = output

The economy will always move towards this point. If aggregate demand is greater than output there is an incentive for firms to produce more. If aggregate demand is less than output, there is an incentive for firms to produce less.
Note: in the Keynesian model, prices are assumed to be constant; i.e. firms change their output not their prices.
The aggregate demand schedule = C + I + G + X − M

The aggregate demand will shift upwards if there is:
• an increase in autonomous consumption
• an increase in investment (e.g. due to lower interest rates)
• an increase in Government spending (e.g. expansionist fiscal policy)
• an increase in exports (e.g. due to a lower exchange rate)
• a decrease in imports (e.g. due to quotas)
The slope of the aggregate demand depends on the marginal propensity to consume.

Aggregate demand

In a two sector economy, aggregate demand is made up of consumption by households and investment by firms.

Investment is drawn as a straight line on this diagram – it is assumed to be unrelated to the level of national income (i.e. exogenous or autonomous of income). Investment tends to be related to interest rates and expectations about the future level of income rather than the *present* income level in the economy.

In a three sector economy, aggregate demand is made up of consumption by households, investment by firms, and Government spending.

Government spending is drawn as a straight line in the diagram. This is because the level of Government spending depends on Government policy and not the level of income. The Government may or may not spend more in a boom or recession, we cannot definitely say, so we assume in this model that it is autonomous of national income.

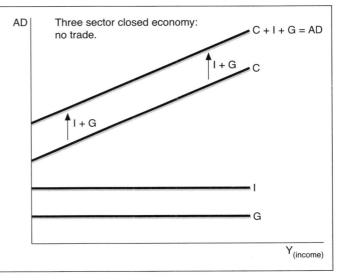

Inflationary gap

This occurs where the level of aggregate demand exceeds the level of output at full employment; this causes upward pressure on prices.

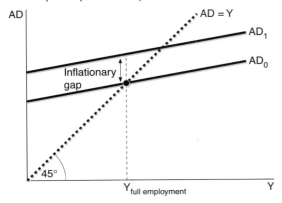

Deflationary gap

This occurs when the level of aggregate demand is below the level of output at full employment.

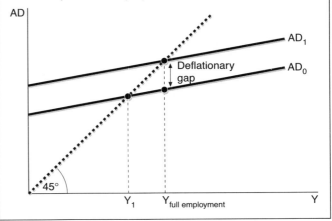

Keynesian cross diagrams continued

National income and the budget position

With an increase in national income, net tax revenue will increase, e.g. the Government will earn more from income tax and VAT and pay out fewer benefits. Assuming Government spending is autonomous, the budget position will move towards a surplus.

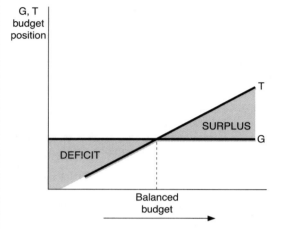

The multiplier

The multiplier shows how an increase in planned injections into the economy leads to a larger increase in output and income. This is because the initial injection sets off rounds of spending. It is based on the idea that 'one person's spending is another person's income'. Imagine the Government spent £100m on building a new road. This £100m is paid to a building contractor who will spend some of this on buying equipment, materials, paying for labour, paying its overheads, and paying out to shareholders. For example, it may spend £80m. The rest is saved. The various groups which have received this money now go and spend some of this £80m. The shareholders might buy a holiday, the employees pay for their food, the suppliers pay their employees, and buy their materials. Of the £80m, £64m may be spent. This then becomes income for another set of people who again go and spend some of it.

The initial £100m creates a series of successively smaller increases in spending throughout the economy (in this case £100m + £80m + £64m +...)
The initial injection has a multiplied effect on the economy.
The size of the multiplier will depend on how much is spent at each stage, i.e. the marginal propensity to consume (MPC). The more that is spent at each stage (i.e. the larger the MPC) the bigger the overall effect.

$$\text{Multiplier} = \frac{\text{change in income}}{\text{change in injections}} = \frac{\Delta Y}{\Delta J}$$

National income and the balance of payments (current account)

With an increase in income, more will be spent on imports. Assuming exports are autonomous, the balance of payments position worsens.

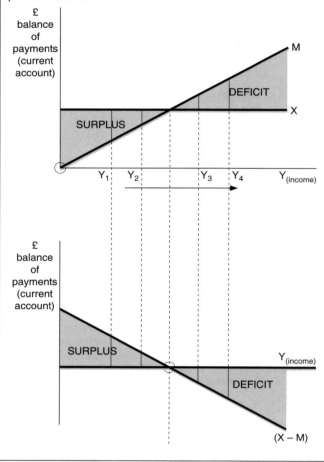

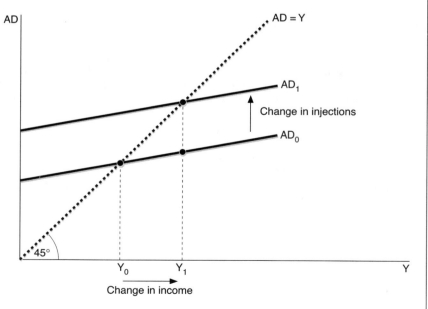

Keynesian cross diagrams continued

Size of the multiplier

The size of the multiplier can be calculated using the equation:

$$\frac{1}{1 - MPC}$$

For example, if the MPC is 0.5, the multiplier is 2. If the MPC is 0.9, the multiplier is 10.

If the multiplier is 2, this means that any injection will have twice the effect on income, e.g. if the Government spends £100m this will lead to an increase of £200m in national income. If the multiplier is 10, this means any injection into the economy will have 10x the effect on national income, e.g. if the Government spends £100m this will lead to an increase of £1000m overall.

The multiplier can also be expressed as

$$\frac{1}{MPS + MPM + MRT}$$

where MRT = marginal rate of tax = amount paid in tax out of each extra pound.

MPM = marginal propensity to import = amount spent on imports out of each extra pound.

MPS = marginal rate of savings = amount saved out of each extra pound.

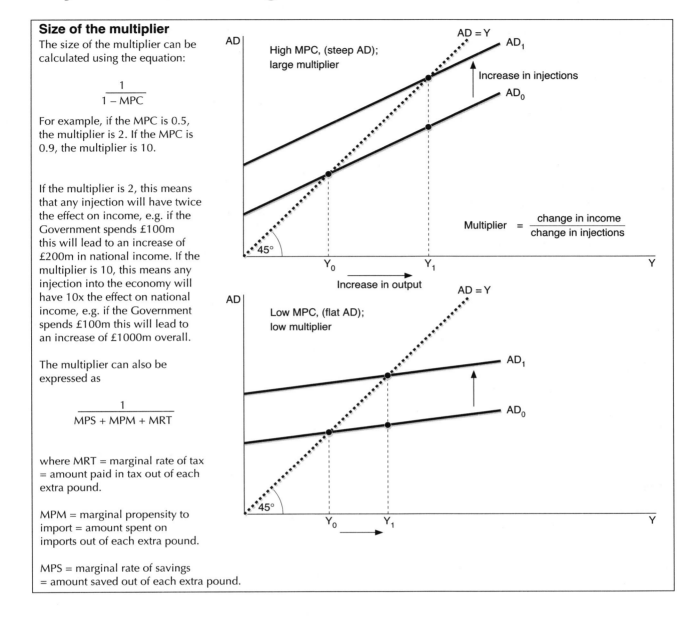

Determinants of the size of the multiplier

- if the economy is open rather than closed, consumers will buy imports – this reduces the amount of money passed on at each stage of the multiplier process within the UK, i.e. it reduces the marginal propensity to consume within the UK so the multiplier is smaller
- interest rates – higher interest rates might encourage more saving and less spending and so reduce the multiplier
- tax rates – with higher tax rates, more of each pound is given to the Government and less is spent on UK goods and services; the multiplier is smaller

Marginal propensity to import (mpm)

Depends on:

- relative prices of UK and foreign goods – this will depend on the exchange rate to a large extent
- quality of goods and services
- income
- interest rates – if overseas interest rates are high, people in the UK will want to save abroad and money will leave the UK
- speculation – if people think the pound will fall, they will sell pounds now and buy foreign currency

Fiscal policy

Involves the use of Government spending and taxation rates to control the economy.

Government spending includes

- health
- education
- law and order
- transport
- social security
- housing
- defence

One of the most significant elements of UK Government spending is social security which often represents over 20% of total spending. After this health and defence are usually the most significant elements of Government expenditure.

Government revenue sources include

- taxes
- privatization proceeds
- rents from Government buildings and land
- profits of nationalized industries
- dividend income from any Government shares in private enterprises

The most significant source of UK Government revenue is usually income tax, followed by VAT and social security contributions.

Public Sector Net Cash (PSNC)

This is the borrowing of the public sector (central Government, local Government and other state institutions such as nationalized industries). In some periods the Government's income is actually greater than its spending (e.g. in the UK in 1988–91 and 1999–2001); this means there is a budget surplus, which is a negative PSNC.

Budget position

- Budget deficit: central government is spending more than it receives in tax revenue
- Budget surplus: central government spending is less than its tax revenue

Key dates in the UK fiscal year

- The budget in March: this is when the Chancellor gives a forecast of Government spending and taxation for the coming year. Changes in taxation are also announced.
- November or December: the Chancellor presents a Pre-Budget Report and Comprehensive Spending Review, also announcing forecast spending and taxation.

Tax

Direct taxes: these take money directly from people's incomes or from companies' profits, e.g.

- income tax – payable on income
- corporation tax – paid by companies on their profits
- National Insurance contributions – these are paid by individuals
- petroleum revenue tax which is charged on the net incomes of North Sea fields

Property taxes

- inheritance tax – paid when money is inherited
- capital gains tax – paid when an asset increases in value and is sold for more than it was bought for
- council tax – this is a local tax paid by households and set by the local government in each area

Indirect taxes: these are paid when goods and services are bought, e.g.

- Value Added Tax (VAT)
- tax on tobacco
- excise duties on alcohol

A good tax system should

- have horizontal equity – people in the same circumstances pay the same amount
- have vertical equity – taxes should be fair in terms of rich and poor
- be cheap to administer
- be difficult to evade; convenient to pay
- be easily understood by the taxpayer
- have limited disincentive effect, e.g. should not discourage people from working

Unemployment trap occurs when people are worse off by working than they are when they are receiving benefits. Because they lose benefits when they start work and are taxed on their income, their total income falls when they start work. This creates an incentive *not* to work.

Poverty trap occurs when people are worse off when they earn more! This is because some benefits are withdrawn.

Tax systems

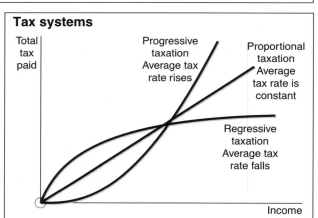

(Note: to find the average tax rate on the diagram, measure the gradient of rays from the origin to different points on the curves)

- Proportional tax – as income rises, the proportion paid in tax stays constant, e.g. if people pay 15% on all their earnings
- Progressive tax – as income rises, the average rate of tax increases, i.e. people pay a greater proportion of their income in tax
- Regressive tax – as income rises, the average rate of income tax falls, i.e. people pay a smaller proportion of their income in tax

Fiscal stance refers to whether the Government is pursuing an expansionist or contractionary policy, i.e. is the Government increasing or decreasing aggregate demand? To find this out, it is important to look at discretionary fiscal policy and ignore automatic effects of changing levels of income.

Reflationary (expansionist) fiscal policies include lower taxes and more Government spending. These increase aggregate demand.
Deflationary contractionary fiscal policies include higher taxes and less Government spending. These reduce aggregate demand.

Fiscal policy continued

Lorenz curve

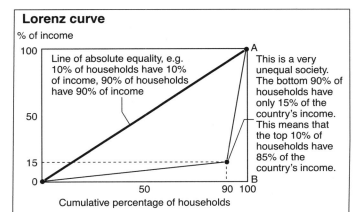

% of income

The **Gini Coefficient** measures the area between the Lorenz curve and the line of absolute equality (the shaded area) compared to the whole of the bottom trangle (OAB). The bigger the Gini Coefficient, the greater the inequality in a country. Fiscal policy can help redistribute income and reduce inequality e.g. through income tax and benefit payments.

Automatic stabilizers

If the income in the economy starts to grow, the progressive tax system acts as an automatic stabilizer. This is because more people will be paying a higher rate of tax, and so the level of disposable income and spending is less than it would be without a Government. This will dampen the effect of the boom. Similarly, the impact of a slump will be reduced because of transfer payments. When incomes fall, some people will become entitled to benefits which will keep their income and spending higher than it would be without a Government.

The tax system also reduces the size of the multiplier – out of each extra pound the consumer will have to pay some tax, so the marginal propensity to consume will fall. This reduces the multiplier, and so any change in injections will have a smaller effect.

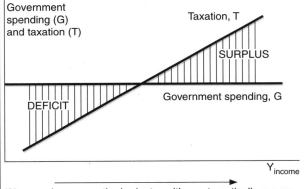

If income increases, the budget position automatically moves towards a surplus

Fiscal rules

In 1998 the Government announced two fiscal rules:

- The **golden rule**: the Government would only borrow money to invest over the whole period of a trade cycle. It could increase borrowing to finance current spending but this would need to be matched by repayments later on. Over the whole cycle, net borrowing for current expenditure would have to be zero. The Government could, however, borrow for capital expenditure such as investment in roads and hospitals. (Note: **current expenditure** is spending on items used up in the current period, e.g. wages, salaries and materials; **capital expenditure** is on long-term assets that provide a benefit over a period of time, such as infrastructure).
- The **public debt rule**: the ratio of public debt to national income would be held at a 'stable and prudent level' over the trade cycle at less than 40% of GDP.

Using tax changes compared to spending changes

Tax changes:

- tax and benefit changes can be introduced and have an effect quite quickly
- tax cuts can increase incentives (to work or to invest) and so have supply side effects

but

- they are an indirect method, i.e. the Government may not be able to predict how consumers will react to a tax cut – they may spend or save the extra money

Spending changes

- Government spending can be targeted at specific industries or regions
- this directly increases aggregate demand and so has full multiplier effects, e.g. £100 spending starts off the multiplier with a £100 increase in demand; if the Government gives £100 back in tax, some will be saved so the initial increase in demand will be lower

but

- there is a time lag before spending actually takes place, e.g. there may be long delay between deciding to increase spending and it actually occurring

Financing a deficit

To finance its deficit the Government can sell

- Treasury bills (short term borrowing by the Government) – these bills are IOUs which are bought back (redeemed) after three months
- Bonds – these are longer term debt, i.e. longer term IOUs
- National Savings certificates

or

- The Bank of England can lend to the Government as the Government's banker

Discretionary stabilizers

Actions deliberately taken by the Government to stabilize the economy, e.g. changes in the rate of taxation, spending on goods and services. In a slump, for example, the Government will usually try to reflate the economy by stimulating aggregate demand; in a boom it will try to deflate the economy by reducing aggregate demand.

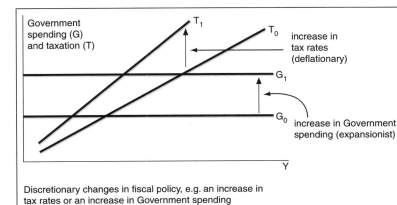

Discretionary changes in fiscal policy, e.g. an increase in tax rates or an increase in Government spending

Fiscal policy continued

The impact of funding a deficit on the money supply

The existence of a deficit means that the Government is putting more money into the economy than it is taking out. This will increase the amount of money in the economy. If, however, the Government sells debt to the non-bank public, or encourages people to use the National Savings, this will take the excess money out again, and the overall effect on the money supply may be neutral. Similarly, if the Government sells long term debt to banks, this will reduce the banks' liquidity (because they have swapped cash for long term IOUs) and may reduce their lending. This might offset the increase in the money supply from the deficit. If the Government sells Treasury bills to banks, these are so liquid that it probably will not affect their lending – overall the money supply will have increased.

The National Debt is the total debt of the Government – it grows whenever the Government has a deficit because the Government is borrowing more money. The Government has to pay the interest of this borrowing back from future earnings.

- If the National Debt consists entirely of borrowings within the country, the Government is simply moving money around from one group to another. To pay off the people it owes interest to, it borrows from another group. When they have to be paid back, it borrows from another group. The money remains within the economy.
- If the Government borrows from overseas, the interest has to be paid to people out of the country and so the National Debt could become a burden.

Problems controlling Government spending

- some items of spending are very difficult to reduce, e.g. education and health spending – demand for these is ever increasing. People expect better standards and it is politically unwise to cut back on these
- factors beyond the Government's control, e.g. an ageing population places a greater burden on the health service. Wars may require political intervention or more defence spending
- commitments to other countries or organizations such as the European Union are not easy to end

Problems of fiscal policy

- time lags – any change in policy will take time to work through the economy, by which time the policy change may not be needed
- information problems – it is difficult to know the exact position of the economy at any moment or to estimate the size of the multiplier or accelerator
- fiscal drag – if the Government keeps spending and taxation rates are constant, it can have a deflationary effect on the economy; as households and firms earn more, they move into higher tax brackets and pay more tax revenue to the Government
- **crowding out** occurs when Government spending 'crowds out' private sector spending (i.e. the Government spends more but the private sector spends less so the impact on overall spending is not great). There are two types of crowding out:
  1. **Resource crowding out:** if the economy is near full capacity and the Government uses resources such as labour and materials that would otherwise have been used by the private sector (this argument does not work if the economy is significantly under-employed, as the Government and the private sector are not then competing for resources)
  2. **Financial crowding out:** occurs when Government spending diverts financial resources away from the private sector. If the Government spends more, it may need to borrow more; to raise this finance it may need to increase interest rates which may deter private sector investment. Also, if the Government borrows from banks they will have less to lend to the private sector, reducing its spending.
- consumption may not be sensitive to tax changes, e.g. consumers may save any increase in disposable income rather than spending a proportion of it
- Government intervention often overshoots or undershoots, i.e. increases aggregate demand too much or too little because of time lags and poor information; this can destabilize the economy

Fine tuning/stabilisation policies

are attempts by the Government to use fiscal policy on a regular basis to increase or decrease aggregate demand, to keep it at a desired level to achieve its objectives. They were common in the 1950s and 1960s.

Fiscal policy v monetary policy

Fiscal policy is likely to be more effective than monetary policy if:

- money demand is interest elastic (so changes in the money supply have little effect on interest rates)
- the marginal efficiency of capital is interest inelastic (so interest rate changes have little effect on investment)

Keynesian fiscal policy

From the 1930s to the 1970s, governments tended to follow Keynesian policies on how to control the economy. This involved a belief that:

- the economy will not necessarily be in equilibrium at full employment, and that the Government needed to intervene to get it to full employment

- fiscal policy was effective
- by having a deficit, the Government can increase aggregate demand to achieve full employment
- fiscal policy can be used to fine tune the economy to stabilize growth

Balanced budget multiplier (equal to 1)

An increase in Government spending accompanied by an equal increase in tax revenue leads to an increase in output. For example, if Government spending increases by £100, and at the same time the Government raises an extra £100 in tax, there will still be a multiplied effect on the economy. Out of every £100 given to households, some is spent and some is saved, e.g. £80 spent and £20 saved. Therefore, if tax revenue is increased by £100, the impact on spending is a fall of only £80 (the rest comes from saving). As a result, if Government spending goes up by £100, aggregate demand rises by £100, but if taxation rises by £100 aggregate demand initially falls by only £80. The overall result is a £20 increase in demand, which sets off the multiplier even though the budget is balanced. The balanced budget multiplier is equal to 1. In this case the multiplier will be 5 (MPC = 0.8); so the overall effect is £20 x 5 = £100 which is equal to the initial injection.

Money and banking

The functions of money:
- medium of exchange – people are willing to change their goods and services for money
- a store of value – people are willing to hold on to money because it generally keeps its value (although not with inflation)
- unit of account – people can measure the value of things in terms of money
- standard of deferred payment – people are willing to accept money as payment in the future, e.g. when the work is completed

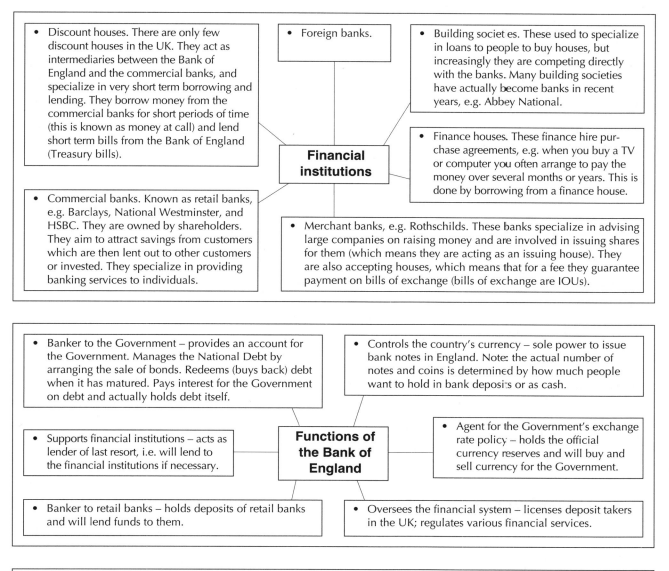

Financial institutions

- Discount houses. There are only few discount houses in the UK. They act as intermediaries between the Bank of England and the commercial banks, and specialize in very short term borrowing and lending. They borrow money from the commercial banks for short periods of time (this is known as money at call) and lend short term bills from the Bank of England (Treasury bills).

- Foreign banks.

- Building societies. These used to specialize in loans to people to buy houses, but increasingly they are competing directly with the banks. Many building societies have actually become banks in recent years, e.g. Abbey National.

- Finance houses. These finance hire purchase agreements, e.g. when you buy a TV or computer you often arrange to pay the money over several months or years. This is done by borrowing from a finance house.

- Commercial banks. Known as retail banks, e.g. Barclays, National Westminster, and HSBC. They are owned by shareholders. They aim to attract savings from customers which are then lent out to other customers or invested. They specialize in providing banking services to individuals.

- Merchant banks, e.g. Rothschilds. These banks specialize in advising large companies on raising money and are involved in issuing shares for them (which means they are acting as an issuing house). They are also accepting houses, which means that for a fee they guarantee payment on bills of exchange (bills of exchange are IOUs).

Functions of the Bank of England

- Banker to the Government – provides an account for the Government. Manages the National Debt by arranging the sale of bonds. Redeems (buys back) debt when it has matured. Pays interest for the Government on debt and actually holds debt itself.

- Controls the country's currency – sole power to issue bank notes in England. Note: the actual number of notes and coins is determined by how much people want to hold in bank deposits or as cash.

- Supports financial institutions – acts as lender of last resort, i.e. will lend to the financial institutions if necessary.

- Agent for the Government's exchange rate policy – holds the official currency reserves and will buy and sell currency for the Government.

- Banker to retail banks – holds deposits of retail banks and will lend funds to them.

- Oversees the financial system – licenses deposit takers in the UK; regulates various financial services.

Departments of the Bank of England

Issue department – responsible for issuing notes and coins
Banking department – acts as banker to the Government and retail banks

In May 1997, the UK Chancellor of the Exchequer announced several changes which made the Bank of England more independent from Government pressure. Interest rates are now set by the Bank's Monetary Policy Committee (MPC), which uses its own judgment about an appropriate level to control inflation. The original operational target for the MPC in 1997 was for an underlying inflation (RPI excluding mortgage interest payments, called RPIX) of 2.5%. MPC sets interest rates with reference to inflation two years ahead.

Credit creation and the money multiplier

When money is deposited in a bank, some is kept in reserve and the rest is lent out; this increases the money supply and is known as 'credit creation'.
If r is the reserve ratio (i.e. the percentage of deposits kept in reserve) the effect of an initial deposit is an increase of $\frac{1}{r} \times$ the initial deposit.

e.g. r = 0.1 (i.e. the banks keep 10% in reserve)
initial deposit = £20
Overall impact $= \left(\frac{1}{0.1}\right) \times 20 = £200$

i.e. with an initial deposit of £20, overall deposits will increase to £200.

Money and banking continued

Measures of the money supply

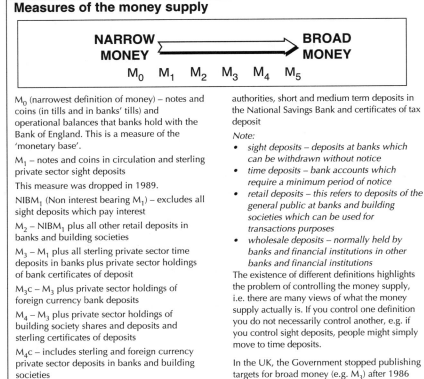

M_0 (narrowest definition of money) – notes and coins (in tills and in banks' tills) and operational balances that banks hold with the Bank of England. This is a measure of the 'monetary base'.

M_1 – notes and coins in circulation and sterling private sector sight deposits

This measure was dropped in 1989.

$NIBM_1$ (Non interest bearing M_1) – excludes all sight deposits which pay interest

M_2 – $NIBM_1$ plus all other retail deposits in banks and building societies

M_3 – M_1 plus all sterling private sector time deposits in banks plus private sector holdings of bank certificates of deposit

M_3c – M_3 plus private sector holdings of foreign currency bank deposits

M_4 – M_3 plus private sector holdings of building society shares and deposits and sterling certificates of deposits

M_4c – includes sterling and foreign currency private sector deposits in banks and building societies

M_3H – includes public corporations' holdings of money

M_5 – M_4 plus other holdings of liquid assets, e.g. bills of exchange eligible for rediscount at the Bank of England, short term loans to local authorities, short and medium term deposits in the National Savings Bank and certificates of tax deposit

Note:

- *sight deposits – deposits at banks which can be withdrawn without notice*
- *time deposits – bank accounts which require a minimum period of notice*
- *retail deposits – this refers to deposits of the general public at banks and building societies which can be used for transactions purposes*
- *wholesale deposits – normally held by banks and financial institutions in other banks and financial institutions*

The existence of different definitions highlights the problem of controlling the money supply, i.e. there are many views of what the money supply actually is. If you control one definition you do not necessarily control another, e.g. if you control sight deposits, people might simply move to time deposits.

In the UK, the Government stopped publishing targets for broad money (e.g. M_3) after 1986 although it still monitored its growth. As building society deposits became more liquid, M_2 and M_4 became the main measures of narrow and broad money rather than M_1 and M_3.

Controlling the money supply

- open market operations – the Bank of England sells Government debt (short term debt is called Treasury bills; longer term debt is called bonds). The buyer pays for these by writing a cheque on their banks. The banks honour the cheque by paying the Bank of England and this reduces their reserves and so reduces their ability to lend.
- liquidity (or reserve) ratios – by forcing a bank to keep more funds in reserve, a central bank can restrict the commercial banks' lending; but banks may find ways around this, e.g. Goodhart's Law (if the Bank of England tries to control one type of lending, banks will find ways of increasing other types).
- cut the amount the Government borrows (Public Sector Net Cash Requirement (PSNCR)) – the PSNCR increases the money supply if it is financed by selling Treasury bills or borrowing from the Bank of England; but cutting the PSNCR may be difficult as it involves cutting public spending and increasing taxes.
- funding – this involves converting short term Government debt to long term debt. By selling longer term debt to banks in return for shorter term debt, the central bank reduces their liquidity and ability to lend. In the mid 1980s the Government undertook 'overfunding', where the value of the bonds sold is in excess of the Government's borrowing requirement.
- special directives and special deposits – banks can be forced to deposit a certain percentage of their liabilities with the Bank of England, e.g. in the 1970s the authorities used Special Supplementary Deposits (this became known as The Corset). Banks had to put a proportion of their deposits at the Bank of England without interest. The Bank of England can also give directives on how much banks are allowed to lend (quantitative controls) or to whom (qualitative controls). These types of control have not been used in the UK since the 1970s.
- moral suasion – the central bank can make it known whether it would like more or less lending; banks will often listen to the central bank's advice or wishes knowing that if they don't listen the Bank of England may force them to change.

Instruments and objectives of monetary policy

- Objectives – what the authorities are trying to achieve
- Instruments – what they are using to achieve their objectives e.g. interest rates.

The objective of monetary policy is usually to control inflation. In 2003, the operational target for monetary policy was set for the Consumer Prices Index (CPI). The target was set at 2%.
In the early 1980s, the Government tried to achieve this by controlling banks' lending.
From the mid 1980s, the Government has used the interest rate as the main policy instrument; this is aimed at controlling demand for money rather than supply.

Monetary and inflation targets

Monetary targets were introduced by the Government in the early 1980s as part of its Medium Term Financial Strategy. These set out the targets for the growth in the money supply. By achieving these, the Government hoped to control the growth of the money supply and control inflation. By announcing money supply targets, they hoped people would believe that inflation would be reduced and so reduce their own wage demands in line. In fact the Government generally missed its targets. The Government now publishes inflation targets.

Bank base rate: the rate which a bank sets to determine its lending and saving rate. It lends above the base rate and pays savers below the base rate.

Key features of UK monetary policy

- The Government sets the monetary policy objective and the inflation target annually.
- The Monetary Policy Committee (MPC) is required to meet the Government's inflation target at all times, e.g. a 2% increase in the 12-monthly Consumer Prices Index.
- Interest rates are set by the Bank's Monetary Policy Committee. The MPC sets an interest rate it judges will enable the inflation target to be met. The Bank's Monetary Policy Committee (MPC) is made up of nine members – the Governor, the two Deputy Governors, the Bank's Chief Economist, the Executive Director for Markets and four external members appointed directly by the Chancellor. The appointment of external members is designed to ensure that the MPC benefits from thinking and expertise in addition to that gained inside the Bank of England.

- The target is symmetric so that deviations below target are treated as seriously as those above target.
- Deviations of more than one percentage point above or below the target require an Open Letter from the Governor of the Bank to the Chancellor to explain the cause and duration of the deviation, and what action the MPC is taking consistent with the Government's wider economic policy objectives.
- When deciding what interest rate to charge, the MPC will consider factors such as:
  1. the rate of increase of average earnings
  2. house prices
  3. the exchange rate
  4. the output gap

However, the indicators do not always give the same messages and are not always completely reliable as they may be very recent figures and have a margin of error. Also different experts may have differing views of exactly where the economy is and what is going to happen next.

Money and banking continued

Changes in the official interest rate

The Bank of England changes the rate it lends to financial institutions; this affects a range of organizations such as banks and building societies. A reduction in interest rates:

- makes saving less attractive and borrowing more attractive (because it is cheaper), which stimulates spending.
- can also increase the prices of assets such as shares and houses. With lower interest rates people buy more assets, increasing the price. Higher asset values increase households' wealth and they may be more willing to spend money. This boosts demand.
- may see outflows from the UK as investors look for higher returns abroad. This may reduce the value of the exchange rate, making UK goods and services cheaper abroad and boosting demand.

Changes in interest rates can therefore affect demand and will also influence wage demands and prices.

In general, there are time lags between interest rate changes and the impact on demand, sometimes up to two years. So interest rate judgements must be made about expected future inflation, not based on inflation today.

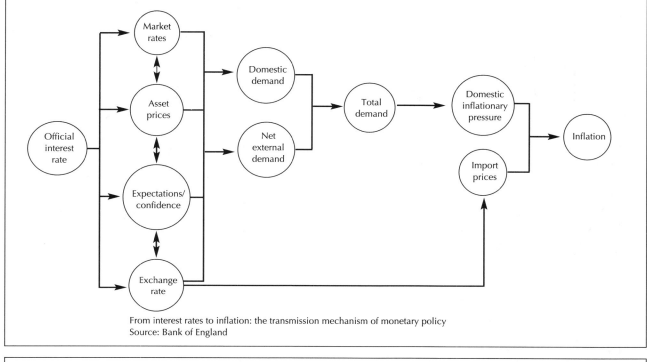

From interest rates to inflation: the transmission mechanism of monetary policy
Source: Bank of England

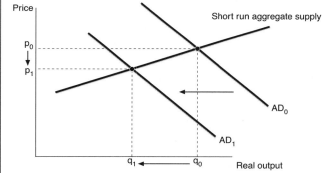

The effect of an increase in interest rates

Higher interest rates lead to less spending by firms and households. With higher rates borrowing is more expensive and there are better returns for saving. As a result aggregate demand decreases. In the diagram on the left prices actually fall. In reality aggregate demand is usually increasing over time so higher interest rates tend to slow up this increase rather than actually decrease aggregate demand; prices still increase but not as fast as they would have otherwise.

Problems of monetary control

- banks may hold in excess of the reserve set by the authorities, so a reserve ratio or special deposits may have no impact.
- Goodhart's Law – attempts to control particular types of lending or lending by certain financial institutions will lead to more lending of a different type or by different organizations.
- disintermediation – lending continues, but banks are no longer the intermediaries, i.e. it is no longer officially organized by banks and so the authorities cannot control it.

Controlling interest rates

Open market operations are often conducted to leave the banks short of cash. The banks then borrow this, which often means they are competing for scarce funds which will make it more expensive to borrow, i.e. increase interest rates. The Bank of England can also change the interest rate by changing its discount rate – this is the rate at which it buys bills. By influencing the interest rate, the Bank of England influences the demand for money.

Problems of using interest rates to influence the economy

Changes in interest rates are likely to affect

- the exchange rate, e.g. using higher interest rates to discourage borrowing may increase the value of the exchange rate and make UK firms uncompetitive
- borrowing by households and firms

Note: changes in the interest rate may take time to have an effect.

The demand for money (liquidity preference)

Why hold money?

People can hold money or they can hold other assets such as houses or bonds (IOUs). According to Keynes, people hold money for three main reasons:

- Transactions demand – money is needed to facilitate transactions, i.e. to buy goods and services. This will increase if:
  a we have more income (because we will buy more goods and services)
  b prices increase (because we will need more money to buy our goods and services)
  c we are paid less regularly

Assume the household receives £2000 every 4 weeks and uses this up at a constant rate. Average holdings will be £1000

- Precautionary demand – this money is held in case of emergency, e.g. people might hold money in case they lose their job. This demand will usually rise with income.
- Speculative demand – this is money which is held rather than invested in bonds or other assets. Money is liquid but it does not earn a rate of return. If people are holding money, they are not earning interest. The interest rate represents the opportunity cost (or price) of holding money. If the interest rate is high, this will reduce the desire to hold money, i.e. it will reduce the speculative demand for money. If the interest rate is low, there will be less incentive to switch out of money into other assets, i.e. it will increase the speculative demand for money.

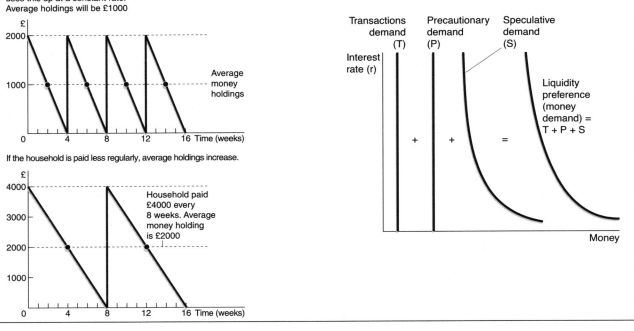

If the household is paid less regularly, average holdings increase.

Active and idle balances

The transactions and precautionary demand for money are called demand for 'active balances', i.e. there is an active reason for holding money.

The speculative demand is called an 'idle balance' – money is held because the individual is worried about holding bonds.

The money market and the bond market

A bond has a fixed return, e.g. £10 a year. If the price of a bond is £100 this represents a 10% return. If the price of the bond is £50 this represent a 20% return, i.e. the lower the price of the bond, the greater the return.

If households and firms feel they have too much liquidity, i.e. they are holding too much money, they will want to switch into bonds. This will increase the price of bonds (and so lower their return). This process will continue until the price of bonds has increased (the rate of return on bonds has fallen) to a point where there is no further desire to switch away from money, i.e. both the money market and bonds markets are back in equilibrium.

At interest rates above r_0 there is excess supply of money; households buy bonds until equilibrium r_0

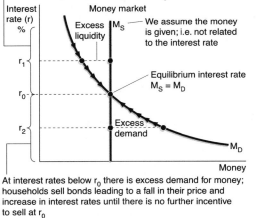

At interest rates below r_0 there is excess demand for money; households sell bonds leading to a fall in their price and increase in interest rates until there is no further incentive to sell at r_0

Keynesians and monetarists and the demand for money

Keynesians see money as an alternative to bonds and financial assets. Monetarists believe money is an alternative to a broader range of alternatives, including physical goods. Any excess liquidity will lead to a direct increase in spending on goods, as well as switching into financial assets, according to the monetarists. However, monetarists also believe that money is NOT a close substitute for other assets and, therefore, changes in the interest rate have relatively little effect, i.e. money demand is interest inelastic.

The monetary transmission mechanism

This shows how changes in money supply or demand can influence the level of national income.

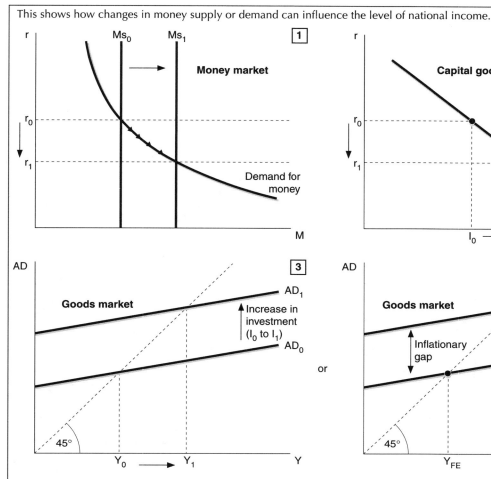

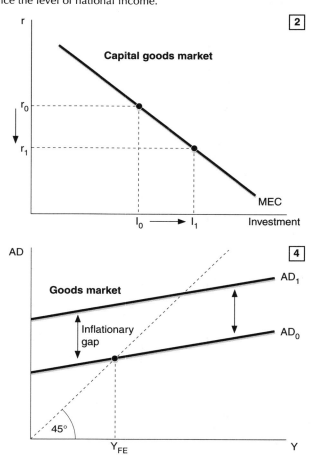

An increase in the supply of money

- **Money market** (diagram 1)
  Imagine there is an increase in the money supply. At the old level of interest rates there is now excess liquidity, i.e. too much money. Households try to shed this liquidity by moving out of money into bonds and other assets. This bids up the price of bonds (and so reduces their return – the interest rate). This process continues until bond prices are so high (interest rates so low) that there is no further incentive to move out of money. Both the money and the bond markets are back in equilibrium.

- **The capital goods market** (diagram 2)
  The lower interest rate will increase the amount of investment – because the cost of borrowing has fallen, there are more investment projects which are now profitable. The extent of the increase in investment will depend on how sensitive investment is in relation to changes in the interest rate, i.e. the interest rate elasticity of investment.

- **The goods market** (diagrams 3 and 4)
  With an increase in investment, there is an increase in aggregate demand.
  If the economy is below full employment, this will lead to an increase in output and employment. (diagram 3)
  If the economy is at full employment, this will lead to an inflationary gap and upward pressure on prices. (diagram 4)

  If prices do increase, this will increase the money value of national income, which will increase the transactions demand for money. This will shift the demand for money outwards which in turn increases interest rates and brings aggregate demand down again, i.e. a one off increase in the money supply will create forces that reduce any inflationary gap and so the inflation. This assumes that the money supply is held constant and not increased again.
  If the money supply is increased at the same rate as prices are increasing, inflation can continue.

An increase in the demand for money

- **Money market**
  At the old interest rate there is now excess demand for money. Households will switch out of assets into money, i.e. they will sell their bonds. This reduces the price of the bonds and increases their rate of return (the interest rate). This process continues until there is no further incentive to move out of bonds.

- **Capital goods market**
  The higher interest rate should lead to a fall in investment, depending on the interest elasticity of investment.

- **The goods market**
  With a fall in investment there will be a fall in the level of aggregate demand.

The monetary transmission mechanism continued

Monetarists and the transmission mechanism

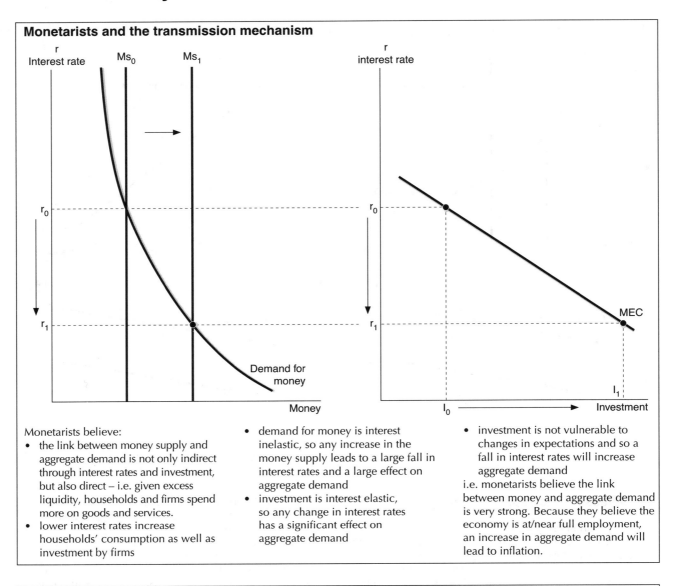

Monetarists believe:
- the link between money supply and aggregate demand is not only indirect through interest rates and investment, but also direct – i.e. given excess liquidity, households and firms spend more on goods and services.
- lower interest rates increase households' consumption as well as investment by firms

- demand for money is interest inelastic, so any increase in the money supply leads to a large fall in interest rates and a large effect on aggregate demand
- investment is interest elastic, so any change in interest rates has a significant effect on aggregate demand

- investment is not vulnerable to changes in expectations and so a fall in interest rates will increase aggregate demand

i.e. monetarists believe the link between money and aggregate demand is very strong. Because they believe the economy is at/near full employment, an increase in aggregate demand will lead to inflation.

Liquidity trap occurs when an increase in the money supply does not affect the interest rate (and so does not affect investment or aggregate demand).

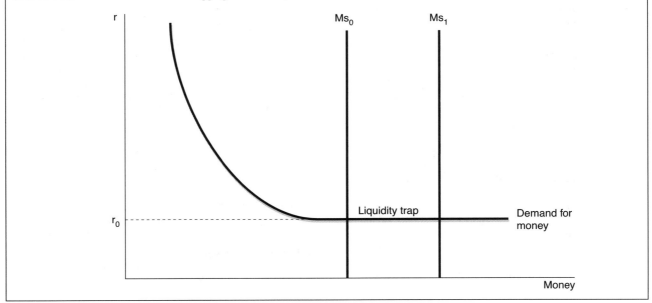

Inflation

Inflation and its causes

Inflation is a sustained increase in the general price level. It is usually measured by the Retail Price Index (RPI) or the Consumer Price Index (CPI). This is a weighted average of retail prices. To calculate it, goods and services are given different weights according to the percentage of income that households spend on them. Weights are determined by results of the Family Expenditure Survey.

Inflation can be caused by:
- too much demand in the economy. This is called demand pull inflation, e.g. the UK in the 1980s. If demand increases and firms cannot produce enough output, they will increase their prices.
- higher costs forcing firms to increase their prices. This is called cost push inflation, e.g. as happened in Western Europe in the 1970s and in 2008 when oil prices increased.
- excessive growth of the money supply

Deflation occurs when prices are falling (inflation is negative). This may be because of an increase in supply and/or fall in demand.

Different price indices

RPI (Retail Price Index) and CPI (Consumer Price Index)

Both of these indices are collected from survey data in which over 100,000 prices are gathered each month for a 'typical' basket of goods. What constitutes a 'typical' basket will change over time as our buying habits change. When calculating the indices items are weighted to take account of their relative importance.

The CPI is based on the average basket of goods bought by all households. The RPI does not include the top 4% of households in terms of income or pensioner households that derive at least 75% of their income from state pensions and benefits.
- RPIX. This measures the RPI but excludes mortgage interest payments. This shows the underlying inflation, which makes it easier to compare inflation figures internationally (since the importance of mortgages and borrowing to buy homes varies considerably between countries; in some countries it is more common to rent than buy). The RPIX is used by the Bank of England for official inflation targets.
- RPIY. This adjusts the RPI to exclude the mortgage interest payments and a range of taxes such as VAT, excise duties, council tax and airport tax.
- Tax and price index. This attempts to measure the income before tax of the average person; this takes into account changes in prices and direct taxes.
- Producer price index. This estimates the prices of goods produced by manufacturers, i.e. at the factory gate rather than in the shops. An increase in the producer price index may signal an increase in the retail price index later on.
- GDP deflator. This attempts to show changes in the level of prices of all goods and services not just consumer goods (e.g. including export items and goods and services consumed by the Government).

Price indices

To work out a price index compare the price of a representative basket of goods today compared to the base year using the equation:

$$\text{Price index} = \frac{\text{present cost of a basket of goods}}{\text{cost of the basket of goods in base year}} * 100$$

Note: when compiling the RPI the goods are given weights according to their relative importance.

Types of inflation
- creeping inflation – slowly increasing rates of inflation, e.g. from 5 to 6%
- strato-inflation – high inflation, e.g. 10 to several hundred %
- hyperinflation – extremely high rates of inflation, e.g. thousands of %, e.g. Zimbabwe 2008
- stagflation – high inflation accompanied by high unemployment

Causes of demand pull inflation
- reflationary policies by the Government
- increased consumer spending, e.g. through greater consumer confidence

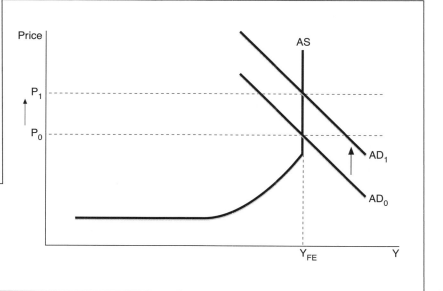

Inflation continued

Causes of cost push inflation

- wage increases to employees which are not linked to higher productivity

- an increase in the cost of imported raw materials, e.g. because of a fall in the value of the pound

- an increase in input prices, e.g. because of the monopoly power of suppliers or higher energy prices

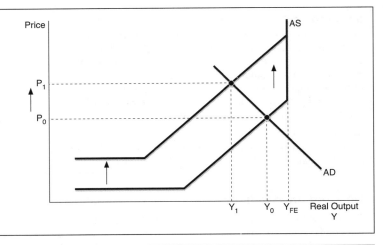

Wage price spiral

Higher wage demands without any increase in productivity lead to higher costs and then prices (cost push inflation); higher prices lead to higher wage demands.

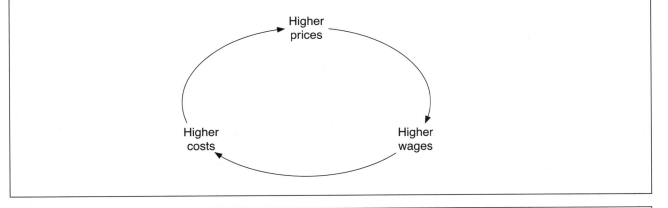

Expectations and inflation

Employees expectations play an important role in inflation. If employees expect high inflation, they are likely to demand high wages which cause the inflation they feared! Governments are eager, therefore, to get employees to believe inflation will fall–they are then likely to put in lower wage claims and this can help reduce inflation in the economy.

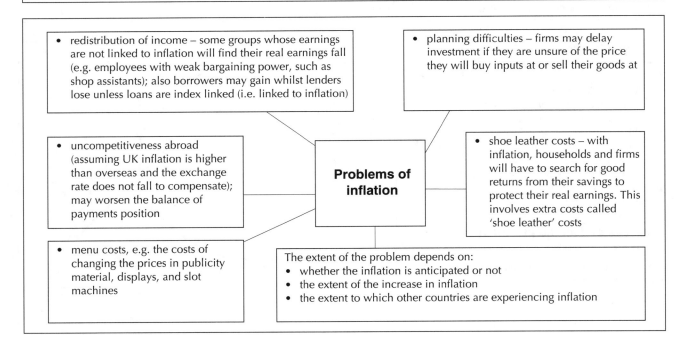

- redistribution of income – some groups whose earnings are not linked to inflation will find their real earnings fall (e.g. employees with weak bargaining power, such as shop assistants); also borrowers may gain whilst lenders lose unless loans are index linked (i.e. linked to inflation)

- planning difficulties – firms may delay investment if they are unsure of the price they will buy inputs at or sell their goods at

- uncompetitiveness abroad (assuming UK inflation is higher than overseas and the exchange rate does not fall to compensate); may worsen the balance of payments position

Problems of inflation

- shoe leather costs – with inflation, households and firms will have to search for good returns from their savings to protect their real earnings. This involves extra costs called 'shoe leather' costs

- menu costs, e.g. the costs of changing the prices in publicity material, displays, and slot machines

The extent of the problem depends on:
- whether the inflation is anticipated or not
- the extent of the increase in inflation
- the extent to which other countries are experiencing inflation

Inflation continued

Fisher equation of exchange
$MV = PY$

where

M = quantity of money, i.e. the supply of money

V = the income velocity of circulation, i.e. the average number of times per year that the typical unit of money must be spent to buy the goods and services bought that year

P = average level of all prices

Y = number of transactions of final products

This is not an equation, it is an identity, i.e. it must be true. MV represents total spending in an economy; PY represents the total amount of money received for the goods and services, i.e. money national income. They show the same things. For example, if there is £100bn in the economy, which is spent 5 times, then total spending must be £500bn. This must equal the value of the money received for goods and services (i.e. £500bn).

Is inflation a monetary phenomenon?
According to monetarists, inflation is 'always and everywhere a monetary phenomenon'. Temporary bursts of inflation may be caused by, for example, costs rising, but if prices are to rise continuously, the money supply must also be increased.

The Quantity Theory of money
states that the price level is directly related to the amount of money in the economy.

Using MV = PY, we can see this is true if V and Y are constant,

i.e. if V and Y are fixed, then the price level is directly proportional to the money supply.

Imagine V = 10 and Y = 30

If the money supply is £60 then prices will be £20; (£60 * 10 = £20 * 30)

If the money supply doubles to £120 and V and Y do not change, then prices increase to £40 (120 * 10 = £40 x 30), i.e. the price level depends on the money supply

Why should V and Y be constant?
* V may be constant because the rate at which money is spent may not change very much over time.
* Y may be constant if the economy is near full employment, which would mean that the output and, therefore, number of transactions in the economy could not change much.

Keynesians and the Fisher equation of exchange
Keynesians believe
* the velocity of circulation can change – with more money people may hold on to it (V falls)
* an increase in the money supply can lead to more output (Y) rather than higher prices

Using MV = PY
If the number of transactions is 200 and the average price level is £20, then the total spent must be 200 * £20, i.e. £4000.

If the total money in the economy is £400, then each pound must have been used 10 times, i.e. the velocity is 10.

Quantity Theory of money and monetarists
Monetarists believe in the quantity theory of money. According to monetarists, the price level is directly related to the money supply. To control prices (and so inflation) the Government should control the money supply.

Curing inflation
The cure depends on the cause, i.e. what type of inflation it is. Policies include:
* demand side policies – reduce aggregate demand, e.g. reduce public expenditure, raise taxes, increase interest rates; this is aimed at demand pull inflation
* supply side policies – to make the labour market more competitive (e.g. reduce trade union power, cut unemployment benefits) or to increase competition (e.g. privatization, encourage small firms and business start ups); this increases aggregate supply
* prices and incomes policies; this is aimed at cost push inflation
* exchange rate policy, e.g. increase value of the currency to reduce import prices and reduce demand for exports

Prices and incomes policies
These are attempts by the Government to control the increase in prices and/or incomes by legislation. They limit the pay increases firms can give and/or the amount prices can be increased.

Problems of incomes policies
* once the legal restrictions are ended, people often try to catch up on the money they did not get before, i.e. there is a surge in wages and prices
* they prevent the market system working, e.g. firms cannot attract the labour they want through higher wages
* they are politically unpopular and can cause industrial relations problems
* firms find ways of avoiding the policy. This is called wage drift – although the wage per hour stays constant, the unit cost of production increases because firms find ways of paying more, e.g. extra benefits (such as cars or cheap borrowing), extra payments for overtime which is not actually worked, or extra holiday pay.

Multi-causal inflation
In reality, inflation is likely to be due to a variety of causes not just one. This means that the 'cure' for inflation may have to be quite complex.

Unemployment

- Unemployed – the number of people who are not employed but who are actively seeking work
- Unemployment rate – the number of people unemployed as a percentage of the labour force
- Labour force – those in a job plus those who are unemployed

Measuring unemployment

- Claimant count – monthly total of those claiming benefit, i.e. those officially registered and able to work but claiming Jobseeker's Allowance; easy to collect but excludes all those not eligible for benefit, e.g. all men aged over 60 who no longer have to sign on to get benefits; it includes those who illegally claim but also work. Governments have been accused of manipulating the claimant count by changing the definitions of who is and who is not included, e.g. in 1988 16–17 year olds were excluded because they were no longer allowed to claim benefit on the grounds that they were guaranteed a place either in education or on a training scheme.
- Standardized unemployment measure: based on quarterly survey of over 60,000 households. Defines unemployment as: those without jobs who say they have actively sought work in the last four weeks or are waiting to take up a job in the next two weeks. This measure is used internationally, enabling comparison between countries, although there is likely to be some sampling error (as only a percentage of households in a country are asked). The International Labour Organization (ILO) administers this survey based measure and its results are referred to as the **ILO unemployment rate**.

The ILO figures can vary significantly from the claimant count; reasons might be:
- many female unemployed workers may be actively looking for work but may be excluded from the claimant count, e.g. because their partners earn so much that they do not qualify for benefit
- older workers may be collecting a pension and so not entitled to benefits but may be looking for work
- workers who are made unemployed cannot claim benefit for a number of weeks even though they would be counted as unemployed in the ILO survey.

Both methods may underestimate overall unemployment because:
- they do not include part-time workers, e.g. if you are working a few hours a week but seeking a full-time job you would not be counted
- anyone on government training and work schemes will not be counted even if they would want to work full time.

The unemployment figure is a stock concept: it measures the number of people unemployed at a particular moment. However there are people moving into and out of unemployment all the time. It is important to consider the rate of flow. Are the same people remaining unemployed for long periods of time – or are people moving through quite rapidly? If people are becoming unemployed and then finding work, this may be less of a problem than a high long-term unemployment figure.

$$\text{Unemployment rate (\%)} = \frac{\text{unemployed}}{\text{labour force}} * 100$$

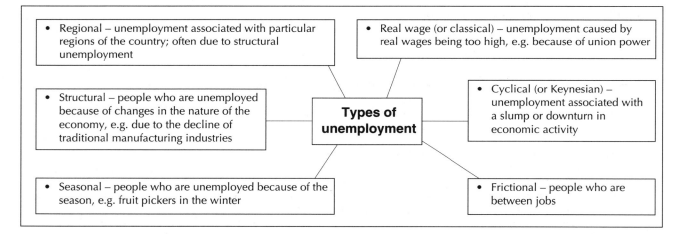

- Regional – unemployment associated with particular regions of the country; often due to structural unemployment

- Structural – people who are unemployed because of changes in the nature of the economy, e.g. due to the decline of traditional manufacturing industries

- Seasonal – people who are unemployed because of the season, e.g. fruit pickers in the winter

Types of unemployment

- Real wage (or classical) – unemployment caused by real wages being too high, e.g. because of union power

- Cyclical (or Keynesian) – unemployment associated with a slump or downturn in economic activity

- Frictional – people who are between jobs

Voluntary and involuntary

- 'Voluntary' unemployment occurs when all those willing and able to work at the given real wage rate are working, i.e. the economy is at full employment. Even at full employment some people will still be unemployed, e.g. due to frictional causes.
- 'Involuntary' unemployment occurs when people are willing and able to work at the given real wage rate but no job is available, i.e. the economy is below full employment. A worker is 'involuntarily' unemployed if he or she would accept a job at the given real wage.

Natural rate of unemployment, or the NAIRU (non accelerating rate of unemployment)

This is the rate of unemployment that occurs when inflation is correctly anticipated. This level of unemployment occurs when the economy is at full employment; i.e. when the labour market is in equilibrium.
The level of the natural rate of unemployment depends on the supply side of the labour market, e.g. training, information, benefit levels, unions.

Full employment occurs when all those willing and able to work at the given real wage are working, i.e. all unemployment is 'voluntary'.

Unemployment continued

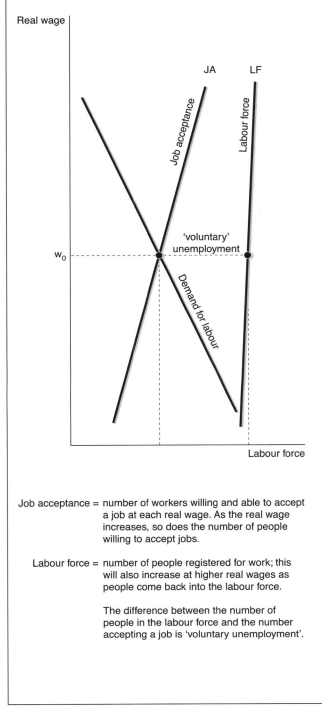

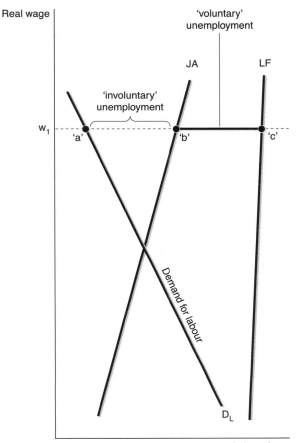

Job acceptance = number of workers willing and able to accept a job at each real wage. As the real wage increases, so does the number of people willing to accept jobs.

Labour force = number of people registered for work; this will also increase at higher real wages as people come back into the labour force.

The difference between the number of people in the labour force and the number accepting a job is 'voluntary unemployment'.

At real wage w_1 there are 'c' people in the labour force; 'b' want to accept a job, so 'bc' is 'voluntary' unemployment; 'ab' is 'involuntary' unemployment–these people are willing and ab le to work but are not demanded at the higher real wage.

This assumes the high real wage is caused by imperfections in the labour market, e.g. money illusion which prevents money wages changing quickly.

Note: If the real wage is above equilibrium because of union power, it could be argued that 'ab' is 'voluntary'–the unions have volunteered workers for unemployment. This is 'classical unemploy ment'

Unemployment continued

Is all unemployment 'voluntary' at full employment?

Arguably yes, for example:
- Frictional unemployment is 'voluntary' because people have decided to look for another job
- Seasonal unemployment is 'voluntary' because people have decided to take a job in which they are only seasonally employed; they could take other work in the 'off' season

- Real wage unemployment is 'voluntary' because workers or their unions have decided to push up wages and have 'volunteered' some workers for unemployment
- Structural unemployment may be regarded as 'voluntary' if workers who have left a job in a declining industry are unwilling to accept a job at a lower wage rate in another industry.

The word 'voluntary' does not mean people actually volunteer to be unemployed.

Why does unemployment matter?
- it is a waste of resources so the economy is underproducing compared to its potential output; it is inefficient

- it can cause social problems, e.g. higher crime rates
- the Government loses tax revenue, e.g. less income tax as fewer people are working and less VAT as there is less spending

Cures for unemployment: demand side policies

To cure 'involuntary' unemployment, the Government can stimulate demand to provide more jobs, i.e. use demand side policies. These include lower taxation, increased Government spending, lower interest rates (all aimed at boosting aggregate demand, AD). An increase in AD will increase output (assuming the economy is not already at full employment). This will reduce cyclical or involuntary unemployment. However, at full employment an increase in AD will simply increase inflation.

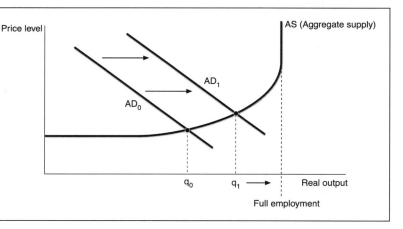

Cures for unemployment: supply side policies

To cure 'voluntary' unemployment, the Government has to make more people willing and able to work. This can be done via supply side policies, e.g.
- more training to give people the necessary skills
- a reduction in income tax so the gains of working compared to collecting benefit are greater (i.e. remove the poverty trap)

- a reduction in unemployment benefits to give people more incentive to look for work
- more information about vacancies and help with applications
- help (e.g. financial) for people who are relocating
- reduce barriers to people accepting jobs, e.g. there used to be 'closed shops' which were factories where only union members could work; this prevented non union members working

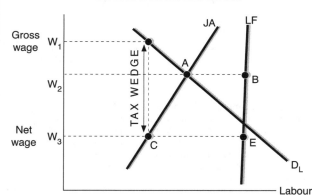

The effect of an income tax cut

With income tax there is a difference between the gross wage paid by the firm and the net wage received by the worker e.g. W_1W_3. At W_3 the natural rate of unemployment is CE; C people want to work at this wage but there are E people in the labour force. If income taxes are removed, the gross and net wage are the same at W_2 and the level of 'voluntary' unemployment falls to AB.

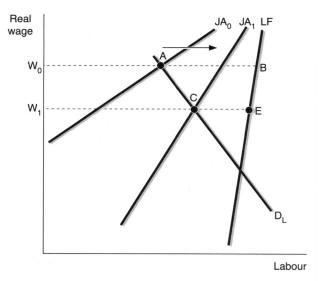

Policies aimed at making people more willing or able to work, shift the job acceptance to the right. 'Voluntary' unemployment falls from AB to CE.

Unemployment continued

Supply of labour depends on

- Changes in migration patterns: when many of the newer member states of the EU joined the EU, countries such as the UK saw an increase in immigrants, and therefore an increase in the labour supply.
- Income tax: when income tax is high, workers may feel that it is not worth working because they take home too little of their pay, and so labour supply may fall, i.e. the value of their leisure time is more valuable than an hour of work, and so they substitute leisure for work. On the other hand, workers may feel that they have to work longer hours to compensate for the reduction in pay, and so labour supply may increase.
- Benefits: if state benefits (e.g. for sickness, disability, unemployment, etc.) are generous, then people are more likely to stay at home rather than work, thus reducing the labour supply.

- Trade unions: because trade unions act to increase wage rates through a process of collective bargaining, this may increase the labour supply as more people are encouraged to join the workforce. However, higher wage rates mean reduced demand for labour, so unemployment might result. A similar outcome may occur as a result of a National Minimum Wage.
- Social trends: the workforce in the UK has increased female participation compared to a few decades ago, as it has become more acceptable for women to work and childcare has become more accessible.

New Deal for Labour

As the UK economy has shifted from the manufacturing sector to the service sector, some low-skilled manual workers have lost their jobs. Schemes such as the Government's New Deal for Labour have been introduced by providing training (although some people cannot afford to spend their time in training rather than work).

Impact of supply side policies on full employment levels

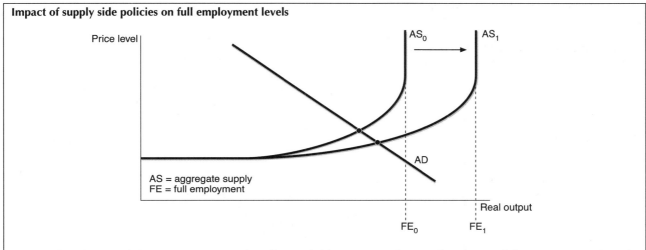

Supply side policies aimed at getting more people willing and able to accept jobs at each real wage shifts aggregate supply to the right. This increases the full employment level.

Employment trends in the UK

- Growth of flexible working: part-time work, temporary contracts, flexi-time
- Deindustrialization – decline in the manufacturing sector

Growth of employment in services

Because:

- high income elasticity of demand for services makes this a growth sector as the economy grows
- UK has comparative advantage in this sector
- import penetration is less easy in the service sector

Decline in employment in manufacturing

- high exchange rates in the early 1980s and late 1990s made many UK manufacturers uncompetitive
- high interest rates made expansion expensive
- technological change replaced some manual jobs
- inefficiency – a need to reduce overstaffing and improve working practices
- the structural decline of certain industries, e.g. coal
- greater competition from abroad

Growth of self employment

due to:

- Government advice and incentives
- inspired by success of others
- redundancies – many use redundancy payments to start up

The poverty trap

The poverty trap occurs when poor people are discouraged from working because it will make them no better off; if they start working the tax rate on their earnings and the loss of benefits means there is little if any net financial gain.

The Phillips curve: inflation and unemployment

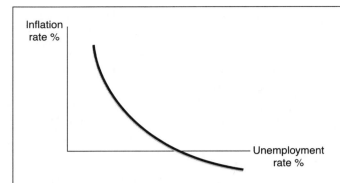

The Phillips curve shows the relationship between inflation and unemployment.
(Note: the original curve showed the relationship between the rate of change of nominal wages and unemployment, NOT the rate of change of prices and unemployment)
The curve was originally produced by A W Phillips in 1958, and suggested a trade off between inflation and unemployment, i.e. if unemployment fell, inflation would rise and vice versa. This fitted in with thinking at the time, i.e. to reduce inflation the Government had to spend more money to boost aggregate demand, and this would probably cause some inflation; the higher levels of demand would pull up prices. Workers would become more confident because the economy was doing well and because it was not as easy for employers to find new employees, and so wages would be pushed up causing cost push inflation. The model suggested that the Government simply had to pick which point on the Phillips curve it wanted the economy to be at and then introduce the appropriate policies.

However, in the 1970s there were high levels of inflation and high unemployment (called stagflation) which did not seem to fit with the original Phillips curve. The new situation was explained by an expectations augmented Phillips curve (Friedman). This model introduced short and long run Phillips curves and suggested that there was a short run trade off between inflation and unemployment but no long run trade off.

Expectations augmented Phillips curve
Each short run curve is constructed based on a level of expected inflation.

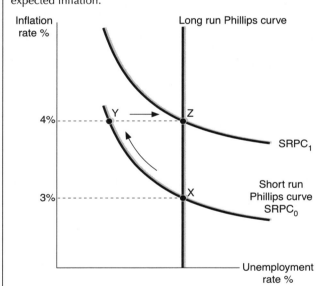

Imagine that the economy is at equilibrium at X. Employees expect inflation to be 3% and it is 3%; the economy is in long run equilibrium; unemployment is at the natural rate. Then an increase in aggregate demand pulls up inflation to 4%. Workers still expect 3% and are often locked into contracts for at least a year. This means in real terms employees are cheaper (they are getting paid 3% but prices are increasing at 4%), and so firms demand more labour. This excess demand for labour gradually pulls up money wages, e.g. to 3.5% and more workers accept jobs because they think they are better off (note: in real terms they are actually worse off because inflation is 4%). Unemployment falls to Y. Over time, however, employees learn that inflation is 4% and bargain for more pay. Prices and wages will once again grow together at 4%; workers are no longer cheap in real terms and so the economy returns to full employment at Z.

Everyone now expects 4%, but if the Government uses expansionist policies which result in 5% inflation, the workers can once again be caught out. They will become relatively cheap because they are paid, say, 4.5% until they realize prices are growing at 5%.

To keep fooling the workers in future, the Government will have to bring about bigger jumps in inflation so employees can never predict what inflation will be next year. This model suggests that in the short run unemployment can be kept below full employment by fooling the employees, but it may require ever accelerating increases in inflation to do it. This assumes employees have 'adaptive expectations' and base their view of future inflation rates on what has happened in the past. Provided the Government keeps increasing inflation by accelerating rates, employees can be fooled.

In the long run there appears to be no trade off between inflation and unemployment; the economy returns to its long run equilibrium. Once employees realize what inflation is and increase their money wages accordingly, the real wage returns to the long run equilibrium and the economy is at full employment.

The short run trade off occurs because of 'money illusion' – employees focus on their money wages and not their real wages, e.g. when money wages rise, more people accept jobs in the short run even though real wages may not have increased; when workers realize what has happened to prices and demand higher nominal wages, the real wage is restored to long run equilibrium.

Rational expectations model:
assumes people do not form expectations of future inflation based on the past, i.e. they do not have adaptive expectations – they look ahead and make an estimate based on all the information they have available at that moment, i.e. they are rational. For example, if workers think the Government will reduce inflation in the future, they will cut their wage demands relatively quickly. This means the economy can adjust to the long run equilibrium fairly quickly and any short run Phillips curve is very short run indeed. In its extreme version, rational expectations mean that workers cannot be fooled at all (i.e. there is no money illusion) and the Government cannot reduce unemployment below the natural rate even in the short run.

Keynesians and monetarists

Keynesians

1950s and 1960s Keynesians argued for demand management policies, i.e. for the Government to control aggregate demand. If the economy grew too fast, the Government deflated; if it grew too slowly it reflated through fiscal policy. This led to a series of stop-go policies, e.g. deflate, reflate, deflate.

Keynesians believe that:
- markets do not clear and are slow to adjust, e.g. the labour market. This means the economy can settle in equilibrium below full employment, so cyclical or 'involuntary unemployment' exists
- the Government should intervene to stabilise the economy

- fiscal policy is more effective than monetary policy
- inflation is often caused by cost push factors.

Extreme Keynesians believe:
- markets do not clear and the economy will not move towards full employment. The Government must expand demand.

Monetarists

In the 1970s the UK experienced stagflation (high inflation and high unemployment). Existing theories struggled to explain it; monetarism grew in appeal.
Monetarism is based on the quantity theory of money, $MV = PY$. V and Y are assumed constant so prices are directly related to the money supply.
Monetarists believe:
- that inflation is due to the money supply growing faster than output growth. Reducing the rate of growth of the money supply will lead to less inflation without more unemployment (in the long run) (see expectations augmented Phillips curve on page 90)
- prices and wages change quite quickly, so the economy tends towards full employment

- inflation makes firms uncompetitive, discourages investment, and so governments must control inflation. To do this they must control the money supply. Apart from this, the Government should intervene very little.

Extreme monetarists are called the **new classical school** – they believe markets clear quickly and expectations adapt very quickly. Faster growth of the money supply will quickly lead to inflation; even in the short run the Phillips curve is vertical.

Moderate monetarists believe:
- markets adjust fairly quickly. An increase in the money supply and therefore demand will lead to some fall in unemployment in the short run. Similarly, a sharp reduction in the money supply may cause unemployment in the short run.

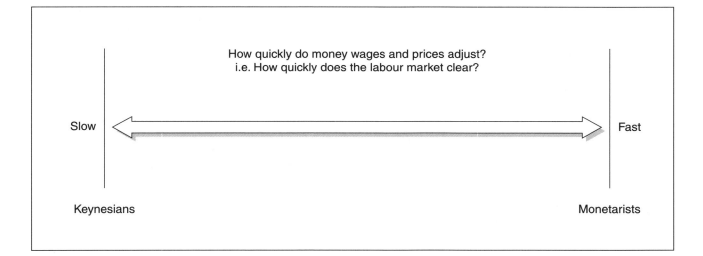

How quickly do money wages and prices adjust?
i.e. How quickly does the labour market clear?

Slow — Fast

Keynesians — Monetarists

The labour market

The labour market is a key element of the economy and its ability to clear (i.e. for supply to equal demand) is important. This depends on the flexibility of wages.
If aggregate demand falls and there is excess supply of labour, in a perfectly competitive world money wages will fall and the labour market will clear – the economy will remain at full employment.

BUT
- unions may fight against a fall in wages
- wages may take time to fall, e.g. they are often negotiated for a year in advance.
If wages do not fall, there will be unemployment for long periods of time and the economy can remain below full employment for long periods of time.

Monetarists believe that money wages and prices are flexible, and so the labour market clears – the economy is at or moving towards full employment.
Keynesians believe money wages and prices are not flexible, and so the labour market does not necessarily clear – the economy can be in equilibrium below full employment.

Exchange rates

The **exchange rate** is the price of one currency in terms of another. It is the external value of a currency (the internal value is what the currency can buy in its own country and depends on the price level). The UK exchange rate is called the 'value of the pound' or 'the value of sterling'.
In a floating exchange rate system, this price is determined by market forces of supply and demand.
In a fixed system the Government intervenes to maintain the external value of the currency.

At any moment in time there are many exchange rates, e.g. the pound in terms of dollars, in terms of yen, in terms of francs and so on. The value of the pound can go up against some and down against others.

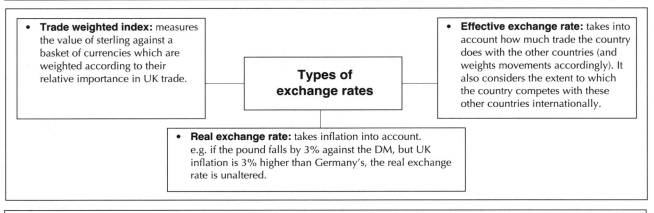

Spot and future exchange rates
- **Spot rate:** this is the current price of a product or a currency
- **Futures or forward market:** a market in which contracts are made to buy and sell products or currencies at an agreed price in the future
- **Future price:** a price that is agreed today for a product or exchange rate to be traded at in the future. Firms that are worried about future changes in the exchange rate may try and set the price today to trade at in the future; this means they can then plan ahead knowing the price at which they will trade.

Changes in the exchange rate
- In a floating exchange rate system, an increase in the exchange rate is an appreciation; a fall is a depreciation.
- In a fixed exchange rate system, if the rate at which it is fixed is increased, this is a revaluation. If a lower rate is fixed it is a devaluation.

- **Trade weighted index:** measures the value of sterling against a basket of currencies which are weighted according to their relative importance in UK trade.

- **Effective exchange rate:** takes into account how much trade the country does with the other countries (and weights movements accordingly). It also considers the extent to which the country competes with these other countries internationally.

Types of exchange rates

- **Real exchange rate:** takes inflation into account.
  e.g. if the pound falls by 3% against the DM, but UK inflation is 3% higher than Germany's, the real exchange rate is unaltered.

The demand for pounds (or sterling)
This refers to the desire to change other currencies into pounds in order to:
- spend on UK goods and services
- save in UK banks and other financial institutions (long term capital movements)
- speculate on the currency in the hope that the pound will become more valuable in the future (these are short term capital movements; called 'hot money')

The demand for pounds will increase if:
- UK goods and services are demanded more, e.g. the quality improves, foreign incomes increase or they are relatively cheaper, more tourism into the UK
- the UK interest rate increases, because there will be a greater desire to save in the UK to earn higher rates of return
- people think the value of the pound will rise in the future so they buy it now

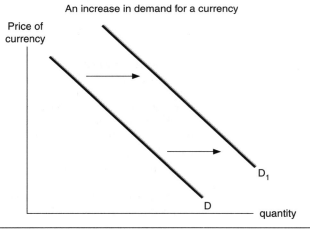

An increase in demand for a currency

The elasticity of demand for pounds
If the pound falls, the price of UK goods or services in foreign currency also falls – demand for UK goods will increase. The extent of the increase and, therefore, the extent of the increase in the quantity demanded of pounds, depends on the price elasticity of demand for UK goods and services. The more price elastic the demand for UK goods and services, the more elastic the demand for pounds.

Exchange rates continued

The supply of pounds (or sterling)

This refers to the desire to change pounds into other currencies in order to:

- buy overseas goods and services; travel abroad

- save in overseas financial institutions

- speculate on a foreign currency in the hope that it will increase in value

The slope of the supply of pounds

If the UK exchange rate falls, the price of imports in UK currency increases – this will reduce the amount of imports which are bought. If demand for imports is inelastic, the total amount spent on imports will increase and the supply of pounds is downward sloping.

If the demand for imports is elastic, then when their price rises in pounds (due to a fall in the value of the pound) the total amount spent on them falls. This means the supply of pounds is upward sloping. We usually assume the supply of a currency is upward sloping.

The supply of pounds will increase (shift to the right) if:
- overseas interest rates increase so saving abroad becomes more attractive
- overseas goods are demanded more, e.g. because they are better quality, UK incomes rise, or foreign goods are relatively cheaper; increased tourism abroad
- people think the pound will fall in the future so they sell it now

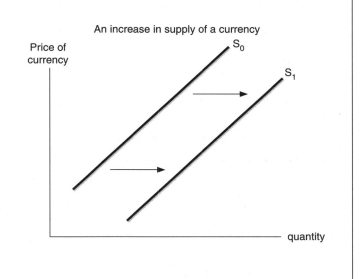

Floating exchange rate system

The exchange rate is determined by demand and supply of the currency in the foreign exchange market. No Government intervention.

Advantages of a floating exchange rate system

- The exchange rate automatically adjusts so that supply of the currency equals demand – this can automatically eliminate balance of payments deficits or surpluses. If imports rise, for example, the supply of pounds increases, leading to a fall in the exchange rate. As the pound falls exports become more competitive and imports become less competitive, which should eliminate the deficit.

- There is no need for the central bank to keep foreign reserves.

- The Government can pursue its own domestic policies, e.g. can adjust interest rates more easily.

- It prevents imported inflation – if one country has higher inflation, then, under a fixed exchange rate system, another country will import those via higher import prices.

- It possibly reduces speculation, because speculators might lose and so do not take the risk.

Disadvantages of a floating exchange rate system

- It causes instability, which deters investment and trade (although business can hedge against exchange rate movements by buying or selling currency at some date in the future in the forward currency markets to reduce the risk).

- It can lead to inflation – if a country has inflation which makes its goods uncompetitive, this will lead to a fall in demand for its currency and a fall in the exchange rate. This makes its goods competitive again but makes imports more expensive, which in the long run will lead to more inflation (cost push).

- Speculation on future movements can lead to major changes in the rate.

- Governments are not forced to control their economies, e.g. they do not have to ensure that domestic inflation is in line with other countries to ensure their firms are competitive (this is because the pound can float downwards).

Exchange rates continued

The Government and the exchange rate

A Government may influence the exchange rate by:
- buying and selling currency
- changing the interest rate to influence capital inflows and outflows from the economy

To increase demand for the currency a Government may:
- buy the currency
- raise interest rates to attract investors

Fixed exchange rate

The Government intervenes to maintain the exchange rate. If the price of the currency is about to fall, the Government may increase demand by buying its own currency (using foreign currency reserves) or increasing interest rates. If the price of the currency is about to increase, the Government may sell its own currency or lower interest rates.

Advantages of fixed exchange rates

- They provide stability for firms and households – this encourages investment and trade.
- They act as a constraint on domestic inflation – if a country has higher inflation than its trading partners, it will become uncompetitive (the currency will not depreciate to offset the inflation). Firms have to control costs to compete.
- In theory they prevent speculation, as there is no point because the value of the exchange rate is fixed.

Disadvantages of fixed exchange rates

- A Government must have sufficient reserves to intervene to maintain the price of its currency.
- A country's firms may be uncompetitive if the exchange rate is fixed at too high a rate.
- The Government must make intervention a priority. This may mean it undertakes policies which damage the domestic economy, e.g. to keep demand for pounds up in the exchange rate market, the Government might increase interest rates. The problem is that this leads to less demand within the country.

Managed exchange rate system

Government intervenes on occasions to influence the price, but does not fix it.

Purchasing power parity (PPP)

The theory that in a floating system exchange rates adjust until a unit of currency can buy exactly the same amount of goods and services as a unit of another currency.

Exchange Rate Mechanism (ERM)

Each member country agreed with the EU to stabilise its currency against a central rate, e.g. the UK joined in 1990 at a central rate of £1: 2.95DM. Each currency could fluctuate within a band around these currencies (usually 2.25% either way, although the pound was allowed to move 6% either way). The central bank intervened to keep the currency within this band. If the central rate needed to be realigned, it could be if all members agreed.

Why join a system like the ERM?

- It may lead to less inflation – firms and workers realize that higher prices will not be offset by a lower exchange rate; this puts pressure on them to control costs and prices.
- Stability – which encourages trade and investment and enables firms and households to plan more effectively.

UK experience in ERM

The rate at which the pound was fixed was too high, and this made UK firms uncompetitive. The Government had to intervene to keep the exchange rate within the set bands – it had to buy currency and increase interest rates. Higher interest rates made borrowing for firms and households more expensive within the UK. The effect of the ERM was to worsen the UK's recession. Speculators sold pounds, putting even more pressure on the Government. The UK left the ERM in 1992. Many members of the EU have now moved to a single currency (see page 107).

Fiscal and monetary policy and exchange rate systems

Under a fixed exchange rate system, monetary policy becomes more difficult – any change in the interest rate is liable to lead to inflows or outflows of currency, and put pressure on the currency, e.g. the Government tries to control the money supply which leads to higher interest rates which encourage inflows on the capital account. These inflows increase the money supply again.

Fiscal policy is effective, e.g. the Government tries to deflate the economy through higher taxes and less spending. This reduces aggregate demand and spending on imports. Lower demand will also reduce demand for money and interest rates. Lower interest rates lead to capital outflow which reinforces the contractionary fiscal policy.

In a floating system monetary policy is more powerful

For example, an expansion of the money supply will reduce interest rates, which will boost spending within the economy. It will also lead to outflows of currency of the capital account. This will lead to a fall in the value of the currency, which will boost exports leading to a further increase in aggregate demand.

Alternatively, a tight (contractionary) monetary policy increases interest rates and reduces aggregate demand. Higher interest rates lead to capital inflows and an appreciation of the pound. This further reduces aggregate demand.

Fiscal policy is less effective, e.g. contractionary fiscal policy reduces income and demand for money. This reduces interest rates and leads to an outflow on the capital account. This in turn leads to a depreciation of the exchange rate which raises aggregate demand.

Balance of payments

Balance of payments

The **Balance of Payments** is a record of a country's transactions with the rest of the world. It shows the country's payments and receipts from its trade. It has two main sections:
1. **Current account:** records payment for the purchase and sale of goods and services
2. **Capital and financial accounts:** record flow of money relating to savings, investment, speculation

The **current account** has three parts:
- Balance of Trade – this measures the value of imports and the value of exports. Exports are goods/services that are made by UK companies and sold abroad. They generate a positive entry in the Balance of Payments because they bring money into the country. Imports are goods/services made abroad and sold to people in the UK. They generate a negative entry into the Balance of Payments because money leaves the country. The Balance of Trade can be split up even further into trade in goods, or visible trade, and trade in services, or invisible trade.
- Income – this comprises income earned by UK citizens who own assets overseas, and it includes profits, dividends on investments abroad (payments made to shareholders by companies who earn a profit) and interest.
- International transfers — these are generally money transfers between central governments (who lend and borrow money from each other) or grants (e.g. as part of the Common Agricultural Policy from the European Union).

If there is a current account deficit then the money leaving the country is greater than the value of money entering the country. If more money comes in than goes out this is a surplus.

The **capital account** involves transfers of money by immigrants and emigrants and Government transfers regarding debt repayments or subsidies with other countries. The capital account refers to transactions in fixed assets and is relatively small. The largest aspect of the capital account refers to flows of capital associated with migration. As immigration into the UK increases, this increases the surplus on the capital account, as immigrants' assets become part of the UK's assets.

The **financial account** records flows of money capital in and out of the country. This is made up of:
- foreign direct investment, e.g. funds coming into a country from abroad to finance a takeover
- portfolio investment: includes money flows to buy shares (where this is less than 10% of the company) and buying bonds and debt issued by firms and governments
- 'other investments' such as purchases of currency and loans

World money capital flows have increased in recent years due to:
- more speculation; with less barriers to movements of money there are more opportunities for speculation
- financing of trade, e.g. borrowing from abroad
- more transfers of money abroad, e.g. as more people work, live or have second homes abroad
- more international takeovers as firms expand overseas
- spreading of risks by firms and households as they diversify their portfolio of investments

Benefits and problems of international money capital flows

International capital flows help facilitate international business. Organizations can gain investment and can invest globally. This promotes world trade and economic growth.

However, it does make economies dependent on each other. Problems in the US banking system, for example, have an impact on UK banks if they have lent or borrowed from the US.

Balance of payments and floating exchange rates

In a free floating exchange rate system, the balance of payments will automatically balance. The exchange rate automatically changes until the supply of pounds equals the demand for pounds, i.e. the number of pounds leaving the country equals the number entering. This does not mean each element of the balance of payments balances, i.e. the current account can be in deficit if the capital and financial account is in surplus or vice versa.

If there is a current account deficit, there must be a surplus on the capital and financial accounts. This is because the country must pay for what is being consumed in some way and so, to fund the current account deficit caused by money leaving the country, assets must be sold to bring money in. This may not be sustainable in the long run because if foreigners invest in the UK, at some point they will want a return on their investment, which will cause a deficit on the financial account.

Balance of payments and fixed exchange rates

If the exchange rate is fixed above the equilibrium rate (e.g. er_0) there will be excess supply of currency, i.e. more money wants to leave the country than come into it. This means that, excluding Government intervention, there is a balance of payments deficit.

If the price is fixed below the equilibrium rate (e.g. er_1) there will be excess demand for the currency, i.e. more money wants to come into the country than leave it. This means that excluding Government intervention there is a balance of payments surplus.

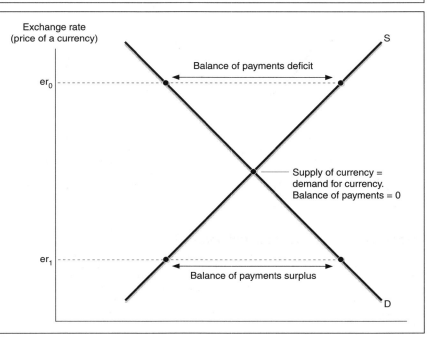

Balance of payments continued

Current account deficit
The UK is spending more on foreign goods and services than is being spent on UK goods and services. Money is leaving the country.

Problems of current account deficit
In the long run this could indicate problems with the competitiveness of a country's industries. Usually more of a problem in a fixed exchange rate system, compared to a floating rate. In a floating system the external value of currency falls, making exports competitive again. In a fixed system the deficit may be offset by inflows on the capital account or the Government will have to intervene to buy up excess currency (this cannot continue indefinitely as the country will run out of foreign currency reserves).

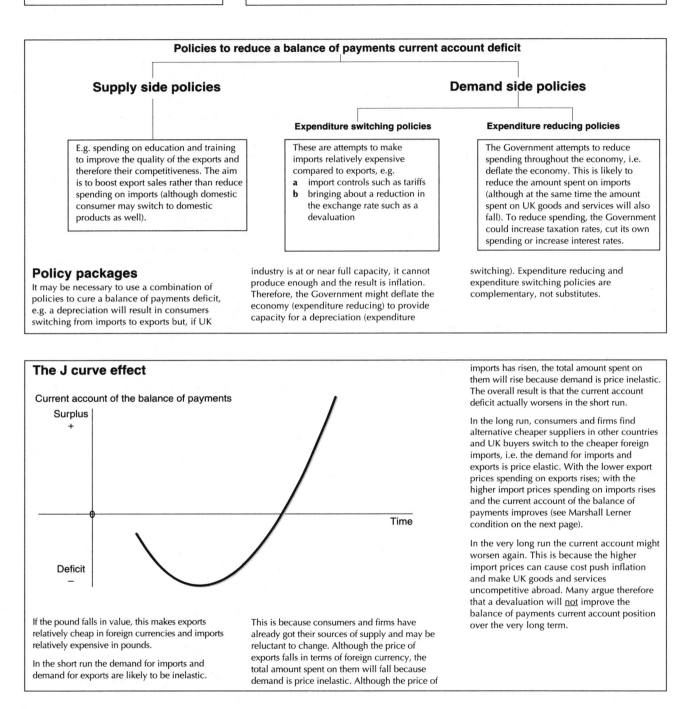

Policies to reduce a balance of payments current account deficit

Supply side policies

E.g. spending on education and training to improve the quality of the exports and therefore their competitiveness. The aim is to boost export sales rather than reduce spending on imports (although domestic consumer may switch to domestic products as well).

Demand side policies

Expenditure switching policies

These are attempts to make imports relatively expensive compared to exports, e.g.
a   import controls such as tariffs
b   bringing about a reduction in the exchange rate such as a devaluation

Expenditure reducing policies

The Government attempts to reduce spending throughout the economy, i.e. deflate the economy. This is likely to reduce the amount spent on imports (although at the same time the amount spent on UK goods and services will also fall). To reduce spending, the Government could increase taxation rates, cut its own spending or increase interest rates.

Policy packages
It may be necessary to use a combination of policies to cure a balance of payments deficit, e.g. a depreciation will result in consumers switching from imports to exports but, if UK industry is at or near full capacity, it cannot produce enough and the result is inflation. Therefore, the Government might deflate the economy (expenditure reducing) to provide capacity for a depreciation (expenditure switching). Expenditure reducing and expenditure switching policies are complementary, not substitutes.

The J curve effect

Current account of the balance of payments

If the pound falls in value, this makes exports relatively cheap in foreign currencies and imports relatively expensive in pounds.

In the short run the demand for imports and demand for exports are likely to be inelastic.

This is because consumers and firms have already got their sources of supply and may be reluctant to change. Although the price of exports falls in terms of foreign currency, the total amount spent on them will fall because demand is price inelastic. Although the price of imports has risen, the total amount spent on them will rise because demand is price inelastic. The overall result is that the current account deficit actually worsens in the short run.

In the long run, consumers and firms find alternative cheaper suppliers in other countries and UK buyers switch to the cheaper foreign imports, i.e. the demand for imports and exports is price elastic. With the lower export prices spending on exports rises; with the higher import prices spending on imports rises and the current account of the balance of payments improves (see Marshall Lerner condition on the next page).

In the very long run the current account might worsen again. This is because the higher import prices can cause cost push inflation and make UK goods and services uncompetitive abroad. Many argue therefore that a devaluation will <u>not</u> improve the balance of payments current account position over the very long term.

Does a current account deficit matter?
The positive effects in the short run are that it enables consumption outside of the **Production Possibility Frontier** (by importing). But it:
• may have a deflationary effect by reducing aggregate demand (with spending leaking from the economy)
• may lead to downward pressure on the exchange rate (as the demand for the domestic currency from abroad is less than the demand for foreign currency); this may improve the current account deficit in the medium term but lead to cost push inflation in the long term (see the J curve effect)
• be financed by financial inflows which may lead to more outflows in the form of profits later.
The significance of the current account deficit depends on the size of it and the duration (large long term deficits may be more of a concern than small short ones)

Balance of payments continued

Marshall Lerner condition

When the pound falls in value, the price of exports in foreign currency falls and the quantity demanded will increase, leading to more pounds being spent (if demand is elastic). The extent of the increase depends on the price elasticity of demand for exports. Meanwhile, the fall in the pound increases the price of imports in pounds; the amount spent on imports will fall provided the demand for imports is elastic.

Overall the current account of the balance of payments will *improve* following a depreciation, provided that:

Elasticity of demand for imports + elasticity of demand for exports > 1

This is known as the Marshall–Lerner condition.

Income effect

If a depreciation leads to a fall in imports the country that produced these goods will suffer a fall in their income. If the UK exports to these countries, it may find its exports also suffer. Also, falling income levels may reduce pressure on prices in these countries so UK goods appear relatively expensive.

Absorption approach

examines the balance of payments from a Keynesian perspective, i.e. the ability of the economy to absorb an increase in demand. For example, if the economy is at full employment, expenditure switching policies will lead to inflation. The economy must be deflated first to provide excess capacity so the economy can meet the higher demand from abroad.

Reducing a balance of payments current account surplus

- reflate to boost demand and so increase imports
- remove import controls
- revalue the currency

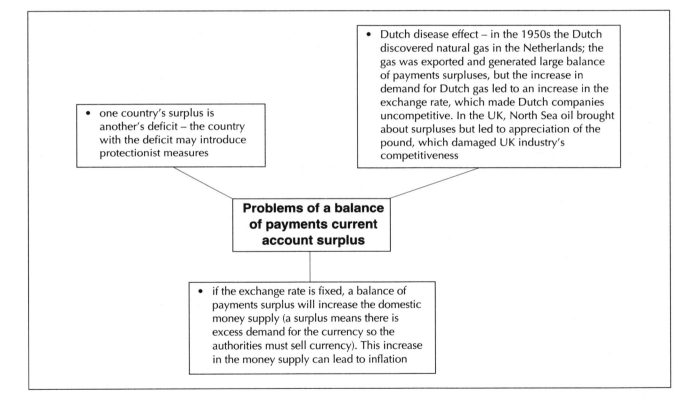

- one country's surplus is another's deficit – the country with the deficit may introduce protectionist measures

- Dutch disease effect – in the 1950s the Dutch discovered natural gas in the Netherlands; the gas was exported and generated large balance of payments surpluses, but the increase in demand for Dutch gas led to an increase in the exchange rate, which made Dutch companies uncompetitive. In the UK, North Sea oil brought about surpluses but led to appreciation of the pound, which damaged UK industry's competitiveness

Problems of a balance of payments current account surplus

- if the exchange rate is fixed, a balance of payments surplus will increase the domestic money supply (a surplus means there is excess demand for the currency so the authorities must sell currency). This increase in the money supply can lead to inflation

International competitiveness

This refers to the ability of a country (or firm) to provide goods and services which provide better value than their overseas rivals.

International competitiveness depends on:
- productivity, e.g. output per worker
- unit costs such as unit labour costs
- state of technology
- investment in capital equipment
- quality of design and production
- research and development and innovation
- entrepreneurship
- exchange rate.

How can the Government improve the UK's international competitiveness?

- lower interest rates to stimulate investment
- tax incentives for research and development and investment
- help entrepreneurs to start up and survive, e.g. reduce regulatory burden and bureaucracy
- encourage the sharing of ideas and 'best practice' (i.e. firms learning from each other the best way of doing something)
- reduce protectionist barriers to stimulate competition

International trade

Trade is based on the principle of comparative advantage, which in turn is based on the concept of opportunity cost. If a country can produce good X with a lower opportunity cost than another country, it has a comparative advantage in the production of X. This means it sacrifices less of other goods to make one unit of X. By comparison, if its opportunity cost of producing good Y is higher than another country it has a comparative disadvantage.

Absolute advantage

A country has an absolute advantage in the production of a good if an equal quantity of resources can produce more of the good than another country. This does not mean it necessarily has a comparative advantage. Although it might be able to make more Xs than another country, it might also involve a greater sacrifice of other goods such as Y.

Free trade - occurs when there are no barriers to importing or exporting (i.e. no protectionism), so trade occurs unhindered.

The benefits of free trade

Imagine resources are allocated between two goods X and Y in two countries A and B and the output is as follows:

	Good X	Good Y
Country A	1	4
Country B	2	3

The opportunity costs of production are as follows:

	Opportunity cost of 1X	Opportunity cost of 1Y
Country A	4Y	$\frac{1}{4}$X
Country B	$1\frac{1}{2}$Y	$\frac{2}{3}$X

If each country specializes in the production of the good in which it has comparative advantage, A will make Y because the opportunity cost is $\frac{1}{4}$X rather than $\frac{2}{3}$X.
B will make X because the opportunity cost is $1\frac{1}{2}$Y rather than 4Y.

If all resources are now diverted into these goods, then, assuming constant returns to scale, the output will double (because there are twice as many resources in the production of these particular goods), i.e.

	Good X	Good Y
Country A	0	8
Country B	4	0

Without trade the economies made 3Xs and 7Ys; with trade they make 4Xs and 8Ys, i.e. there are more of both goods. Trade allows countries to benefit from more goods and services by specializing in goods and services where they have comparative advantage. International trade is always beneficial if there is a difference in the opportunity cost ratios between two countries. Through trade consumers can have a wider range of goods at a cheaper price than is possible if they do not trade.

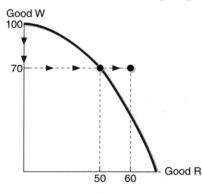

Trade enables countries to consume outside of their production possibility frontiers, e.g. without trade if the country gives up 30 units of W it achieves 50 units of R in return. With trade it may be able to export its 30W for 60R.

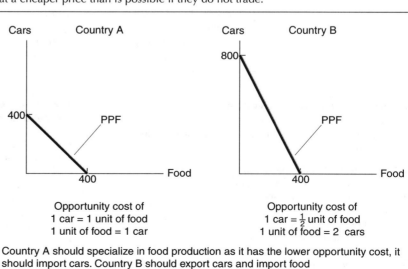

Opportunity cost of
1 car = 1 unit of food
1 unit of food = 1 car

Opportunity cost of
1 car = $\frac{1}{2}$ unit of food
1 unit of food = 2 cars

Country A should specialize in food production as it has the lower opportunity cost, it should import cars. Country B should export cars and import food

International trade continued

Further gains from trade
- economies of scale – by specializing, countries may increase their output and gain lower unit costs
- efficiency – the competition which arises from trade acts as an incentive to domestic firms to increase their competitiveness
- political, social and cultural gains from bringing countries closer together

Limits to the benefits from free trade
- increasing costs of production – firms may suffer from diseconomies of scale
- transport costs may make it more expensive to trade, even if a country has comparative advantage

---

The terms of trade refer to the rate of exchange of one good for another between trading partners. This depends on the opportunity cost ratios, e.g. country A can make 1X for 4Y; country B can make 1X for 1.5Y.

Trade will occur if

1.5Y < 1X < 4Y for example, trade might occur if 1X = 2Y

At this rate B sells Xs for more than it costs to make them; A buys them for less than it could produce them itself. Trade is therefore mutually beneficial.

The terms of trade are measured by:

$$\frac{\text{average export prices (index)}}{\text{average import prices (index)}} \times 100$$

If export prices increase compared to import prices, the terms of trade improve (this is called a 'favourable' movement in the terms of trade).

If export prices fall relative to import prices (e.g. do not increase as much) the terms of trade worsen (an 'adverse' movement).

UK trade
- Most UK trade is with industrialized countries; it is increasingly within Europe.
- In recent years the balance of manufactured goods for the UK has been in deficit (due to the decline of manufacturing and a decline in competitiveness).

- from the 1970s (peaking in the mid 1980s) North Sea oil has made a positive contribution to the UK balance of payments – without North Sea oil there would have been an even larger current account deficit.
- Most of the twentieth century there has been a deficit on the balance of visible trade and surplus on invisibles. The UK has lost

competitive advantage in many manufacturing industries, but has comparative advantage in services, e.g. finance. Invisibles have also gained from net property income from abroad – the UK has invested heavily overseas and these investments are now paying dividends.

Globalization
Globalization occurs with greater integration of the world's economies into a single market. It can be seen by the greater freedom of movement across borders of:
- goods and services
- people
- money
- technology

Globalization is 'The ability to produce any goods (or service) anywhere in the world, using raw materials, components, capital and technology from anywhere, sell the resulting output anywhere, and place the profits anywhere.' (Peter Jay)

Causes of globalization include:
- improvements in transport infrastructure and operations, making trade easier;
- improvements in communications technology and IT, making it easier to find suppliers and customers and to trade globally;
- a reduction in protectionist measures, enabling the freer movement of people, money and products.

The effects of globalization
- Businesses producing globally, making use of the cheapest and best resources worldwide.
- Greater choice for customers, who are able to choose products from all over the world .
- Businesses selling globally, accessing more customers, boosting their sales.
- Changing prices, e.g. greater demand by growing economies for some products such as steel and oil is increasing world prices; the ability to produce in low-cost locations is reducing the price of some goods for customers (such as consumer electronics).
- Increases in income; by participating in the global economy countries can earn more.
- Changing employment patterns; the location of production facilities has increased employment in some regions such as China and India but this has taken jobs from the more developed regions.
- Environmental impact; global growth has led to greater demands on natural resources and, in some cases, damage to the environment; however, there is increasing pressure on governments to control the environmental damage from growth.

More interdependent economies
Economies across the world are increasingly dependent on each other.
- Interdependence through trade: countries trade with each other and so changes in their domestic economies will affect other nations. If the USA economy slows up, for example, this will affect the demand for exports from their trading partners. The more open an economy is the more vulnerable it is to changes in the state of economies abroad.
- Financial interdependence: there are enormous financial flows across borders; changes in monetary policy will lead to movements worldwide, e.g. higher US interest rates will lead to outflows from some countries into the US to benefit from higher returns.

International trade continued

Protectionism: involves barriers to trade

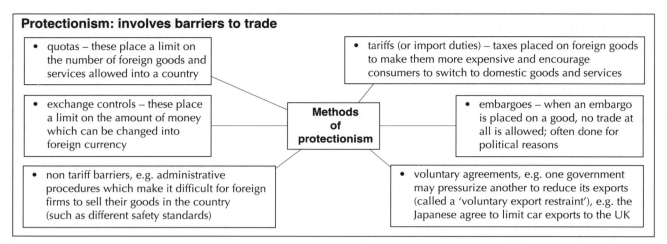

- quotas – these place a limit on the number of foreign goods and services allowed into a country

- tariffs (or import duties) – taxes placed on foreign goods to make them more expensive and encourage consumers to switch to domestic goods and services

- exchange controls – these place a limit on the amount of money which can be changed into foreign currency

Methods of protectionism

- embargoes – when an embargo is placed on a good, no trade at all is allowed; often done for political reasons

- non tariff barriers, e.g. administrative procedures which make it difficult for foreign firms to sell their goods in the country (such as different safety standards)

- voluntary agreements, e.g. one government may pressurize another to reduce its exports (called a 'voluntary export restraint'), e.g. the Japanese agree to limit car exports to the UK

Reasons for protectionism

- infant industry argument: small firms need to be protected to give them time to expand and gain economies of scale, which will allow them to compete on an international basis
- dumping: to prevent foreign firms selling goods at a loss to destroy the domestic industry. If the foreign firms are going to sell at the low price indefinitely, the other country should welcome the cheap goods. If, however, it is simply a policy to destroy a domestic industry, then anti-dumping tariffs might be justified
- to raise revenue for the Government through tariffs
- to prevent overspecialization and diseconomies of scale
- to remove a balance of payments deficit (but this does not solve the underlying cause of the deficit)

Non-economic reasons for protectionism

- strategic interests – some industries (such as defence and agriculture) may need to be kept in national hands for strategic reasons (e.g. in case of war)
- political reasons, e.g. a country may not want to trade with another because of political differences
- to prevent the import of harmful goods, e.g. a country may want to ban the import of certain literature or drugs
- way of life – a country may want to keep its existing way of life, e.g. protect farming
- protection against low wage economies. Some countries use protectionism to combat the low wages paid elsewhere. This is <u>not</u> an economic argument for protectionism. If one country has a comparative advantage because it pays low wages, the other country should welcome the cheaper goods and services and concentrate on producing items where it has a comparative advantage.

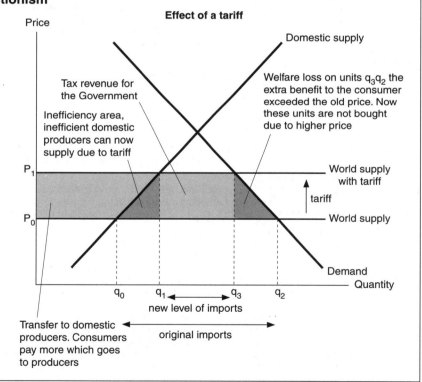

Problems of protectionism

- Difficult to decide/predict which industries are likely to survive in the long term (i.e. which ones should you help?).
- Membership of international organizations limits power to protect industries (would mean breaking treaties).
- Industries may not become efficient (therefore subsidize inefficiency).
- There may be retaliation.

International trade continued

Alternatives to protectionism

Even if some of the arguments for protectionism are valid, the same results may be achieved more efficiently. For example, the Government could subsidize domestic production – this would have the effect of making more goods and services available at a cheaper price rather than restricting consumer choice to fewer goods at a higher price. Politically this is less popular, since the subsidies may have to be financed out of higher taxes, and imposing a tariff on foreign producers looks more aggressive.

Types of trading bloc include:

- **Free trade area:** free trade between member countries; members are allowed to charge whatever tariffs they wish against non-member countries.
- **Customs union:** free trade between member countries; members must charge a common external tariff against non-member countries.
- **Trading blocs:** a group of countries that has an agreement to reduce or eliminate protectionist measures such as tariffs and quotas.
- **Preferential trade agreements:** protectionist measures are reduced on some goods traded between member countries but not on all products.

Trading blocs

- NAFTA – North American Free Trade Association: powerful trading bloc created in 1994 and made up of USA, Canada and Mexico. Tariffs are being phased out and new non-tariff restrictions not allowed (although some existing ones will remain). NAFTA is at best a free trade area; there is no attempt to harmonize laws and regulations (unlike the EU).
- ASEAN – Association of South East Asian Nations: Brunei, Indonesia, Malaysia, Philippines, Singapore, Thailand, Laos, Myanmar, Vietnam, and Cambodia. Aims to increase economic cooperation within the region and remove tariffs over time. It hopes that other countries such as China, Japan, India and Australia will join the free trade area by 2013. Unlike NAFTA it does have political aims, e.g. agreements on the environment and energy.
- EU – European Union: customs union of 27 countries (see pages 107–108).

Gains of customs unions

- internal economies of scale – firms operate in a larger market and may be able to increase output and sales and reduce the unit cost
- greater competition can improve efficiency
- the union as a whole can have more bargaining power and get better terms of trade

BUT consider

- the cost of administering the union
- the possibility of diseconomies of scale

International institutions

- International Monetary Fund
  Aim: to provide finance to maintain exchange rate stability – countries pay into the fund, which will lend to them when they need additional finance to support their currency, e.g. the UK in 1976. IMF loans are given with certain conditions, e.g. that the Government must control the growth of its money supply or cut its spending.
- The World Bank, also called the International Bank for Reconstruction and Development (IBRD)

Funds development projects such as dams and roads, especially in the developing world.
Interest is charged so the projects must pay their way.

- World Trade Organization (WTO); previously the General Agreement on Tariffs and Trade (GATT)
  Set up in 1945. Member countries try to reduce the level of protectionism between them. The first GATT meeting was in 1947. Since then there have been various 'rounds' of negotiations to reduce barriers to trade, such as the Tokyo round and the Uruguay round.

International competitiveness

The competitiveness of UK firms abroad will depend on the following.

- Relative unit labour costs: these in turn depend on factors such as wage rates, productivity and pension costs. High unit labour costs are likely to make a business less competitive.
- The exchange rate: a strong pound, for example, will (with other things unchanged) make UK products more expensive in foreign currencies.
- Domestic market conditions: competitive local markets help force local firms to become more innovative and provide better products and services; this in turn helps these firms to compete abroad.
- Regulations: regulations such as tariffs and quotas can limit UK firms' ability to compete abroad; domestic regulations can also increase firms' costs, e.g. by imposing higher standards or greater restrictions on their production.
- Taxation: high taxation rates on company profits will reduce the funds a firm has available for investment and therefore its ability to develop new products and processes and to compete effectively.

- Innovation: firms that produce innovative products through research and development may be more competitive; this requires a long-term view so firms are willing to invest. Research and development spending may also be affected by government policy, e.g. government subsidies.

Productivity gap: UK productivity levels are lower than some other leading economies such as USA and Germany. This means that, on average, UK firms are less efficient than their international competitors (lower output per worker). This could lead to a higher price per unit due to higher labour costs and lack of competitiveness.

UK productivity may be lower than some other countries due to:

- poor management
- less effective training
- poor working practices
- less investment in technology and less innovation

The Government may help via:

- tax allowances for research and development
- more funding of education and training
- encouraging the sharing of information and best practice

Economics in developing countries

Categorizing countries
- **First World countries:** a small group of rich highly industrialized countries, e.g. United States, Canada, France, Italy, Germany, the UK and Japan (this group are known as G7). Also called **Developed Economies**.
- **Second World** countries include the nations of Eastern Europe and the Soviet Union. Given the end of the Cold War, the distinctive identity of the Second World has largely disappeared and the term is not used much.
- **Third World countries:** generally relatively poor countries often in Asia, Africa and Latin America. Mostly in the southern hemisphere. Sometimes called **Developing Economies** or **Less Developed Countries (LDCs)**. Within these there are some countries, e.g. countries like Singapore, South Korea and Mexico, which are called **emerging economies** because they are growing fast to become First World Economies. These are also called **Newly Industrialized Countries** (NICs) for the same reason.

Some analysts do not distinguish between First, Second and Third World countries; instead they focus on the differences between economies in the Northern v Southern hemispheres.

Other ways of classifying countries:
- The IMF divides countries into three categories:
  - industrial countries
  - developing countries
  - transitional economies
- The World Bank and the United Nations divide them further into high income, middle income and low income.
- A **low income** economy has an income per capita below $875. This is the largest group of countries with the lowest levels of development. Living standards are low and they suffer from the greatest levels of deprivation.
- **Transition economies** are those former command economies that have adopted market systems. These are predominantly the ex-Soviet bloc countries but also include a small number of Asian economies. Their standards of living are higher; they are usually middle income countries and some are developing rapidly towards western European standards. They are more technologically advanced and internationally competitive.

Note: There can be substantial differences between so-called Third World countries. e.g. countries like the United Arab Emirates have a relatively high income per capita compared to the UK and US, i.e. not all 'Third World' economies are poor.

Typical problems of Third World economies
- High birth rates, relatively high death rates and a low life expectancy
- Low income per capita; 85% of the world's population lives in the Third World but it only has 22% of the world's total income
- Less capital per person than First World countries, e.g. fewer machines, less equipment and infrastructure per person
- Human capital; lower levels of investment in human capital, e.g. lower proportion of people enrolled in education. Less investment in education today is likely to lead to slower growth in the future due to lower productivity and innovation.
- High population growth; this means more money needs to be invested to provide jobs and goods for this growing population. Fast population growth tends to bring a high dependency ratio, i.e. a high percentage of the population is dependent on those who are working. It may be difficult to provide the dependants with a suitable standard of living unless those working are taxed very heavily, which in turn may discourage work and investment
- Poor health: Third World countries tend to have poorer health. This may be due to poor nutrition, lack of access to facilities such as clean water and proper sanitation. Also health care provision is often poor, e.g. the government spending on health is a low percentage of GDP.

Structure of the economy
Third World economies tend to be more reliant on the primary sector. In many cases Third World countries are heavily reliant on the export of certain primary commodities, although in recent years the export of low-technology products has increased. Several LDCs rely on a single commodity for more than half their export earnings. If export earnings fluctuate, the whole economy is affected. These fluctuations occur due to the fact that supply and demand for primary commodities tend to be price inelastic so any shift in either demand or supply has a more significant effect than in the case of manufactured goods.

Also:
- these countries tend to be affected by the development of synthetic substitutes for natural products which reduce demand for their products
- demand for foodstuffs is typically income inelastic, i.e. will not grow as fast as income so long-term growth is unlikely.

International Commodity Agreements
To stabilize commodity prices LDCs have sought to organize International Commodity Agreements (ICAs); these are essentially buffer stock schemes on a global scale. It requires producers and importers to agree; however, these two groups often disagree on the buffer stock price. If the intervention price is set too high, the excess supply must be bought up each year. This happened with the 1985 Tin Agreement.

Economics in developing countries continued

Measuring economic welfare

GDP is one measure of the welfare of a country and is often used to determine whether or not a country is developing or developed. However may also want to consider *non-monetary indicators*. In 1990 the United Nations Development Programme (UNDP) introduced a **Human Development Index (HDI)**. This is used by the United Nations as a measure of economic development. It is based on three indicators of development:

a Life expectancy at birth

b The level of education in a country measured by adult literacy and the number in education compared to the population size of education age

c The standard of living as measured by real GDP per person at purchasing power parity.

These components are combined to give a single value between 0 and 1. The HDI can be adjusted to take into account income distribution and can be disaggregated for individual groups of regions. However, some feel that it still has important omissions, such as:

- the percentage of adult male labour in agriculture
- combined primary and secondary school enrolment figures
- access to clean water
- energy consumption per person
- access to mobile phones per thousand of the population.

UNDP also calculates the **Human Poverty Index (HPI)** which measures deprivation in four areas; specifically it measures:

a Percentage of people not expected to survive until the age of 40

b Illiteracy

c Percentage of people lacking access to health services and safe water

d Percentage of children under five moderately or severely underweight.

Growth in developing economies

Harrod Domar growth model

This was developed in the 1930s. This theory stated that investment, savings and technological change were the key variables in growth. Increased investment shifts out the production possibility frontier.

Policy implications of the Harrod Domar model: increasing the rate of growth involves increasing savings (to finance growth) or increasing technology to increase the output per unit of capital.

The residual: The Harrod Domar model emphasized the need for more physical capital. Since then there has been an emphasis on human capital. However even then this does not explain all growth – there remains a 'residual' element which is due to innovation and entrepreneurship.

Lewis model of growth

Focused on the role of migration in the process of development.

Lewis argued growth could be sustained by gradual movement of workers from agriculture (which is low productivity) in rural areas to secondary and tertiary industries (which are higher productivity) in urban areas. Industrialization therefore leads to development. The argument was that the marginal rural workers had limited productivity and so could be transferred into the secondary sector (the rate of transfer depending on the rate of capital accumulation).

However:
- it is possible that workers transferring may add little to productivity
- the model assumes stable urban wages which may not be true
- new technology in developing countries has often been imported and required a small highly skilled workforce. This has meant there has been relatively little job creation. In some cases suitably skilled local labour has not been available.

Rostow

identified five stages of development in an economy:

1 Traditional society where barter is common and agriculture is very important.

2 An economy which has the preconditions for take-off into self-sustaining growth. Savings rise to around 15 to 20% of income.

3 Take-off. The economy begins to grow at a positive rate.

4 The drive for maturity. The economy moves towards a developed economy.

5 Mass consumption. The economy is now developed and citizens achieve a high standard of living.

According to Rostow savings were important to move to stages 3 and 4. First World economies were encouraged to give aid to Third World economies to provide the funds for growth.

Balanced growth theory: argues that Third World countries should aim to encourage industries to grow at a similar rate to create

Economics in developing countries continued

Unbalanced growth theory: argues that Third World governments should focus on certain key industries and aim to get these growing; the growth of these industries will stimulate the economy overall.

Dependency theory: argues that failure of Third World economies to grow is due to external rather than internal factors. First World countries have often exploited Third World countries and even after their independence many Third World countries remained tied to the First World through trade and aid. Also Third World countries are often dependent on primary products and it is argued that First World countries have encouraged this and held back the Third World with poor advice, unfair trading restrictions and poor investment.

What can governments do to promote growth?
- Provide stable macroeconomic climate, e.g. stable rates of inflation and GDP growth. This encourages savings and investment.
- Invest in human capital, e.g. in education and training.
- Provide an effective financial system, e.g. to provide funds to enable investment, to encourage savings to gather the funds to allocate to investment.
- Invest in technology to ensure capital is productive.
- Have policies to encourage productive use of land, e.g. fertilizers and irrigation systems.

- Have policies to encourage development of infrastructure, e.g. roads, railways.
- Have policies to encourage trade.

Other issues may involve:
- Preventing corruption so business people have faith in the system as do foreign investors.
- Selective intervention, e.g. to promote exports.
- Increasing the role of women in society to provide more skills in the economy.

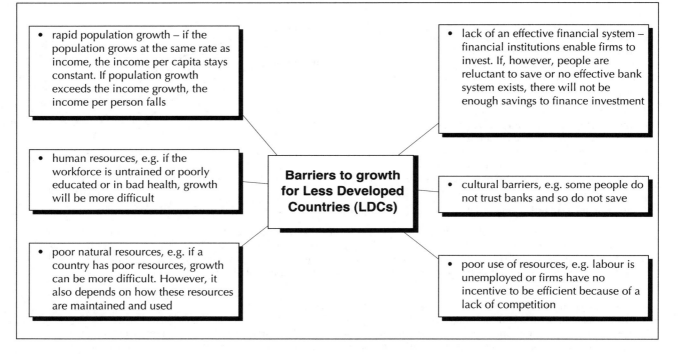

- rapid population growth – if the population grows at the same rate as income, the income per capita stays constant. If population growth exceeds the income growth, the income per person falls

- human resources, e.g. if the workforce is untrained or poorly educated or in bad health, growth will be more difficult

- poor natural resources, e.g. if a country has poor resources, growth can be more difficult. However, it also depends on how these resources are maintained and used

Barriers to growth for Less Developed Countries (LDCs)

- lack of an effective financial system – financial institutions enable firms to invest. If, however, people are reluctant to save or no effective bank system exists, there will not be enough savings to finance investment

- cultural barriers, e.g. some people do not trust banks and so do not save

- poor use of resources, e.g. labour is unemployed or firms have no incentive to be efficient because of a lack of competition

Third World trade
- Developing economies do not tend to trade with each other; they tend to trade with developed economies.
- Trade of developing economies has grown most quickly in recent years in East Asia and the Pacific, e.g. the Tiger economies of Taiwan and South Korea.
- Most Third World trade is in goods, not services.
- Developing countries have diversified to reduce their dependency on exports of primary products and are beginning to export more low- and medium-technology goods. Nevertheless many developing economies can still be significantly affected by movements in primary products. This has caused problems as real commodity prices have fallen over the last twenty years (and within these price falls there are significant fluctuations (causing instability).

Economics in developing countries continued

Boosting growth in Third World countries
1. Import substitutions
Many Third World countries have responded to the decline in primary products by protectionism. It was believed the best way to protect jobs and create growth was by keeping foreign goods out. They built high tariff walls to keep out foreign goods. Their policies focused on **import substitution**, i.e. trying to replace foreign imports with domestically produced goods.

But import substitution removes the benefits of free trade; countries may end up producing goods less efficiently and so at a higher cost than they could buy them in from abroad. Also producers have no incentive to produce more efficiently because they know they are protected. There is often a very high opportunity cost – firms use up resources which could be used more efficiently elsewhere.

These strategies of protectionism and import substitution are 'inward-looking development strategies'.

2. Export-led growth
An alternative to import substitution is an **export-led strategy** (an 'outward-looking development strategy'): rather than becoming less dependent on foreign goods a country may seek to encourage trade. This forces domestic industry to become more efficient. Resources will be allocated to those sectors where the country is most efficient and can benefit from specialization and the principles of comparative advantage.

Export-orientated growth/export led growth has been very successful for countries such as South Korea and Hong Kong, Taiwan and Singapore. (These are called the Asian tigers.) Also noticeable in these countries is the shift away from primary products towards manufactured items.

3. Tourism
Tourism can often be a source of foreign exchange for developing countries. This increases exports. However, it may also involve the import of products to meet customer expectations, e.g. foreign drinks and services. Also likely to be seasonal.

May also create negative externalities, e.g. pollution, destruction of the environment and congestion.

4. Foreign aid
- can help Third World countries by filling in the savings gap. In Third World countries the marginal propensity to consume is high so the level of savings is low and likely to be insufficient to generate the growth required.
- can help finance the import of technology.

Types of aid:
- grants, e.g. a donation for a particular project.
- loans, e.g. a sum is given to the Third World country which has to be repaid with interest.
- tied aid, e.g. grants or loans are given on the understanding that the Third World country will use the money to buy certain goods or services from the First World economy.
- bilateral and multilateral aid: bilateral aid is given directly from one country to another, i.e. country X gives to country Y. Multilateral aid occurs when donor countries give money to an agency which then distributes the aid.
- help with education: help for foreign students wanting to study abroad; technical assistance, e.g. technical experts provided to assist developing countries.

Motives for foreign aid:
- a genuine desire to help others
- to win favour with particular governments and gain political advantage
- to benefit from return business, e.g. aid given in return for products being bought from the donor country. Also in the long term if it helps the economy develop this will lead to more imports which may benefit the donor.
- to fulfil the 'savings gap'; i.e. provide the savings needed to finance the investment required to provide growth
- to provide the foreign reserves needed to import foreign goods and services, e.g. equipment, machinery and technology

Problems with foreign aid:
- foreign aid can remain in the hands of a few and may not be used to improve the economy as a whole.
- some foreign aid investments have been unproductive and unsuccessful; it may be that the donor governments or even the Third World governments do not always know how best to use the finance.
- some policies can harm the local economy, e.g. donating large quantities of food may depress the domestic price of the food and make it difficult for the local producers to survive.
- loan repayments can be difficult for the Third World country to repay. May lead to complacency and a failure to address the fundamental problems within the country.
- often focused on urban areas and not necessarily of tremendous use to the economy as a whole.

Foreign aid is often cut in times of recession. Citizens of First World countries demand that their governments make looking after their own citizens a priority.

Non-governmental organizations include voluntary organizations and charities such as Oxfam and World Vision. They provide support on a small, relatively focused scale and with a minimum of conditions. Help often takes the form of skilled personnel. Official aid is from governments and may come with conditions; politically, some countries may not want to accept aid from abroad.

5. Debt relief
In the 1980s and 1990s many LDCs could not pay their debts to financial institutions due to high interest rates and an increase in the value of the dollar (most loans were denominated in dollars). The IMF set up Structural Adjustment Programmes to lend countries money to pay off the debt if they agreed to various fiscal and monetary regimes. Alternatives are debt forgiveness, where loans are called off (not popular amongst lenders!), or debt rescheduling, where the repayment terms are renegotiated.
Jubilee 2000, a pressure group, actively campaigns for debt cancellation.

6. Fairer trade
Some LDCs claim that developed economies protect their own producers, e.g. their own farmers, making it difficult for them to compete. The Fair Trade movement aims to help producers in LDCs by guaranteeing them a certain income so they are not exploited by the big buyers from developed economies, e.g. in cocoa and cotton.

Economics in developing countries continued

Third World debt crisis

In the 1970s there was a major oil price increase. Some oil-exporting economies deposited their extra revenues in Western banks. Western banks looked to lend this out to make a profit; a major source of lending was to non oil-exporting Third World countries. This created a huge Third World debt, leading to large interest repayments for these countries to Western banks.

The situation was made worse in the 1980s when there was a huge increase in the government deficit (due to major tax cuts) in the US. To finance this the US Government had to sell large amounts of Government debt; to do this it had to offer much higher interest rates (which had a knock on effect on interest rates elsewhere). High US interest rates increased the value of the US dollar.

This caused major problems for the Third World countries:
- higher interest rates made it more expensive for them to repay loans.
- the strong dollar made it more difficult for them to repay the loans which were denominated in dollars.
- developed economies entered a major recession hitting Third World exports.

In 1982 Mexico started the Third World Debt crisis by defaulting, i.e. not paying its loans. Other countries soon followed.

The 1997–8 Asian crisis

At the end of 1997 Thailand was unable to pay its debt. Western banks became extremely reluctant to offer new loans to Thai borrowers. They also cut back loans to other Asian countries which they thought would be affected, e.g. Indonesia and Malaysia.

The cause was partly due to overborrowing by countries and also by banks being too willing to lend and not being cautious enough.

Many firms had to be bailed out by the Thai government. Asian countries recovered quickly due to government action and loans from the International Monetary Fund (IMF).

Structural Adjustment Programmes (SAPs)

These refer to conditions imposed by the World Bank and the International Monetary Fund when they lend to developing countries. They are intended to ensure that the money is spent efficiently and effectively and to help improve the economy. Generally they aim to liberalize economies and promote competition.

The G8, debt cancellation and the environment

The G8 is an informal grouping of the USA, Japan, Germany, France, UK, Italy, Canada and Russia, whose leaders meet regularly to discuss problems in the world economy. In 2005 the G8 summit at Gleneagles in Scotland agreed to boost aid to developing countries by $50bn (£28.8bn). The debt of the 18 poorest nations in Africa was also cancelled. Among the countries benefiting were Benin, Bolivia, Burkina Faso, Cambodia, Ethiopia, Ghana, Guyana, Mali, Nicaragua, Niger, Rwanda and Tanzania. Twenty more countries, with an additional US$15 billion in debt, would be eligible for debt relief if they met targets on reducing corruption and met structural adjustment conditions to encourage private investment, privatize industries and make their economies more open. The agreement came into force in July 2006 and has been called the Multilateral Debt Reduction Initiative (MDRI).

Campaigns before the meeting included a Live 8 concert organized by Bob Geldof, and demonstrations by the Jubilee Debt Campaign (including the Make Poverty History organization).

In **2008** G8 leaders aimed to set a global target of cutting carbon emissions by at least 50% by 2050 in an effort to tackle global warming. Five of the world's biggest emerging economies (China, India, Mexico, Brazil and South Africa) said the G8 should increase its targets to more than 80% by 2050).

Jubilee Debt Campaign

This campaign was set up to reduce the debt of developing economies; it calls for 100% cancellation of this debt. Its literature claims: 'The world's most impoverished countries are forced to pay over $100 million every day to the rich world in debt repayments, while poverty kills millions of their people. Meanwhile, creditors use their power over indebted countries to force them to privatize their services, open up ther markets or cut essential spending.' According to the World Development Movement, 'On average, debt payments cost many poor countries almost twice what they spend on education and more than three times the amount spent on the population's health care'.

Millennium Development Goals

At the United Nations Millennium Summit in September 2000, eight Millennium Goals were agreed. Nearly 190 countries have subsequently signed up to them. The goals are:

- Eradicate extreme poverty and hunger
- Achieve universal primary education
- Promote gender equality and empower women
- Reduce child mortality
- Improve maternal health
- Combat HIV, AIDS, malaria and other diseases
- Ensure environmental sustainability
- Develop a global partnership for development.

In July 2007, the UK's Prime Minister Gordon Brown launched the Millennium Development Goal Call to Action, seeking to accelerate progress on achieving them.

The European Union

> **The EU** is a customs union, i.e. free trade between member countries and common external tariffs with non-members.

Aims of the European Union

Treaty of Rome 1957: established a customs union with arrangements for phased withdrawal of tariffs and a common external tariff on goods coming into the European Community.

The aims of the EU include:
- elimination of customs duties and quotas on the import and export of goods between member states
- the establishment of a single customs tariff and common commercial policy towards non-member states
- abolition of obstacles to free movement of people, services and capital between member states
- establishment of common policies for agriculture and transport
- the prohibition of business practices which restrict or distort competition within the common market in ways considered to be harmful.

Treaty of Maastricht 1992: represented a further move towards economic and monetary union and political union. It set out a common foreign and security policy, a common justice and interior policy and a common social policy. It also outlined a detailed programme and timetable for monetary union.

Key EU institutions

- **The European Commission:** based in Brussels; its role is to draft policies and present them to the Council of Ministers. Also administers and implements the EU's policies.
- **Council of Ministers:** takes policy decisions. Members represent national governments. Unanimity required for major decisions; in some areas only a majority vote needed – these rules were reviewed in Nice in 2000. The actual ministers sent by each country depend on the issues being discussed, e.g. for agricultural issues may send agriculture minister; when discussing finance may send finance minister, and so on.
- **The European Parliament:** the Council and Commission are answerable to the Parliament; it has the power to veto the EU budget. Based in Strasbourg. Made up of elected representatives (called MEPs).
- **Court of Justice:** based in Luxembourg; settles any dispute about the interpretation and application of the Treaty of Rome and Maastricht. Individuals, institutions and member governments can appeal to the Court. Ultimate court of EU law.
- **European Central Bank:** main aim is price stability. Decides on and implements monetary policy including exchange rate policy. National central banks must operate the monetary policy within countries.

Common Agricultural Policy (CAP)

Aims of CAP include:
- to increase agricultural productivity
- to achieve a reasonable standard of living for the agricultural community
- to stabilise markets in agricultural products
- to provide adequate supplies of food
- to ensure supplies to consumers at reasonable prices.

Target prices in CAP

Each year the Council of Ministers sets a target price for the product for the next agricultural year. This is the price which is regarded as the most appropriate to meet the above objectives.

An intervention price is then set just below the target price. If the market price falls below the intervention price, farmers can sell to the EU which stores these supplies. In theory these supplies are used in years when there is a shortage. In reality the EU has had to buy up supplies far more often than it has distributed them so it has built up huge stores of food.

Assessment of CAP

- it has ensured adequate supplies by giving farmers an incentive to produce more

BUT

- it is costly to administer; spending on the CAP is the biggest element of the EU budget
- it can lead to surpluses and high storage costs.

EU budget

The EU budget comes from various sources:
- customs duties on imports from non-EU countries. These are the proceeds from the Common External Tariff (CET) and are paid by all EU member states
- agricultural duties on foods
- a percentage of each country's GDP
- a contribution from each country's VAT

EU expenditure includes spending on:
- CAP
- the regional development fund which aims to reduce regional differences in income and employment
- the European Social Fund (ESF) which promotes improvements in the labour market conditions and employment opportunities
- the Community Fund
- EU foreign aid
- administration

The European Union continued

The Social Charter (1989): proposed to guarantee workers' rights. This Social Charter became the **Social Chapter** in the Maastricht Treaty in 1992.

The Social Charter was an agreement on social policy. The objectives include: the promotion of employment, improved living and working conditions, proper social protection, improved dialogue between management and labour, combating social exclusion and developing human resources with the aim of maintaining high employment.

The social provisions include a minimum wage, equal pay for male and female workers for equal work, minimum standards for health and safety at work and the establishment of works councils (forums for employer – employee discussions).

Joining the EU

Joining the EU may lead to:
- **Trade creation:** the removal of trade barriers may lead to greater specialisation according to the principles of comparative advantage; without tariffs and other trade barriers a country may be able to export more goods than before.
- **Trade diversion:** consumption shifting from lower cost producers outside the EU to higher cost producers inside; with the introduction of a tariff on non-EU members a firm may find it now has to trade within the EU, buying goods which are more expensive than the products it used to buy from outside the EU before a tariff was placed on them.

Gains of EU include:

- greater specialisation and economies of scale; access to a greater 'home' market enables more efficient producers to produce and sell on a larger scale and hence benefit from lower unit costs
- greater competition: more efficient firms will be able to compete more fairly and more successfully in a bigger market
- more exports: the benefits of greater economies of scale and greater competition may make EU firms more competitive and enable them to export more to countries outside the EU
- more financial assistance: the growth of the EU as a whole may enable more funds to be available for the poorer regions
- trade creation i.e. can switch to cheaper supplies with the EU tariffs now removed

BUT:
- possible diseconomies of scale due to overexpansion and problems within firms such as control, communication and coordination
- unemployment: less efficient firms or high-cost regions may suffer as competition increases
- administrative costs: of running the EU institutions
- trade diversion – because of the common tariffs against non-members a country may switch away from a previous supplier to one within the EU and be paying more than before, i.e. than it was paying without the tariff
- impact of EU policy, e.g. social policy may affect employer costs

The members of the European Union by 2008

Austria, Belgium, Bulgaria, Cyprus, Czech Republic, Denmark, Estonia, Finland, France, Germany, Greece, Hungary, Ireland, Italy, Latvia, Lithuania, Luxembourg, Malta, Netherlands, Poland, Portugal, Romania, Slovakia, Slovenia, Spain, Sweden, United Kingdom

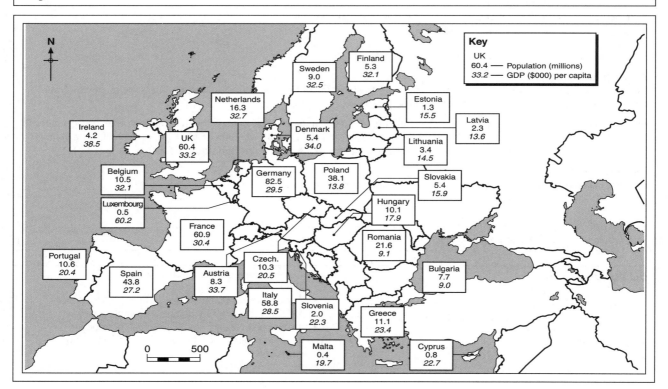

The European Union continued

Migration
In 2004, ten more countries joined the EU. This has led to a major migration into the UK from many of these regions, especially Poland. Consequences of labour migration include:
- an increase in the supply of labour; should lead to lower wages and prices
- an increase in aggregate supply and economic growth.

However, the benefits of immigration into the UK depend on:
- who comes, e.g. what skills?
- the impact on housing, benefits and the infrastructure
- the context, e.g. is it a young workforce coming in to an ageing population?

Entry of other countries
Existing members of the EU are worried that the entry of other countries may mean:
- markets will be swamped by cheap imports from the new members
- the contributions of the richer countries will have to increase to finance the new poorer ones
- they would lose power to the newer ones.

Economic and Monetary Union (EMU)
1989 Delors Committee outlined a three-stage route to monetary union
- *Stage 1:* freeing movements of capital, strengthening competition and increasing policy coordination
- *Stage 2:* transition period in which countries were urged to work towards greater monetary convergence by avoiding excessive budget deficits, keeping inflation rates and interest rates in line with each other and maintaining stable exchange rates
- *Stage 3:* introduction of a single currency (which occurred in January 1999); eleven countries joined the euro system forming the 'euro area'; Denmark, Sweden and the UK decided not to join immediately. The European Central Bank operates the monetary policy which includes determining exchange rate policy, managing exchange reserves, controlling the money supply and taking decisions on interest rates. 1 January 2002 was when notes and coins of the new currency were first distributed. After this notes and coins of member countries in the euro-zone were withdrawn.

Five tests for the UK to join the euro
In 1997 Gordon Brown, then the Chancellor, set out five tests that had to be passed if Britain was to join the euro.
1. Convergence. The economies and their position in the economic cycle need to be compatible, e.g. changes in interest rates must have similar effects on economies.
2. Flexibility. There must be sufficient flexibility to cope with economic problems.
3. Investment. Would having the euro encourage firms to invest in the UK?
4. Financial services. Will the financial markets benefit from euro membership?
5. Employment, stability and growth. Will joining the euro create jobs and lead to economic stability and growth?

Convergence criteria
These are tests that national economies have to pass to join the economic and monetary union (EMU). They consist of five criteria, laid out in the Maastricht Treaty:
- the budget deficit has to be below 3% of GDP
- the total amount of money owed by a government (i.e. the public debt) has to be less than 60% of GDP
- a country should have an inflation rate within 1.5% of the three EU countries with the lowest rate
- long-term interest rates must be within 2% of the three lowest interest rates in the EU
- exchange rates must be kept within 'normal' fluctuation margins of Europe's exchange-rate mechanism.

Benefits of joining the euro
- Reduced transaction costs: firms within the members of the euro-zone which trade with each other do not need to convert their currency; this saves time and commission.
- Removes exchange rate risk; firms trading in euros do not have to be concerned about the impact of an appreciating or depreciating currency. This makes planning easier for businesses and may encourage investment.
- Economies of scale: the removal of exchange rate risk may encourage trade which might lead to economies of scale and a cost advantage.
- Greater price transparency: it will now be easier to compare prices of suppliers; this might lead to greater price competition and lower input prices. These may be passed on the final consumer. Also there will be greater transparency for the customer choosing between brands.
- Inward investment: the existence of a euro-zone may encourage foreign firms to base themselves in this zone to avoid the problems of exchange rate fluctuation and uncertainty.
- The intervention of the independent European Central Bank may lead to lower long-term inflation, and this may require lower interest rates which could stimulate investment and consumption.

The problems of a single currency (the euro)
- Transition costs: there will be various costs as countries transfer to the euro, e.g. producing new price lists, altering vending machines, etc.
- European monetary policy: monetary policy such as interest rates will be determined on the basis of what is appropriate for the euro-zone as a whole rather than one country. Therefore interest rates might be increased at a time when a particular domestic government might want them to fall. This could cause political problems.
- Reduced freedom over fiscal policy: although members of the euro do have considerable freedom over their fiscal policies, they are constrained by the fact their deficit can only be up to 3% of GDP.
- Loss of the option to devalue the domestic currency to provide a short-term boost to international competitiveness.
- The richer countries within the euro-zone may have to finance the poorer ones to reduce structural economic inequalities.

Growth and economic cycles

Economic growth

This can be measured in two ways: an increase in real GDP or an increase in potential GDP. The first can be measured relatively easily (although it is not always easy to do so accurately). The second measure shows what is happening to the capacity of the economy (as opposed to actual output), which is not so easy to estimate.

The output gap is the difference between the actual level of GDP and the estimated long-term trend value. If actual GDP is below the trend line there is a negative output gap. If it is above the trend it is a positive output gap.

Benefits and problems of economic growth

- Higher incomes may lead to better material welfare, health, education and opportunities.
- Poverty may be reduced as extra tax revenue raised may be used to, e.g., increase benefits, spend on schemes to train the unemployed.

But

- Income growth may be achieved by some groups being exploited and suffering from poor living standards and working conditions.
- The additional income may not be used to benefit households directly, e.g. may be spent on military hardware.
- Income may be kept by a few, leading to bigger differences between high and low income groups.
- How beneficial economic growth is depends on whether it is sustainable or not. If an economy is growing by depleting non-renewable resources and/or creating pollution, future generations may not be able to benefit from the same rate of economic growth.
- A steady rate of economic growth may be more beneficial than one that fluctuates. This is because it makes it easier to plan and is likely to encourage investment.

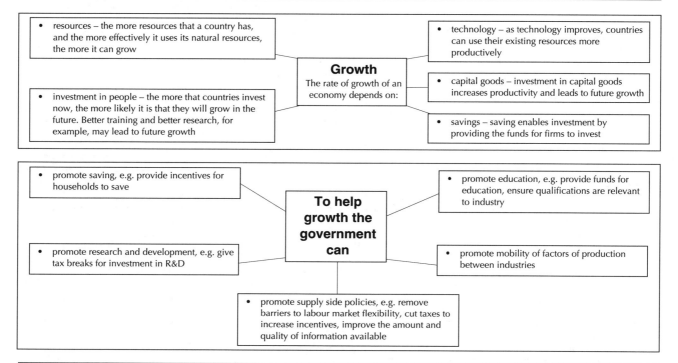

- resources – the more resources that a country has, and the more effectively it uses its natural resources, the more it can grow
- investment in people – the more that countries invest now, the more likely it is that they will grow in the future. Better training and better research, for example, may lead to future growth

Growth
The rate of growth of an economy depends on:

- technology – as technology improves, countries can use their existing resources more productively
- capital goods – investment in capital goods increases productivity and leads to future growth
- savings – saving enables investment by providing the funds for firms to invest

- promote saving, e.g. provide incentives for households to save
- promote research and development, e.g. give tax breaks for investment in R&D

To help growth the government can

- promote education, e.g. provide funds for education, ensure qualifications are relevant to industry
- promote mobility of factors of production between industries
- promote supply side policies, e.g. remove barriers to labour market flexibility, cut taxes to increase incentives, improve the amount and quality of information available

Arguments against economic growth

- causes external costs, e.g. pollution
- may reduce quality of life, e.g. more income growth may involve less leisure time, pollution, movement away from the countryside towards the towns

The 'zero growth proposal' argues that because of the external cost of growth, governments should aim for zero growth.

Economic cycles (also called the business or the trade cycles)

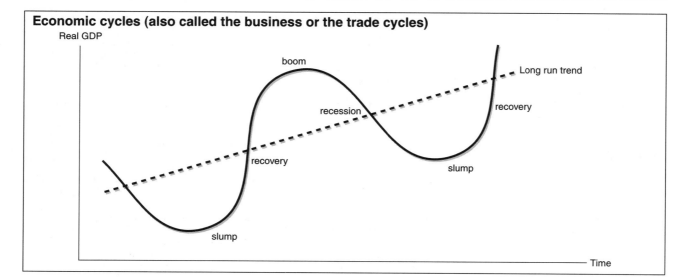

Growth and economic cycles continued

Term	Characteristics
Slump or depression	heavy unemployment, low levels of aggregate demand
Recovery	economy picks up; demand increasing; firms begin to invest
Boom	more confidence in the economy, investment high but beginning to be shortages of supply (e.g. of labour)
Recession	downswing of the economy – technically two successive quarters of negative GDP growth; associated with falling demand and rising stocks of unsold goods; some firms will close and unemployment will rise

Possible causes of a recession

- Lack of aggregate demand, e.g. due to a lack of investment perhaps because of a lack of confidence in the economy and/or higher interest rates deferring borrowing. A recession may also be caused by contradictory government policies, e.g. the Government increases taxes too much. A government may intervene to slow up a boom and end up causing a recession.

- Supply side shock, e.g. higher energy prices shifting aggregate supply to the left, leading to higher prices but less output.

Reasons for the economic cycle:

- Political – in the run up to an election, the Government will want the economy to grow, and is likely to increase the level of demand. This causes growth and falling levels of unemployment. Post election, the Government may face demand pull inflation due to there being too much demand in the economy and may have to deflate the economy.

- Multiplier accelerator model – the multiplier and accelerator can work together to create booms and slumps. For example, an increase in injections can set off the multiplier, which leads to an increase in output. To produce this output, firms increase their level of net investment which sets off the multiplier. At some point the economy begins to reach full capacity and output cannot easily be increased. Output may rise but by less than before – this causes a fall in the level of net investment (accelerator) and so a downward multiplier. However, there is a limit to how much investment will fall, i.e. a floor to the recession – some firms will always be investing, e.g. to replace equipment.

- Inventory stock cycle – firms are often slow to adjust to changes in the level of economic activity. When they do change, their decisions can often exaggerate the economic cycle. For example, if demand falls, firms may be reluctant to cut output in the short run until they are convinced the fall in demand will last. In the short run they build up stocks because they continue producing at the old level, even though demand has fallen. At some point firms realize that demand has fallen and cut back on output. Given that they have built up stocks, firms will cut output below the level of demand. This causes a further fall in aggregate demand, i.e. it worsens the slump.

Similarly, when demand picks up, firms use up stocks in the short run. In the long run, firms will expand their capacity, invest and produce more. Given that they have used up their stocks, they will increase output to a level above demand, so they can rebuild them. This gives an additional boost to the boom.

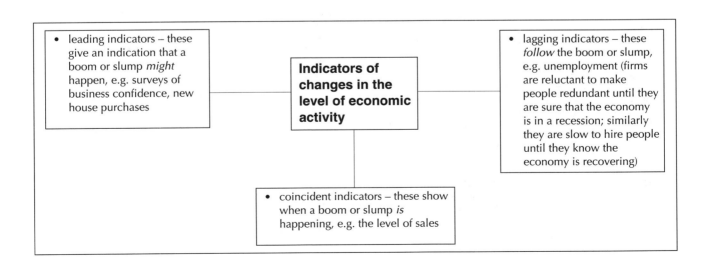

- leading indicators – these give an indication that a boom or slump *might* happen, e.g. surveys of business confidence, new house purchases

Indicators of changes in the level of economic activity

- coincident indicators – these show when a boom or slump *is* happening, e.g. the level of sales

- lagging indicators – these *follow* the boom or slump, e.g. unemployment (firms are reluctant to make people redundant until they are sure that the economy is in a recession; similarly they are slow to hire people until they know the economy is recovering)

UK economy and economic history

The UK economy:
- has a population of 60.6 million (source: ONS, 2007)
- was the second largest recipient of foreign direct investment (FDI) globally in 2007 (source: UNCTAD, 2008)
- is a leading global trading nation, being the second largest exporter and third largest importer of commercial services, and the seventh largest exporter and fourth largest importer of merchandise (source: World Trade Organization, 2007). Leading destinations for UK products and services include the USA (16% of all exports), Germany (9.9%) and France (9.7%). Exports of goods and services to the European Union as a whole accounted for around 55% of all UK exports (source: ONS, The Pink Book, 2007).
- is a member of the European Union, the world's largest trading entity, with nearly 500 million consumers and a GDP of approximately US $19,000 billion (source: Eurostat, 2008)
- is one of the most competitive locations in Europe for business and personal taxation, has low unemployment (with an unemployment rate well below the European Union average), and London is the best European city in which to do business (source: Healey & Baker, European Cities Monitor, October 2007)
- has interest rates set by the Bank of England to meet the Government's inflation target of 2% for the 12-month increase in the Consumer Price Index (CPI)
- has a highly skilled, flexible and dynamic labour market, with less labour regulation than most other European countries
- had an employment level in March 2008 which was at record levels with over 29.46 million people in work, comprising 21.9 million in full-time work and 7.56 million in part-time work (source: ONS, 2008). The employment level (the proportion of working age people in work) was also high in the UK at 74.8%, compared with the European Union average of 66% (source: ONS, 2007).

• 1950 to mid 1970s
Focus was on fiscal policy as a means of influencing aggregate demand. The belief was that the Government could 'fine-tune' the economy using fiscal policies, e.g. in a recession the Government would cut taxes and boost spending.

The Government took a Keynesian view of the economy: believed the economy settled below full employment and that they should use demand management policies.

Monetary policy seen as less significant; where it was used the Government tended to use direct controls on financial institutions to regulate their lending.

1966: Incomes policy to control pay increases
1967: Devaluation of the currency
1972–3: Barber boom – expansionist fiscal policy and loose monetary policy by the Government led to very rapid growth in the economy
1973–4: Oil price increases caused cost push inflation and recession throughout Western Europe. Caused stagflation (rising inflation and unemployment), also led to a worsening balance of payments and falling output.

• Mid 1970s onwards
Move away from Keynesian techniques and towards classical or monetarist approach. Belief that the economy was at or moving towards full employment. Believed that expansionist fiscal policies would simply lead to inflation.

- **1979** Margaret Thatcher elected. Role of fiscal policy was now seen mainly as a means of affecting supply in the economy (e.g. reducing income tax to increase the incentive to work). Fiscal policy was not intended to be used for demand management. Targets set for growth of the money supply. There was a belief that inflation was a 'monetary phenomenon' and could be reduced by controlling the rate of growth of the money supply. The 1980 government introduced the Medium Term Financial Strategy setting out monetary targets. However, the government failed to achieve the targets due in part to deregulation of financial institutions (so it was more difficult to control their lending), abolition of exchange controls, and abolition of the 'corset' which was a direct control on bank lending.
- **1980–1:** Oil price increase – severe recession; stagflation; unemployment more than doubled and manufacturing hit particularly badly. The exploitation of North Sea oil increased the exchange rate, dampening demand for UK exports and by high interest rates and taxes.
- **1986–89:** Lawson boom – rapid expansion of money supply plus income tax cuts. Particularly noticeable was the increase in house prices which further fuelled consumer confidence and spending. Major increases in spending led to current account deficit.
  By mid 1980s government basically abandoned attempts to control the money supply.
- **1987:** Attempted to shadow the Deutschmark – belief that this would force UK firms to be competitive as they could not rely on depreciating currency to make UK exports more competitive amd imports less competitive.
- **1990:** UK joined Exchange Rate Mechanism – fixed pound to other currencies; fixed too high and government had to keep interest rate high to maintain external value of the pound. Caused recession.
- **1992:** UK left ERM (on Black Wednesday, 16 September); Government could finally cut interest rates and this helped economy out of recession along with a fall in the value of the pound.

- **1992+:** Period of growth without any major external shocks.
  – There was the Asian crisis in 1997–8 when several Asian economies went into recession and their currencies depreciated; however, these economies recovered quickly and the fast growth of the US economy helped UK exporters.
  – Interest rates throughout the mid to late 1990s were used as and when required to control inflation and hit target of 2.5%.
  – UK Government kept control of fiscal policy and with the help of the Monetary Policy Committee ensured growth without increasing inflation.
- **2000+:** Belief that public finances should broadly balance over the trade cycle. In a recession spending can rise (as benefits rise and tax receipts fall); in a boom budget position can move into surplus. Main role of fiscal policy is achieving objectives such as rectifying market failures (e.g. public and merit goods), redistributing income, improving aggregate supply; not seen primarily as tool to control aggregate demand. Interest rates are set by Monetary Policy Committee to ensure inflation is controlled. Strong pound of late 1990s and 2000 made exporting difficult.
- **2008:** It became clear in 2008 that US and UK banks had been lending to high-risk borrowers in what was called the 'sub prime market'; this left them very exposed when the borrowers could not repay. This hit several banks hard; their profits fell and what they thought were assets (their lending) turned out not to be worth much. Banks became wary of lending to households, firms and even to each other and this became known as the 'credit crunch'. This led to a slowdown of growth in the US and other countries such as the UK as households and firms borrowed less. This hit sectors such as leisure, tourism, consumer durables and construction. It also led to less demand for property and a fall in house prices. This reduced the wealth of households, which further contributed to a fall in spending. The central banks of the US and the UK cut interest rates to encourage spending. UK economic growth slowed after 15 successive years of growth. Inflation also reached over 4% and the pound hit a 12 low against the euro.

Useful websites for information on the UK economy
For more information on the UK economy you can visit:
- the Office for National Statistics (www.statistics.gov.uk)
- Eurostat/European Commission (www.europa.eu.int/comm/eurostat)
- the Organisation for Economic Development and Co-operation (www.oecd.org)
- the World Trade Organization (www.wto.org)
- the United Nations Conference on Trade and Development (www.unctad.org)
- the Bank of England: (www.bankofengland.co.uk)
- UK Trade and Investment: (www.uktradeinvest.gov.uk)

A-Level revision questions

Key terms in Economics
1 What are the fundamental economic problems?
2 Define "profit".
3 State three economic agents.
4 State three resources.
5 What are sustainable resources?
6 Distinguish between normal profit and abnormal profit.
7 What is meant by the division of labour?
8 Explain one advantage and one disadvantage of the division of labour.
9 What is the difference between the short term and the long term in economics?
10 What is meant by equilibrium?

Introduction to Economics
1 Distinguish between normative and positive economics.
2 What is meant by "the basic economic problem"?
3 Explain how the basic economic problem is solved in
   (a) a free market and
   (b) a command economy.
4 What is meant by the phrase "the division of labour"?
5 What is meant by "opportunity cost"?
6 Explain what is meant by the "production possibility frontier".
7 Explain two benefits of the free market system compared with a planned economy.
8 Explain two benefits of a planned economy compared with a free market economy.

Demand
1 What is the law of "demand"?
2 Draw a demand curve and explain why it is downward sloping.
3 Distinguish between a movement along a demand curve and a shift in demand.
4 Explain three reasons why demand might shift outwards.
5 What is an inferior good?
6 Why might a demand curve be upward sloping?
7 Explain the difference between the income and substitution effects.
8 What is a Giffen good?
9 What is a normal good?
10 What is meant by "marginal utility"?

Elasticity of demand
1 Distinguish between price, cross and income elasticity of demand.
2 Examine the possible reasons why demand for a product might be price inelastic.
3 What is meant by the "price elasticity of supply"?
4 Examine the factors which might make supply more price elastic.
5 Discuss the usefulness of the concept of elasticity to
   (a) producers (b) the government.
6 Is the cross price elasticity for substitutes positive or negative? Explain your answer.
7 Is the income elasticity for an inferior good negative or positive? Explain your answer.
8 Is the price elasticity for a normal good positive or negative? Explain your answer.
9 If the price elasticity of demand is –0.8, is this price elastic or inelastic? Explain your answer.
10 If demand is price elastic, will a price increase lead to an increase or decrease in revenue? Explain your answer.

Supply
1 What is meant by "supply"?
2 Draw a supply curve and explain why it is upward sloping.
3 Distinguish between a movement along a supply curve and a shift in supply.
4 Explain three reasons why supply might shift outwards.
5 What is meant by "joint supply"?
6 If the price elasticity of supply is +2, what does this mean?
7 Explain three factors that influence the price elasticity of supply.
8 Is supply likely to be more price elastic or price inelastic? Explain your answer.
9 Does a change in price lead to a movement along the supply curve or a shift in supply?
10 What is the law of supply?

Market mechanism
1 What is a "market"?
2 What is meant by "equilibrium"?
3 What is meant by "excess demand"? How would the price mechanism restore equilibrium in a free market?
4 What is meant by "excess supply"? How would the price mechanism restore equilibrium in a free market?
5 Examine the role of the price mechanism in the free market.
6 Examine the effect of an increase in demand on the equilibrium price and quantity in a market.
7 Examine the effect of an increase in supply on the free market equilibrium.
8 What is meant by "consumer surplus"?
9 What is meant by "producer surplus"?
10 What is meant by "allocative efficiency"?
11 What is meant by "productive efficiency"?
12 Examine the effect of an increase in indirect taxes on a market.
13 Examine the effect of an increase in subsidies on a market's equilibrium.
14 Examine the effect on a market of a maximum price set below the equilibrium.

Marginals, average and totals
1 What is the law of diminishing returns?
2 What is meant by "marginal product"?
3 What is meant by "average product"?
4 If the marginal product is above the average product, what will happen to the average product?
5 What is meant by "productivity"?
6 Explain two ways in which productivity might be increased.
7 Why do the average total cost and the average variable cost converge?
8 If the marginal cost is below the average cost, what happens to the average cost? Explain your answer.
9 What is the difference between the average cost and the total cost?
10 Why does the average fixed cost fall as output increases?

Long run cost curves
1 What is meant by the "long run" in economics?
2 Explain what is meant by "average cost".
3 What is the minimum efficient scale?
4 What is the difference between internal and external economies of scale?

A-level revision questions continued

5 What is the difference between a short run average cost curve and the long run average cost curve?
6 Explain two internal economies of scale.
7 What is meant by "decreasing returns to scale"?
8 What is the least cost combination of factors?
9 Explain two possible internal diseconomies of scale.
10 Explain one external economy of scale.

Price and output decisions
1 What is meant by "profit"?
2 What is the profit maximising condition?
3 What is the difference between abnormal profit and normal profit?
4 What is the difference between economic profit and accounting profit?
5 What is meant by "contribution"?
6 What is meant by a "loss"?
7 Under what circumstances will a firm produce in the short run?
8 Under what circumstances will a firm produce in the long run?
9 What is allocative efficiency?
10 What is productive efficiency?

Business objectives
1 What is a multinational?
2 Explain the possible reasons why a firm might want to become a multinational.
3 What is meant by "horizontal integration"?
4 What is meant by "vertical integration"?
5 What is a conglomerate merger?
6 Examine the possible reasons why a firm would want to increase in size.
7 Examine the possible objectives of organizations apart from profit maximization.
8 What is meant by "satisficing"?

Income and wealth
1 Distinguish between income and wealth.
2 Examine reasons why inequality might exist within the UK.
3 Explain what is meant by the "Lorenz curve".
4 Examine ways in which the government can reduce inequality in the UK.
5 Distinguish between absolute and relative poverty.
6 What is meant by "horizontal equity"?
7 What is meant by "vertical equity"?
8 What is non-marketable wealth?
9 What is unearned income?
10 Why might one individual's wages be greater than another's?

Consumption
1 What is the Keynesian consumption function?
2 What is meant by the "marginal propensity to consumer"?
3 What is meant by the "average propensity to consume"?
4 Explain two factors that determine the marginal propensity to consume.
5 Explain what is meant by "autonomous" consumption.
6 What is meant by "discretionary savings"?
7 Explain how expectations may affect consumption.
8 Explain the permanent income hypothesis.
9 Explain the life cycle hypothesis.
10 How does an increase in consumption affect aggregate demand?

Investment
1 Is investment an injection or a withdrawal?
2 What is the difference between gross and net investment?
3 What is the difference between autonomous and induced investment?
4 Explain three factors that might affect the level of investment in the economy.
5 Explain the difference between a movement along the MEC schedule and a shift in the MEC schedule.
6 What is meant by the "accelerator"?
7 Explain two limitations of the accelerator model.
8 What is meant by "cost benefit analysis"?
9 How does the interest rate affect aggregate demand?
10 Explain one problem of cost benefit analysis.

Aggregate demand and supply
1 Explain with a diagram what is meant by "aggregate demand".
2 Explain two possible reasons why aggregate demand might increase.
3 Discuss the possible effects of an increase in aggregate demand on the economy.
4 Explain what is meant by the "multiplier".
5 What is meant by "aggregate supply"?
6 Examine the possible factors which might cause aggregate supply to shift outwards.
7 Distinguish between short run and long run aggregate supply.
8 Discuss the impact of a fall in aggregate demand on the economy.
9 Why might aggregate supply be price elastic?
10 Explain two ways of increasing aggregate supply.

Keynesian cross diagrams
1 What is the equation for aggregate demand?
2 What is a four sector economy?
3 What is an inflationary gap?
4 What is a deflationary gap?
5 Explain two factors that can increase aggregate demand.
6 What is meant by the "multiplier"?
7 What is the equation for the multiplier?
8 What determines the size of the multiplier?
9 What is the marginal propensity to import?
10 How does an increase in income affect the government's budget position?

Fiscal policy
1 Explain what is meant by "fiscal policy".
2 Explain two sources of government revenue.
3 Explain two elements of government spending.
4 What is a direct tax?
5 Explain two features of a good tax system.
6 What are reflationary fiscal policies?
7 What is a progressive tax system?
8 What is a regressive tax system?
9 What is meant by the "government's fiscal stance"?
10 What is meant by "crowding out"?

Money and banking, the demand for money and the monetary transmission mechanism
1 Explain two functions of money.
2 Explain two functions of the Bank of England.
3 What is meant by the "money multiplier"?
4 Explain how changes in interest rate affect the economy.
5 Explain two problems of monetary control.

6 Explain two problems of using interest rates to influence aggregate demand.
7 What is the role of the Monetary Policy Committee?
8 Explain two ways the Bank of England could control the money supply.
9 Explain two elements of the demand for money.
10 What is meant by the "liquidity trap"?

Inflation

1 What is meant by "inflation"?
2 What is the Retail Price Index?
3 Examine the possible causes of inflation.
4 Outline the Quantity Theory of Money.
5 Explain the significance of Fisher's Equation of Exchange.
6 Discuss the ways in which a government might want to reduce inflation in an economy.
7 Explain what is meant by the Phillips curve. According to this is there a trade-off between inflation and unemployment?
8 What is the CPI?
9 What is deflation?

Unemployment

1 Explain how unemployment might be measured.
2 What is meant by the non accelerating rate of unemployment?
3 Examine the possible causes of unemployment.
4 Examine the possible effects on an economy of an increase in unemployment.
5 Discuss the possible ways in which a government might try to reduce unemployment.
6 What is full employment?
7 What is the difference between voluntary and involuntary unemployment?
8 Explain what is meant by demand side policies to cure unemployment.
9 Explain what is meant by supply side policies to cure unemployment.
10 Explain two factors that influence the supply of labour.

Exchange rates

1 Explain how the exchange rate is determined in a free floating exchange rate system.
2 Explain what is meant by a "strong pound".
3 Explain three reasons why demand for a currency might increase.
4 Examine the possible effects of a depreciating currency on an economy.
5 What is meant by an exchange rate?
6 Explain two factors that influence the demand for a currency.
7 Explain two factors that influence the supply of a currency.
8 Explain what is meant by a trade weighted index.
9 What is meant by the spot rate for a currency?

International trade

1 Distinguish between comparative and absolute advantage.
2 Outline the possible benefits of free trade to an economy.
3 What is meant by the "balance of payments"?

4 Examine the possible effect on an economy of a current account deficit.
5 Discuss the ways in which a government might attempt to reduce a current account deficit.
6 Explain what is meant by the Marshall Lerner condition.
7 What is globalization?
8 What is the role of the WTO?
9 Distinguish between a tariff and a quota.
10 Discuss the case for and against a government introducing greater protectionist measures to protect an industry.
11 Examine the factors which influence a firm's international competitiveness.

Economics in developing countries

1 What is the Human Development Index?
2 What were Rostow's five stages of development in an economy?
3 How can economic growth be shown using a Production Possibility Frontier?
4 Explain two typical problems of developing world economics.
5 What is export led growth?
6 What is the Harrod Domar model of growth?
7 What is the Lewis model of growth?
8 What are the barriers to growth in less developed countries?
9 What is meant by "import substitution"?
10 Discuss three possible ways of boosting growth in developing countries.

The European Union

1 What is the European Union?
2 Outline the role of three European Union institutions.
3 What is the Common Agricultural Policy (CAP)? Explain how the CAP operates.
4 Examine the case for and against the Common Agricultural Policy.
5 Discuss the possible advantages and disadvantages for the UK of being a member of the European Union.
6 What is meant by the "European Monetary Union"?
7 Consider the possible impact on the UK of joining the single currency area in the European Union.
8 Explain the purpose of the Social Charter.
9 How does the European Union raise money?
10 What are the convergence criteria?

Growth

1 What is meant by "economic growth"?
2 What is meant by "GDP"?
3 Examine ways in which a government might seek to increase growth in the economy.
4 Explain the possible problems for a country of fast economic growth.
5 Discuss the problems of using national income to measure a country's standard of living.
6 What is a recession?
7 Outline two arguments against economic growth.
8 What is the zero growth proposal?
9 What is meant by a "leading indicator"?
10 What is the multiplier accelerator model?

GLOSSARY OF ESSENTIAL TERMS

Microeconomics

Abnormal profit Occurs when the total revenue is greater than the total costs.

Ad valorem tax A tax placed on the producer that is a percentage of the price.

Allocative efficiency Occurs when the price paid by the customer equals the social marginal cost of producing the good.

Asymmetrical information Occurs when one individual/organization knows more about an issue than another, e.g. the seller has information not available to the buyers.

Average cost The cost per unit (also called the average total cost).

Average fixed cost The fixed cost per unit.

Barriers to entry Anything that makes it difficult for other firms to enter a market.

Breakeven point This is the output at which the total revenue equals total cost.

Buffer stocks These are stocks held by the Government to be used in a price stabilization scheme.

Cartel This occurs when the firms in an oligopoly collude when setting prices and outputs.

Collusive oligopoly This occurs when several firms that dominate an industry act together, e.g. when setting the price or quantity.

Company A business organization that has its own legal identity; it is owned by shareholders who have limited liability.

Complementary demand Occurs when one good is demanded in conjunction with another.

Composite demand Occurs when there are competing demands for a product or service.

Concentration ratio The 'n' firm concentration ratio measures the market share of the largest 'n' firms in a market

Consumer surplus The difference between the price charged for a product and the utility that consumers derive from it.

Cost Benefit Analysis A method of investment appraisal that takes account of social costs and benefits.

Cross price elasticity of demand Measures the responsiveness of demand for one product in relation to changes in the price of another.

Demand curve Shows the quantity demanded at each and every price, all other factors being unchanged.

Derived demand Occurs when the demand for something is derived from the demand for something else, e.g. employers demand labour because their products are demanded.

Diminishing returns Occurs when the extra output produced falls as more units of the variable factor are added.

Diseconomies of scale (external) Occur when a firm's unit costs increase at every level of output due to an increase in the size of the industry as a whole.

Diseconomies of scale (internal) Occur when there are increases in the long-run average costs as the scale of production increases.

Economic rent Occurs when an individual earns more than his/her transfer earnings.

Engels curve This shows the relationship between demand and income.

Entrepreneurship Occurs when individuals are willing to take the risks to produce new ideas or introduce new processes.

Equilibrium Occurs when there is a state of balance and there is no incentive for change.

External economies of scale Occur when a firm's unit costs fall at every level of output due to an increase in the size of the industry as a whole.

Externality Occurs when there is a difference between private and social costs and benefits.

Fixed costs Costs that do not change with the amount of products produced.

Free rider problem Occurs when it is not possible to exclude individuals from the consumption of a product.

Game theory Involves the study of alternative strategies oligopolists may choose depending on their assumptions about each other's actions.

Giffen good These have a negative income elasticity of demand, i.e. demand falls as income increases, and a positive price elasticity of demand, i.e. a higher price, leads to a higher quantity demanded.

Hit and run competition Occurs when firms enter a market attracted by high profits and then leave when they are competed away.

Horizontal integration Occurs when two or more firms at the same stage of the same production process are integrated (e.g. takeover or merger).

Imperfect competition Refers to market structures that are not perfect competition, e.g. monopoly and oligopoly.

Income elasticity of demand Measures the responsiveness of the demand for a product in relation to changes in income.

Inferior goods These have a negative income elasticity of demand, i.e. demand falls as income increases, and a negative price elasticity of demand, i.e. a higher price leads to a lower quantity demanded.

Internal economies of scale Occur when there are reductions in a firm's long-run average costs as the scale of production increases.

Joint supply Occurs when the supply of one product is linked to the supply of another, e.g. an increase in the supply of beef increases the supply of hides.

Kinked demand curve This is a model of oligopoly; demand is assumed to be price elastic above the existing price and price inelastic below the existing price.

Lender of the last resort The Bank of England acts as a guarantee of the UK banking system.

Liquidity trap This occurs when any increase in the money supply is held as idle balances and does not affect aggregate demand.

Long run The period of time when all of the factors of production are variable.

Marginal cost The extra cost of producing an extra unit.

Marginal revenue The extra revenue earned by selling another unit.

Marginal revenue product Measures the value of the output produced by employing an extra worker.

Marginal utility This is the extra satisfaction gained from consuming another unit.

Merit good This is a product that is underconsumed in the free market because its external benefits are not appreciated or known by customers.

Minimum Efficient Scale This is the first level of output at which the average costs of the business are minimized.

Mixed economy An economy that has both the private sector and public sector, i.e. goods and services are provided by both the free market and the Government.

Monopolistic competition A market structure in which there are many firms but each offers a differentiated product.

Monopoly A firm that dominates a market.

Monopsony Occurs when there is a single buyer in a market.

Multinational A company that has production bases in more than one country.

Non-excludability This occurs when it is not possible to prevent someone from consuming a product.

Normal goods Normal goods have a negative price elasticity of demand and a positive income elasticity of demand.

Normal profit Occurs when the total revenue equals the total costs.

Objective This is a target, e.g. to profit maximize.

Oligopoly A market structure in which a few firms dominate the market.

Opportunity cost Benefit foregone – in the context of a production possibility frontier, this is the amount of one product that has to be given up to produce more of another product.

Pareto optimality Occurs when it is not possible to make someone better off without making someone worse off.

Perfect competition This is a market structure with many firms, freedom of entry and exit, where firms produce identical products and where firms are price takers.

Price discrimination Occurs when different prices are charged to different customers for the same product.

Price elasticity of demand Measures the responsiveness of the demand for a product in relation to changes in its price.

Price elasticity of supply Measures the responsiveness of the supply for a product in relation to changes in its price.

Producer surplus The difference between the price paid to producers for products and the cost of producing the items.

Production possibility frontier Shows the maximum combination of products that an economy can produce given its resources.

Productive efficiency Occurs when more of one product can only be produced if less of another product is produced. It also occurs when a firm produces at the minimum of the average cost curve, that is, at the lowest cost per unit possible.

Profit maximizing condition Profit maximization occurs at the output level where marginal revenue equals marginal cost.

Progressive tax A tax system where the average rate of tax increases as income increases.

Proportional tax A tax system where the average rate of tax is constant as income increases.

Public good A product that is non-diminishable and non-excludable.

Sales revenue maximization Occurs at the output where the marginal revenue is zero.

Short run (short term) The period of time when at least one factor of production is fixed.

Shut down point Occurs when price is the minimum of average variable cost; a firm would shut down if the price fell below the average variable cost.

Social costs The private costs plus external costs.

Specific tax A tax placed on products; a fixed amount per unit.

Supernormal profits These are the same as abnormal profits. They occur when the price is greater than the average cost.

Supply curve Shows the quantity that producers are willing and able to produce at each and every price, all other factors being unchanged.

Sustainability This refers to the ability of the economy to survive to produce in the long term, e.g. using renewable resources.

Takeover This occurs when one business buys control of another.

Total cost The total cost at any level of output equals the fixed costs plus the variable costs.

Total revenue The value of sales (calculated as the price of a product multiplied by the quantity sold).

Trade union This is an organization that represents employees; it aims to protect employees' rights and promote their interests.

Transfer earnings Occur when an individual earns the amount required to keep them in that job.

Utility The satisfaction that a consumer would receive from consuming a product.

Vertical integration Occurs when two or more firms at different stages of the same production process are integrated (e.g. takeover or merger).

Macroeconomics

Absolute advantage A country has an absolute advantage in a product if it can produce it with fewer resources than another country.

Accelerator Shows the relationships between the level of net investment and the rate of change of national income.

Actual growth rate The percentage annual increase in the output of an economy, e.g. an increase in GDP.

Aggregate demand The total planned demand for final goods and services in an economy.

Aggregate supply The total output of goods and services producers are willing and able to supply in an economy.

Appreciation of the exchange rate This occurs when the external value of a currency increases; it becomes stronger.

Automatic fiscal stabilizers When tax revenue rises and spending falls automatically as national income rises.

Average propensity to consume This measures the percentage of disposable personal income spent on consumer goods. It generally varies with the level of income.

Balance of payments This is a record of all the transactions between one country and the rest of the world over a given period.

Budget deficit This occurs when government spending is greater than its income.

Budget surplus This occurs when government spending is less than its income.

Business cycle (or economic cycle) The fluctuations in national income over time around the long run trend.

Coase Theorem The creators and sufferers of negative externalities can internalize the externality by charging those who create it or bribing those who suffer.

Comparative advantage A country has a comparative advantage in the production of a product if it has a lower opportunity cost than other countries.

Consumption Shows the level of planned spending by households on final goods and services.

Cost-push inflation Occurs when higher costs force producers to put up their prices.

Current account on the balance of payments This records the transactions of one country in goods and services with other countries.

Customs Union This is an area of free trade in which members adopt a common trade policy with non-members, such as a common external tariff or quota.

Cyclical unemployment Occurs when people are unemployed due to a lack of demand in the economy.

Deflationary gap This measures the extent to which aggregate demand is below the level required for full employment.

Demand for money Shows the amount of money that people want to hold at each and every interest rate, all other things being unchanged.

Demand-pull inflation Occurs when the aggregate demand is greater than the aggregate supply, thereby pulling up prices.

Depreciation of the exchange rate This occurs when the external value of a currency falls.

Economic cycle (or business cycle) The fluctuations in national income over time around the long run trend.

Exchange rate The price of one currency in terms of another.

Financial crowding out Occurs when government spending diverts money away from the private sector.

Fiscal policy Uses government spending and taxation and benefit rates to influence the economy.

Forward exchange rate market A market where a price is set today to trade currencies at a future date.

Frictional unemployment Occurs when people are between jobs.

Game theory An approach to oligopoly in which each firm's strategy depends on its expectations of how the others in the market will behave.

Gini coefficient Measures the extent of income inequality in an economy.

Gross domestic product (GDP) Measures the value of final goods and services produced in an economy.

Human Development Index (HDI) This is a measure of economic development based on three indicators of development: life expectancy at birth, the level of education in a country, and real GDP per person at purchasing power parity.

Infant industry A new industry that has not yet expanded and benefited from economies of scale or developed its comparative advantage.

Inflation Occurs when there is a persistent increase in the general price level. This can be measured using various price indices such as the RPI, RPIX or CPI.

Inflationary gap Measures the extent to which aggregate demand is above the full employment output.

Injection Spending into the economy in addition to consumption; injections increase the aggregate demand.

Interest rate The opportunity cost of money; it measures the reward offered to savers and the cost of borrowing.

Involuntary unemployment Measures the number of people who are willing and able to work at the given real wage but who are not in employment.

J curve The J curve effect shows how depreciation of a currency can make the balance of trade worse in the short run before it improves.

Laffer curve Shows the relationship between the tax rate and the level of tax revenue.

Less-developed country A less-developed country is an economy with low income and is usually associated with low life expectancy and low levels of literacy.

Liquidity preference This is the demand for money; shows the amount of money that people want to hold at each and every interest rate, all other things being unchanged.

Lorenz curve Shows the proportion of income earned by a given proportion of the population in an economy.

Marginal efficiency of capital (MEC) Shows the expected rate of return on investment projects.

Marginal productivity theory The theory that the demand for labour depends on the marginal revenue product.

Marginal propensity to consume This measures the proportion spent on consumption out of each extra pound of income.

Marginal propensity to import This measures the proportion spent out of each extra pound of income on imports.

Marshall Lerner condition States that, provided the price elasticity of demand for exports plus the price elasticity of demand for imports is greater than 1, then a depreciation in exchange rate will improve the current account.

Menu costs The costs associated with changing menus and price lists when inflation occurs.

Monetary policy This is government policy to affect the economy by controlling the money supply or using interest rates.

Monopoly This occurs when one firm dominates a market. In the UK a monopoly occurs when one firm has a market share of more than 25%. A 'pure' monopoly has a market share of 100%.

Multiplier Shows how an increase in the aggregate demand leads to a greater increase in national income.

National debt The total debt of the Government.

Net investment This is gross investment minus depreciation.

Paradox of thrift This occurs when households attempt to save more but end up saving a greater proportion of their incomes but the same total amount.

Phillips curve Shows the short-run and long-run relationships between inflation and unemployment.

Potential economic growth Occurs when there is an increase in the capacity of the economy.

Poverty trap This occurs when individuals are worse off if they work than if they remain unemployed due to a loss of benefits and because of the tax that has to be paid.

Precautionary demand This is the demand to hold money in case of an emergency.

Progressive tax This occurs when the average rate of taxation increases with income.

Protectionism Occurs when a government protects its domestic firms against foreign competition.

Public sector net cash requirement (PSNCR) The deficit between government spending and revenue.

Purchasing Power Parity (PPP) The theory that the exchange rate changes to offset difference in countries' inflation rates so that the same quantity of goods and services can be bought abroad as at home with a given amount of domestic currency.

Quantity theory of money The quantity theory of money states that $MV = PT$.

Quota A limit to the amount that a firm can produce.

Recession A period of six months or more during which national income growth is negative.

Regressive tax This occurs when the average rate of taxation decreases with income.

Regulatory capture Occurs when the regulator starts to act in the interests of the industry being regulated.

Special deposits Deposits that banks may have to make at the Bank of England.

Speculative demand The demand to hold money rather than invest in less liquid assets.

Tariff This is a tax placed on imported products.

Terms of trade Measure the prices of exports from a country compared to the prices of imports into the country.

Trade creation This occurs when a customs union leads to a shift from trade with higher cost countries to lower cost countries.

Trade diversion This occurs when a customs union leads to a shift from trade with lower cost countries to higher cost countries because of the protectionist measures on non-members.

Transactions demand This is the demand for money to finance day-to-day transactions.

Unemployment The number of people who are actively looking for work but currently are without a job.

Unemployment rate The number of people who are actively looking for work but currently are without a job as a percentage of the labour force.

Velocity of circulation The number of times that money, on average, is spent on goods and services over a given time period.

Vertical equity This occurs when there is redistribution of income and/or wealth from the rich to the poorer.

Voluntary unemployment Occurs when people who are looking for work are not yet willing to accept work at the given real wage rate.

Withdrawal A leakage from the economy; it reduces the aggregate demand.

INDEX